Table of Contents

Introduction

We are living in very challenging times. Many believe the end of the age has come or is really close. Others continue to doubt. But even those hardened to the message of Christ know something's up. Jesus warned us about the end and gave us signs to look out for before His coming. Yet those who claim to belong to Him are often unaware as though they didn't get the memo. And despite all the best-selling books and Bible prophecy teachings over the years, confusion still abounds in the church. But what is the source of the confusion? Why are there so many different voices? With all that the Bible has to say on the subject, what is the problem? How could there still be so much mystery? How could so many questions still be unanswered? Why don't all the pieces fit? Could it be that there is something missing? Have the passages been misinterpreted? Have the ancient clues been misread? Is there wisdom yet to be discovered? Were there keys hidden by God that have not been found? The answer is, amazingly, yes!

This book contains revelation that came as a flood into my understanding nearly twenty years ago. After teaching on the subject for many years prior, I came to the conclusion that there was much I did not understand. So I sought the Lord afresh and studied the Scriptures for a period of two years. It was then that I discovered the hidden keys to the End-Time passages and began to present them to others. All who have been willing to listen have discovered them as well. The result has been the restoration of hope and clarity regarding the day we live in and the biblical scenario to be played out. Though difficult days are coming my heart is filled with excitement and joy for the future! What about you? Are you filled with excitement about the return of Christ? Do you long for His appearing or are you scared the end will come? Do you have questions about the end of the age that have not been answered? Have you been told that none of it matters, yet you know in your heart it really does? If the answer is yes, then this book is for you!

Chapter One
Mysteries of the End

I have always found mysteries exciting. Since childhood I have followed the famous detective Sherlock Holmes and been intrigued with the writings of Agatha Christie. Today these stories continue to be popular being repackaged for a new generation. Besides this, the various CSI series collecting evidence from ghoulish places, and the many mystery novels flying off the shelves, testify that I am not alone. Indeed, most people love solving a puzzle and unraveling a complicated plot. There is something in all of us attracted to a treasure hunt with or without a map. I remember the suspense in the theatre as Indiana Jones searched for the Lost Ark. Just when it seemed he had escaped one pitfall, he found himself in another. Then there was National Treasure. I remember the intrigue of doors opening and closing and secret codes and passageways. Could this be the place? Was the key behind this stone or statue? And all the while there was the reminder that someone else had lost their way and missed the signs or had fallen to their death trying to unlock the code. Some had quit altogether, concluding that there was no treasure. Others just went in circles looking in all the wrong places. But once the keys were found, the mystery was easily solved. And so it is with all mysteries.

The Mysteries of God

"For nothing is hidden, except to be revealed; nor has anything been secret, but that it should come to light." Mark 4:22

The Bible is full of mysteries. This is especially true when it comes to the end of the age. But did you ever wonder why? Why did God hide so many things? Jesus told us they were hidden that they should come to light. In other words God wants to reveal them and will reveal them to certain people. God hides a thing that it may be found. "What's the point of that," you ask? Well, it's not about the hidden things themselves but about those who want to know. In other words, God wants to reveal them, but only to those who want Him. He does not throw His pearls before swine or reveal His secrets to those who don't have His interests at heart. He wants us to want Him and He wants us to want to know His mysteries. That's why He gives us so many signs so that we will search them out. Our God is the revealer of mysteries.[1] Jesus told His followers that they had been given the keys of the kingdom. He also told them that they had been granted the knowledge of the mysteries of the kingdom that were hidden from the rest.[2] It was the Father's pleasure, He said, to hide things from the wise and intelligent and reveal them to babes.[3] This implies that not all believers have the mysteries revealed to them, but only those who humble themselves and line up with his will. This is clear from Jesus' teaching in Matthew 13. Many hear the message but can't comprehend because their heart is dull.

Mystery Stewards

This does not mean that God reveals everything to believers. Some things He still hides for another season. Timing matters as well. There are times when God reveals things and when He hides them. Daniel was shown many things that he did not understand because they were for the future – for our day. God is now revealing them to those who love Him and are fitting into His plan. But He is still hiding them from those who have their own agenda, be they believers or not. Paul said that the apostles were stewards of the mysteries of the kingdom. Indeed, all the Bible authors were stewards of these mysteries as they carefully wrote them down and passed them on. They opened up what was revealed to them and

---

[1] Dan 2:29
[2] Mt 13:11
[3] Mt 11:25

passed it on to us who live at the End-Time. Surely this compels us to seek it out. If God wants to reveal mysteries how can we not want to know them? We too must be good stewards of these things. But to be a steward of the mysteries does not mean that one keeps them hidden. On the contrary, we are to search them out and reveal them as the Father intends and keep them from being twisted or stolen by others. We are to unfold them to God's people as they are unfolded to us by the Holy Spirit. He promised to teach us all things and disclose to us what is to come.[4] Therefore, if we are good stewards and receiving from the Holy Spirit, we should be unraveling the mysteries concerning the end of the age.

The Lost Keys

All of the mysteries of the end of the age are contained in the Bible. It is the treasure map. The first century church had the keys to unlock these mysteries, but a century and a half later they were lost. Believers stumbled over the Gentile stumbling[5] stone and lost the keys. Consequently, they remained lost for nearly two thousand years.

Though much has been restored to the church, the End-Time scenario remains shrouded in confusion. Some things have come into focus, yet ignorance prevails. This is partly because of indifference and partly because of frustration. Those who have attempted to unveil the secrets of the End-Times without the lost keys have contributed to this. We commend them for their heart to unfold these truths to God's people, but without the keys, they have only created more mysteries. They only had pieces of the map. Besides this, many false treasure hunters have gone out to throw us off course. Yet, there are a multitude of signs and signals as to where the treasure is hidden. But one has to know how to interpret

---

[4] John 16:13

[5] The Jewish stumbling stone is Christ and His cross. The Gentile stumbling stone is Israel. Gentile believers became arrogant toward Israel and invented Replacement Theology which is how the keys were lost.

them. Some have concluded that there are no mysteries at all to be unfolded or treasures to find and that they disappeared long ago. Others say they are there but cannot be discovered until Christ comes. This they say is the wise and intelligent conclusion. But didn't the Lord say He would hide from the wise and intelligent and disclose to His trusting children what is to come? The Lord's promise is not yes and no – it is yes in Him. Of course it is! Therefore the mysteries regarding the End-Time are for the people of the End-Time to whom they were given. The treasure chambers of End-Time revelation are full of riches but they can only be opened by the lost keys. Where then are those keys? Surely they can clear up the myths and dispel the rumors? Surely they will open the granaries of wisdom and feed the starving souls for whom they were stored? Could it be that these keys are now available to the church? What if I told you they have been there all along but we did not have eyes to see? But now as our hearts are being healed and our worldview is lining up with His, they are in our hands again. "Oh come on," some of you are saying. "Is this for real?" I understand your skepticism. Trust me, I've been there. But if I'm right and the mystery vaults open up, what will you say? Either they are real or they are not. Either they will work or they will not. Come with me through the secret passageways and watch as we open the forgotten chambers. Let us believe the words of the Lord who promised that he who seeks will find and to him who knocks the door will be opened![6]

Seven Hidden Doors

There are seven hidden doors and seven lost keys. The doors were once visible but now they are hidden. Because the keys have been lost, the doors are lost also. They appear as impenetrable walls. Those who have no keys just walk in circles around and around. For them, the mystery may one day be resolved, or maybe never. Meanwhile, they are satisfied to have a promise that might come to

---

[6] Mt 7:7

pass. But those who have discovered keys have begun to open doors. Some have found the first key and have gotten inside the first chamber. But they are now stuck speculating about what might be inside the next door if it can be found, or if it's even there. Others have already gone through but have become stranded again, staring at the next impenetrable wall. They have decided that God alone can unlock the next chamber and take them into deeper revelation. But if God has already given the keys in His word, what are they waiting for? Why have they stopped searching? Why have they stopped asking and knocking? Since all indications are that time is very short, shouldn't they keep going? Don't they understand why the revelation is given? God didn't give warnings to be ignored, or revelation to stay locked away. He gave it to us for our instruction and preparation. He wants us to be ready. He wants us to be equipped. He wants us to know what is coming – the how, when and where. Jesus told us that He would speak plainly to us and that the Holy Spirit would disclose to us the mysteries of the coming days! If you agree, then we are ready to begin our journey.

Throughout this book, we will enter the seven hidden doors. Before each chapter, we will expose the hidden door and then unveil the key that opens it. Sometimes it will be one chapter, and other times it will take two. But once we have the key, we will use it to unlock the mysteries within. Then we will proceed to the next door. It is important to follow the sequence, since one chamber is inside the other. Finding the key will do you no good if you are not at the right door. It will take some time and it will require all of your attention. Remember, treasure hunting is not for the fainthearted. He who endures to the end will be delivered, and he who overcomes will reign with Him. So be ready to endure, and consider it a small price to pay for a Biblical understanding of the End-Time Mysteries!

The First Door

You might be surprised to discover that many Christians are unconvinced that we are at the end of the age. Many pastors will say that we may or may not be. Often they will say, "No one knows for sure" and go on to speak of future generations after us. They use Peter's words out of context[7] and say that there may be a hundred or even a thousand years left. This causes great confusion among God's people. It makes them think that all End-Time teaching is useless and there is no way to know if it's true. It is a great wall or stronghold built up in their minds that seems impenetrable. But there is proof that we are at the end of the age. There is even proof that this is the last generation. We are not talking about speculation, but proof. Take a hold of the First Key and open this door. Once you have seen inside, you will never go back to eschatological indifference!

The First Key

The Restoration spoken by the Prophets of Israel unveils the last generation.

The End-Time scenario begins with and is anchored in the prophets of Israel. Jesus and His apostles pointed us to the writings of the prophets for the background and framework of Eschatology.[8] All that they have spoken will continue to come to pass! When the restoration they spoke of starts, we are in the last generation. This is where our adventure begins! Are you ready?

---

[7] 2 Pet 3:8
[8] Study of last days!

Chapter Two
The Restoration of Israel – Proof of the End

"Therefore repent and return, so that your sins may be wiped away, in order that times of refreshing may come from the presence of the Lord; and that He may send Jesus, the Christ appointed for you, whom heaven must receive until the period of restoration of all things about which God spoke by the mouth of His holy prophets from ancient time."Acts 3:19-21

In the above passage, Peter said that Jesus the Messiah, who was appointed for the Jewish people, would remain in heaven <u>until</u> the restoration of Israel at the end of the age. This restoration was foretold by all the prophets including Moses! This is not the restoration of "all things" as many say, but the restoration of "all things about which God spoke by the mouth of His holy prophets." While it is true that God is restoring the church and will restore the heavens and the earth, this is not the focus of this verse. When we study the prophets, it is abundantly clear that the restoration they spoke of, was the restoration of the Jewish people to their ancient homeland after having been scattered throughout the earth. Thus, we can conclude that the emergence of the State of Israel in the twentieth century is the event that ushers in the last generation when Christ will come back! As we begin to illustrate this amazing fulfillment of prophecy, let us look at some verses that speak of the scattering and re-gathering of God's ancient covenant people. Please note these are but a sampling.

"I will lay waste your cities as well and will make your sanctuaries desolate, and I will not smell your soothing aromas. I will make the land desolate so that your enemies who settle in it will be appalled over it. You, however, I will scatter among the nations and will draw out a sword after you, as your

land becomes desolate and your cities become waste. Then the land will enjoy its Sabbaths all the days of the desolation, while you are in your enemies' land; then the land will rest and enjoy its Sabbaths." Lev 26:31-34

"So it shall be when all of these things have come upon you, the blessing and the curse which I have set before you, and you call them to mind in all nations where the LORD your God has banished you, and you return to the LORD your God and obey Him with all your heart and soul according to all that I command you today, you and your sons, then the LORD your God will restore you from captivity, and have compassion on you, and will gather you again from all the peoples where the LORD your God has scattered you. If your outcasts are at the ends of the earth, from there the LORD your God will gather you, and from there He will bring you back." Deut 30:1-4

"Then it will happen on that day that the Lord will again recover the second time with His hand the remnant of His people, who will remain, from Assyria, Egypt, Pathros, Cush, Elam, Shinar, Hamath, and from the islands of the sea. And He will lift up a standard for the nations and assemble the banished ones of Israel, and will gather the dispersed of Judah from the four corners of the earth." Is 11:11-12

These promises concerning the scattering of Israel, and her re-gathering at the end of the age, are repeated throughout the prophets and are re-iterated by Christ Himself in Luke 21. As He exited the Temple for the last time during Passion Week, the Lord confirmed that Jerusalem would be destroyed and the Jewish people scattered to the nations. Then He added that the Holy City would be trampled underfoot by Gentile rulers until their time of dominance would end.

"…because these are days of vengeance, so that all things which are written will be fulfilled……for there will be great distress upon the land and wrath to this people; and they will fall by the edge of the sword, and will be led captive into all the nations; and Jerusalem will be trampled underfoot by the Gentiles until the times of the Gentiles are fulfilled." Luke 21:22-24

This destruction of Jerusalem foretold by Christ took place in 70AD when the Roman legions burned the city and scattered the Jews throughout the earth. From that time on the city was dominated by Gentile Empires from the Romans to the British. But in 1967 the Old City and the Temple Mount were captured by the new nation of Israel and came back under Jewish control. This is the most amazing fulfillment of prophecy bringing to an end the Times of the Gentiles as predicted by Jesus and beginning the generation that would see all the End-Time events take place (Luke 21:28,32 – "begin to take place"). Thus, the Times of the Gentiles ended in 1967 and the last generation began.

Captivity of Israel – Prophecy of Ezekiel
In Ezekiel Chapter 4, the prophet is given a time frame concerning God's punishment of Israel for their sins and their restoration at the end of the age. Careful examination of this prophecy reveals that the time of Israel's restoration was predicted.

"As for you, lie down on your left side and lay the iniquity of the house of Israel on it; you shall bear their iniquity for the number of days that you lie on it. For I have assigned you a number of days corresponding to the years of their iniquity, three hundred and ninety days; thus you shall bear the iniquity of the house of Israel. When you have completed these, you shall lie down a second time, but on your right side and bear the iniquity of the house of Judah; I have assigned it to you for forty days, a day for each year." Ezek 4:4-6 NASU

The Lord told Ezekiel that 430 years had ben decreed for the punishment of Israel and Judah at the end of which they would be restored. From that number we must subtract the 70 years of the Babylonian exile which was the beginning of this punishment. This leaves us with 360 years remaining.

In 606BC, Nebuchadnezzar came up against Judah and captured it. He took Jehoiachin the king captive along with many of the Jewish nobility. Ezekiel himself was in this number, along with Daniel and his friends. Then Nebuchadnezzar appointed Zedekiah (Jehoiachin's uncle) as king and went back to Babylon. However, Zedekiah rebelled against the king of Babylon and the word of the Lord through Jeremiah and Babylon came against him. In 586BC, Jerusalem and Solomon's Temple were destroyed and Zedekiah and the rest of the nation were taken captive. Only a tiny remnant of very poor Jews was left. Then seventy years later in 536BC, in fulfillment of the words of Jeremiah, the first exiles returned under Ezra the priest. Thus the exile in Babylon was from 606BC to 586BC – 70 years.

~~~~~

Jewish Exile - 606 BC - 536 BC = **70 years**
Temple Destroyed - 586 BC
Temple Rebuilding Finished - 516 BC
586 BC - 516 BC = **70 years**

~~~~~

Another interesting aspect of the exile in Babylon is the 20 year lag between the return of the people and the restoration of the Temple which was completed in 516BC. The exiles returned after 70 years and the Temple was rebuilt after 70 years – 586-516BC. This same 20 year lag between the people and the Holy Place occurs again after the beginning of the State - 1947/48 to 1967.

Israel and Judah

Some will argue that the northern kingdom of Israel was separated from Judah since they were exiled by Assyria many years before the Babylonian exile. However, what is not taken into account is that many from the northern tribes had already migrated south into Judah and Benjamin long before the Babylonian exile and thus were represented in Judah. For instance, Anna the prophetess, who appears in the gospels,[9] was from the tribe of Asher, and Paul was from the tribe of Benjamin.[10] Thus all Israel was represented in Babylon and after the exile all were called Jews.

2520 Years of Punishment

Now that we understand Israel was punished for seventy years in Babylon let us go back to the prophecy of Ezekiel. According to the prophecy, four hundred and thirty years of punishment are decreed. When we subtract seventy years from that, we conclude that after the exile three hundred and sixty years of punishment remain. Adding this number to the end of the exile in 536BC brings us to 176BC.

~~~~~

430-70 = 360 years remaining
(Subtract the 70 years of exile as part of the punishment)
Return was in 536 BC
-536 BC + 360 = 176BC

~~~~~

Thus, according to the prophecy, Israel's punishment should have been over in 176BC. However, at that time they were about to enter one of their most difficult periods of persecution under Antiochus Epiphanes. What then are we to do with the prophecy? The answer to this mystery seems to come from Moses himself.

"Yet if in spite of this, you do not obey Me, but act with hostility against Me, then I will act with wrathful hostility against you; and I, even I, will punish you seven times for your sins ......I will lay waste your cities as well, and will make your sanctuaries desolate; and I will not smell your soothing aromas. And I will make the land desolate so that your enemies who settle in it shall be appalled over it. You, however, I will scatter among the nations and will draw out a sword after you, as your land becomes desolate and your cities become waste." Lev 26:27-33

---

[9] Luke 2:36
[10] Rom 11:1

The people did not come back from Babylon in full repentance. In fact, only a small remnant returned and they had to be admonished by the prophets Zechariah, Haggai and Malachi to complete the work on the Temple. Thus, we can conclude that the remnant was lukewarm and had to be punished seven times more for their sins. When we multiply 360 years by 7, we get 2520yrs. These 2520 years for the punishment of Israel must be converted from biblical prophetic years[11] to our calendar years. When we add this to 536BC, we arrive at 1948. The punishment of Israel ended with her re-gathering from all the nations to her ancient homeland in 1948.

~~~~~

The Captivity of Israel
390 days for Israel - 40 days for Judah - 1 day = 1 year
390 years + 40 years = 430 years
430-70=360
360 x 7 = 2520 years
2,520 x 360 (days) = 907,200 days
907,200 days / 365.25 = 2483.8
-536 B.C. + 2483.8 = **1948**

Captivity of Jerusalem (Holy Place)
-516 B.C. (Temple Restored) + 2483.8 = **1967**

~~~~~

A Parallel Restoration of Israel and the Church

In 66AD, the Roman legions entered Israel and began what has come to be known as the War of The Jews. They began in the Galilee and worked their way to Masada. They massacred the people and took many as prisoners who were sold into slavery and scattered to the nations. In 68AD they laid siege to Jerusalem and two years later the city fell and was destroyed. Many Jews fled to Masada and held out there until 72AD when Masada fell and all its inhabitants were

---

[11] The Biblical prophetic year has 360 days as per the ancient Jewish calendar and the Genesis account – Gen 7:1,24 & Gen 8:4 – 5 months = 150 days

found to have committed suicide. This began the long exile of Israel throughout the nations until their return in 1948.

When Israel went into exile, this also began the decline of Jewish influence in the early church. In addition, when the false Messiah Shimon Bar Kokhba was defeated in 135AD, the decline was all but complete. Thus the church became almost exclusively Gentile, and within a short while, Anti-Semitic as well. Subsequent generations of church leaders would concoct the heretic doctrine of Replacement Theology, which reinterpreted all of the prophecies spoken to Israel as now applying to the church – the positive ones, of course. However, from our perspective as believers today, we can trace the decline of the church to this period and this teaching. Indeed, what we understand now is that not only did Israel go into exile, but the church did as well. Israel was exiled for her rejection of the prophets and the Messiah. The church was exiled for her rejection of Israel! However, just as God has been restoring Israel, he has also been restoring the church. In fact, it appears that there is a parallel restoration taking place.

The Reformation

The Reformation was an incredible event, which turned the church and the world around! People began to read the Bible again and to discover truth! The subsequent revivals of the seventeenth, eighteenth, and nineteenth centuries brought the church back to Christ and the world prospered as a result! The revivals in England and the New World facilitated the return of the Jews to their land! Then while Theodore Herzl was crisscrossing the world looking for a home for the Jews, God began to pour out His Spirit on the church, culminating in the Pentecostal revival in Azusa St, Los Angeles, California. In addition, as Christians were discovering the gift of tongues once again, God was restoring the Hebrew language to the Jews. In 1967, while Israel was being reunited with its ancient capital, the Holy Spirit was falling afresh on the church in what came to be known as the Charismatic Renewal. The Messianic Jewish Movement was also born at this time!

The Jewish State

In 1897, a Jew named Theodore Herzl was moved to write the book "The Jewish State." Later that year, in response to Anti-Semitism, he founded the World Zionist Congress in Basel, Switzerland. This conference marked the official beginning of the regathering of Israel, which took place exactly seventy years later. At the same time, in England, godly believers had found their way into the government of that land, and began to work for the creation of the Jewish State. Their efforts resulted in the Balfour Declaration of 1917.

After the formation of the World Zionist Congress, Herzl made many attempts to forge a deal with the Ottoman Turks to allow the Jewish people a homeland. He made five trips to the Sultan, yet his efforts failed. World War I began shortly thereafter, which resulted in the defeat of the Ottoman Turks and their removal from Palestine by the British.

Fishermen and Hunters

"Therefore behold, days are coming," declares the LORD, "when it will no longer be said, "As the LORD lives, who brought up the sons of Israel out of the land of Egypt,' but, "As the LORD lives, who brought up the sons of Israel from the land of the north and from all the countries where He had banished them. For I will restore them to their own land which I gave to their fathers. Behold, I am going to send for many fishermen," declares the LORD, "and they will fish for them; and afterwards I will send for many hunters, and they will hunt them from every mountain and every hill and from the clefts of the rocks." Jer 16:14-16

This prophecy of Jeremiah said that God would first send many fishermen who would fish for the Jewish people to bring them back to the land. However, after that, He said He would send many hunters who would hunt them from every mountain and every hill and from the clefts of the rocks, and drive them back to the land of Israel. In the years after the founding of the Zionist movement, the "fishermen," such as Herzl and many others, pleaded with the Jews of Europe to take up the cause and return to Palestine and begin building there. However, only a small number heeded the call and were successful in their efforts in the land. Then came World War II and the Nazis. These were the "hunters" of the prophecy who hunted the Jews out of Europe, forcing them to go to Palestine, since there was nowhere else for them after the war.

Though we know there were other causes for World War I and II, both of these worldwide conflicts were allowed by God to bring the Jews home. Indeed that was their primary purpose!

~~~~~

World War I - Defeat of the Ottoman Turks
British got control of "Palestine."
God raised up the British to open the way for the Jews to come home.

World War II - The Hunters – driving them home.
It took the horrific events of the Holocaust to uproot the Jews of Europe! Thus, two world wars were fought to bring the Jewish people back to their land fulfilling the promise of God!

~~~~~

Two Stage Restoration

God promised to restore Israel in two stages. In Stage 1, He promised to bring the people back to the Land - period! Their spiritual state was of no consequence! In Stage 2, He promised to bring the people back to Himself and fill them with the Holy Spirit.

*(**Stage 1**) "For I will take you out of the nations; I will gather you from all the countries and bring you back into your own land (Stage 1). I will sprinkle*

*clean water on you, and you will be clean; I will cleanse you from all your impurities and from all your idols. (**Stage 2**) I will give you a new heart and put a new spirit in you; I will remove from you your heart of stone and give you a heart of flesh. And I will put my Spirit in you and move you to follow my decrees and be careful to keep my laws. You will live in the land I gave your forefathers; you will be my people, and I will be your God." Ezek 36:24-28 NIV*

Since the people and the city had to be re-united for the physical return to be complete, Stage1 ended in 1967. Stage 2 also got underway then. Consequently, we are now more than half-way through Stage 2.

~~~~~
Beginning of the Physical Restoration **1897**
Completed 70 years later - the Capture of Jerusalem **1967**
~~~~~

The Last Generation

In Luke 21, while answering the question of His disciples regarding the stones, Jesus said that Jerusalem would be trampled underfoot by the Gentiles until the times of the Gentiles were fulfilled.[12] The "until" implies that once the city was back under Jewish control the Times of the Gentiles (trampling it) had ended. He then said that the generation to see this would see all of the prophetic events, including the return of Christ, in their lifetime!

"But when these things <u>begin</u> to take place, straighten up and lift up your heads, because your redemption is drawing near." Luke 21:28

Jesus said that the generation to see the End-Time scenario begin will see all of the End-Time events including His return. The "until" in Luke 21:24 takes us from 70AD to 1967. Thus the last generation

---

[12] This is not to be confused with the Fullness of the Gentiles referred to in Rom 11. The Times of the Gentiles refers only to the trampling of Jerusalem by Gentile powers.

began in 1967. Then Jesus emphatically stated that this specific generation would be the last.

"Truly I say to you, this (specific) generation will not pass away until all things take place." Luke 21:32

Of course, this does not mean that all the Jews have come back. They will continue to come back until Messiah comes and at that time they will all be gathered again. It is the same as it was in the re-gathering from the Babylonian exile. At that time, when the remnant had come back to Jerusalem, then the nation had come back. The same is true today. When the Jewish state took possession of Jerusalem, the Jews had officially come back from the nations. That is the completion of the first stage. The second stage is their returning to God and to the Messiah, being sprinkled with water and filled with the Holy Spirit. Now, if this first stage ended officially in 1967, then it is reasonable to conclude that the second stage began then. This means that, since 1967, God has been at work bringing the nation of Israel back to Himself and preparing them for Jesus' return.

Now if the official re-gathering ended in 1967, then we might well ask, "When did it begin?" If we know when the first stage officially began and officially ended, then it is reasonable to conclude that the second phase will be of similar length. However, do we know when the official beginning of the re-gathering took place? I believe so. Most would agree that it started with the foundation of Zionism and the World Zionist Conference, which began in Switzerland in the year 1897. From 1897 to 1967 is exactly seventy years. Therefore, if the first phase took seventy years is it unreasonable to assume that the second phase will also take seventy years? The people born in the late 1890s saw the re-gathering of Israel, and the generation born in the late 1960s will not pass away until the restoration is complete.

Does this mean that I have just predicted the year Jesus will come back? Perhaps! Yet I did not give the day or the hour. The end may come sooner, but it certainly will not take longer than seventy years from 1967, which brings us to 2037. Although you may not yet realize it, we are in the second phase of the restoration spoken of by all the prophets and re-emphasized by Peter as the time of Messiah's return.[13]

How long is a Generation?

There has been much speculation about this. Some have thought it to be forty years, since Israel wandered in the wilderness for forty years. However, this does not imply that a generation is forty years. The people wandered forty years because God did not want any of that older generation that came out of Egypt to enter the land. Thus, that generation was more than forty years old since it is the adults who are being spoken about. Besides, nowhere in human history has a generation been forty years. When we examine Jesus words spoken to the first century Jews the answer to this question seems clear.

"Because of this, God in his wisdom said, 'I will send them prophets and apostles, some of whom they will kill and others they will persecute." Therefore, this generation will be held responsible for the blood of all the prophets that has been shed since the beginning of the world, from the blood of Abel to the blood of Zechariah, who was killed between the altar and the sanctuary. Yes, I tell you, this generation will be held responsible for it all. Luke 11:49-51 NIV

Jesus told that generation (His generation), that all the destruction spoken by the prophets would come upon them. That specific generation would suffer cruelly like no other, because of the blood of the prophets that had been shed by previous generations and because they rejected Him. There can be no dispute about this

---

[13] Acts 3:19-21

meaning. It was all to come on that generation which He was part of. At that time, Jesus was approximately thirty three years old. The fulfillment of the word took place forty years later, in 70 A.D. Therefore, I believe a generation, biblically and prophetically speaking, is seventy years. The Bible is very specific about times, dates, and numbers. Every number has a meaning. Had Jesus not died on the cross, He would have been seventy three in the year 70 A.D. Therefore, His generation would have been in their sixties and seventies, perhaps even eighties. This does not make a generation approximate, but seventy years is the biblical number and people live to different ages. This is substantiated by the following verse from Psalm 90:

"The length of our days is seventy years-- or eighty, if we have the strength."
Ps 90:10

The Number for Jerusalem
Seventy is the number related to Israel and Jerusalem. Seventy persons went into captivity in Egypt. The mourning for Jacob was seventy days (Gen 50:3). When the people went into exile in Babylon it was for seventy years. The angel told Daniel that seventy periods of seven years had been decreed for the people and the city. The city was destroyed in 70 AD, which was a biblical generation after the birth of Messiah.

Parallel Restoration

1890's – 1905
Pentecostal Movement

1947-1948
Healing Revival
Latter Rain Movement

1967
Jesus People
Charismatic Movement

1897
World Zionist Congress

1948
Restoration of Israel

1967
Jerusalem under Jewish
Control
Times of the Gentiles Ended

The Second Door

The second door has to do with two prophecies spoken about Israel and the land and the Holy Place.[14] Both are pivotal in the End-Time scenario. The first has to do with Daniel's visions of four world empires that would overrun Israel. The fourth empire was to disappear and come back to life at the end of the age and again overrun Israel. Since the fourth empire was Rome, and there have been many empires since then that overran the Holy Land, where do they fit in? Did we get the fourth one wrong? How do we know which ones to leave in or take out? Some are now suggesting that the Ottoman Empire was the fourth empire. But if this is so, what about all the others? For most of the church today this continues to be a mystery that fuels speculation. Without the key it is just guesswork!

The second prophecy has to do with something called the Seventieth Week or Last Shemitah Cycle (more on this later). Daniel prophesied that Israel would have seventy periods of seven years (490 years) to finish the age. Then he revealed that sixty nine of these periods (483 years) were completed when Jesus was rejected by the Jewish nation. This left one seven year period remaining which contains the End-Time scenario. The mystery has to do with all the years in between. When does this seven year period begin and how are we to know?

The Second Key

Prophecies concerning Israel and the Land or the Holy Place are suspended when either are separated. In other

---

[14] The Holy Place is the site in Jerusalem where the Temple was and where the Holy of Holies was. It is known today as the Temple Mount.

words, when the people were exiled, the prophecy was suspended until they came back. Likewise, the second prophecy (covered in Chapter 4) is suspended until they consecrate the Holy Place. Did you get that? We have one key, but two prophecies or doors. Don't be concerned; just take the key in your hand and it will all become clearer as we go!

Chapter Three
The Prophet Daniel & World History

Through a series of visions and angelic visitations, the prophet Daniel received the future history of the Gentile nations as it relates to Israel. It is very important to understand however, that when Israel is not in the land, the Gentile history is not pertinent to them and is ignored by the prophecies. This is a most important point. Failure to see this has resulted in mass confusion in Eschatological teaching.

The revelations that Daniel received in Chapters 2, 7, and 8, are different details on the same events. They must be put together to be understood. The dream of Nebuchadnezzar, which is covered in Chapter 2, summarizes the future of the four Gentile empires which will directly control Israel. They are explained again in Chapter 7 with more detail. Then Chapter 8 focuses in on two of them, namely Media Persia and Greece. The future wicked king Antiochus Epiphanes comes out of Greece. He is a type of the End-Time Antichrist. The chart on page 291 illustrates this (chart 1), and the passages in Revelation 13, 17, and 18, which correspond, are shown as well.

~~~~~

Daniel 2 – The Statue

Head of Gold - *Babylon* (also the name of statue)
Breast & Arms of Silver - *Media-Persia*
Belly & Thighs of Bronze - *Greece* (Alexander the Great- Kingdom given to 4 Generals – Two prominent - *Selucid & Ptolemies)*
Legs of Iron - *Roman Empire* - West & East
Revived Roman Empire - Alliance (Iron & Clay)

~~~~~

The Roman Empire destroyed Jerusalem and scattered Israel in 70 AD. The subsequent empires that conquered the land are irrelevant to the prophecy because the people were not there! But when Israel was reborn as a nation in her ancient homeland, the Roman Empire, or the fourth beast, began to come back to life.

~~~~~

Key Points in End-Time Prophecy
As far as the Bible is concerned:
a. The Gentile nations are always dealt with on the basis of their relationship with Israel!
b. Israel is the center of the world!
c. The "Great Sea" is always the Mediterranean
d. Most Bible prophecy applies when the Jewish people are in the land of Israel! When the people are out of the land, Gentile history is excluded from prophecy!

~~~~~

The European Union
In Nebuchadnezzar's dream of a statue the feet of iron and clay come together in the end as Ten Toes to fulfill the purpose of the Beast. The European Union, which began with the WEU and the Treaty of Brussels in 1948, is this final Empire, which is the embodiment of all the others.[15] In addition, the stone cut out of the mountain without hands is the Messianic Kingdom, which strikes the statue on the toes, shattering it. Then the kingdom of Christ fills the whole earth!

"The Brussels Treaty was signed on 17 March 1948 by Belgium, France, Luxembourg, the Netherlands, and the United Kingdom. The Brussels Treaty Organization, as it was then called, provided for collective self-defense and economic, social and cultural collaboration between its signatories. On 23 October 1954, the

---

[15] Rev 13:1-2

Brussels Treaty was modified to include the Federal Republic of Germany and Italy, thus creating the Western European Union. In November 1988, a Protocol of Accession was signed by the WEU Member States with Portugal and Spain. The ratification process was completed in March 1990. Greece followed a similar process in 1992 and 1995 thus bringing the total WEU membership to 10." (See chart 2 on page 291)

In June 2000 the WEU created the post of High Representative and Common Foreign Security Policy Chief, giving him or her a 5 year term. This person filling this office is the representative of the EU and eager to broker a treaty with Israel. Though the WEU has disbanded or submerged, it is easy for these ten nations to re-emerge for a purpose, such as brokering a treaty with Israel. One or more of these nations could drop out, but others can take their place. Since this has already happened once, it is not difficult for it to happen again.

The Four Beasts (Empires - Kings) - Daniel Chapter 7
In Daniel Chapter 7, the prophet has another alarming vision. Yet, it is essentially the same as the statue of Nebuchadnezzar only with more detail. The vision presents the same four kingdoms that will arise on the earth and persecute the Holy People (the Jews). Again, as in the first vision, the Roman Empire and the Empire of Antichrist at the end of the age are pictured as one.

"I was looking in my vision by night, and behold, the four winds of heaven were stirring up the great sea (Mediterranean). And four great Beasts were coming up from the sea, different from one another." Daniel 7:2-3

The Beast of the Revelation is the same as that of Daniel. That is why John gives so little explanation. Students of Scripture were expected to know these things. The book of Daniel was and is the "Revelation" of the "Old Testament" (Mt 24:15).

"And he stood on the sand of the seashore. And I saw a Beast coming up out of the sea, having ten horns and seven heads, and on his horns were ten diadems, and on his heads were blasphemous names." Rev 13:1

"Thus he said: 'The fourth Beast will be a fourth kingdom on the earth, which will be different from all the other kingdoms and will devour the whole earth and tread it down and crush it. <u>As for the ten horns, out of this kingdom ten kings will arise; and another will arise after them, and he will be different from the previous ones</u> <u>and will subdue three kings.</u> He will speak out against the Most High and wear down the saints of the Highest One, and he will intend to make alterations in times and in law; and they will be given into his hand for a time, times, and half a time." Dan 7:23-25

~~~~~

Four Great Beasts - 4 Kings or Kingdoms that will arise
from the earth (Vs 17)
Lion - Wings of an Eagle - Babylon (Nebuchadnezzar)
Bear - Raised up on one side - *Media / Persia*
Leopard - 4 Wings - 4 Heads - *Greece*
(The Kingdom Divided into 4)
Different than all others - it's a conglomeration of all 4 - (Vs 12) – Roman Empire & *Revived Roman Empire - Ten Horns*

~~~~~

"And the ten horns which you saw are ten kings, who have not yet received a kingdom, but they receive authority as kings with the Beast for one hour. These have one purpose and they give their power and authority to the Beast. These will wage war against the Lamb, and the Lamb will overcome them, because He is Lord of lords and King of kings, and those who are with Him are the called and chosen and faithful." Rev 17:12-14

Little Horn

In Daniel Chapter 7, verse 8, a Little Horn rises up and subdues three of the 10 kings. At this time, we can only speculate as to who and what these three kingdoms are that are subdued by the

Antichrist. Perhaps they are the Benelux Union countries of Belgium, the Netherlands, and Luxembourg. These countries between them share the European Union headquarters and government as well as the home of the UN's International Court of Justice. Also, since Switzerland is the only European country not a member of the EU, and the capital of the banking system, perhaps the Antichrist will operate from Switzerland and take over the Benelux countries which would also be part of his capital.

The 'Mid-East Beast' Myth

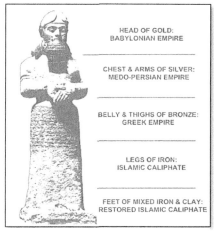

For more than a century, and especially since 1948, the majority of premillennial[16] scholars have understood that the last empire spoken of in Daniel Chapters 2 and 7 was the Revived Roman Empire. This was not dreamed up because they were located in the West, or because they had a Western mindset, as is suggested by the proponents of this new "Mid-East Beast" theory. On the contrary it is solidly based on the visions given to

Chart from "Mid-East Beast" by Joel Richardson

Daniel and their fulfillment in history. Why then would such "scholars" be willing to take us back to a Middle Ages understanding? Actually the answer is quite simple and it is one I have been preaching for the last twenty years. They fail to understand that the prophecies of Daniel have to do with Israel and not just the land. These prophecies predict the occupation and domination of Israel by Gentile empires. Once Israel was removed from the land by God through the Roman Empire in 70AD, the prophecies were no longer in operation until they were united as a nation with the land in 1947/48. This is a most essential

---

[16] Those who believe Christ is coming and will reign for 1000 years.

understanding and it is true for all Biblical prophecy regarding the end of the age. Without Israel in the land, the prophecy does not apply - period. This is also the primary proof we are at the end of the age, and the prophecies are once again being fulfilled, because Israel is back in her ancient homeland.

Daniel's interpretation of Nebuchadnezzar's dream (Dan 2:36-45) makes it clear that the statue represents four consecutive kingdoms beginning with Babylon. These four kingdoms would govern the Middle-East, and more importantly, Israel. Then there is a fifth kingdom that comes out of the fourth, represented by the feet and toes, but it is different than any kingdom that has gone before. It is a revival of the fourth but with very different characteristics, since it is an alliance of nations and peoples who come together for a purpose but do not adhere – like iron and clay.

In Daniel Chapter 7, the prophet is given another picture of these kingdoms as four great beasts. The first three are identified by name as Babylon, Media-Persia, and Greece. The last one is not identified since it is so different, and the prophet was unable to compare it to anything. This last beast takes up where Greece left off and ends out the age as the Antichrist kingdom with ten horns. It is very clear from history, and even the New Testament, that Rome conquered Greece, dominated Israel, crucified the Messiah, destroyed the Temple, and banished the nation to exile in 70AD. This destruction under Rome was prophesied throughout Israel's history. To suggest that this empire was not the fourth beast, because it came from the West rather than the East, is truly absurd. But even worse is the claim that the fourth beast was an Islamic Caliphate, which came on the scene nearly six hundred years later, when Israel no longer occupied the land. To ignore the Roman Empire, which conquered Greece and terrorized Israel more than any other, fulfilling a host of biblical prophecies, is not only absurd, it is irrational. It is hard to imagine how any biblical scholar can take this seriously. Yet many of them do because they have not been able to understand the role of the Middle-East empires that have come and gone after Rome. Now someone comes along and gives them an alternative that seems to fit the current situation and they are all ears. Since they have not been able to understand the mystery of the toes, they are ready to abandon Rome as the fourth kingdom and jump ahead to an Islamic Caliphate that began in the seventh century. However, besides the glaring omission of the Roman Empire in this scenario, and even if we assume that all the various Islamic Caliphates throughout history were one entity, what do we do with the Crusader Kingdom and the British Empire?

There are many other problems with the Antichrist kingdom being an Eastern Islamic Caliphate, such as the fact that it is an alliance (Dan 2:41-43, Rev 17:12-13), and the Book of Daniel clearly connects the Antichrist with the Roman Empire (Dan 9:26, Rev 17:9-13, 18). Yet, the foundation of this theory is the notion that Rome was not the fourth kingdom. On this it stands or falls to the ground. There can be no doubt that Rome is the fourth beast, a revival of which began the same year Israel became a nation once again in her own land – 1948. The emergence of the EU and its development into the United States of Europe, with a goal to swallow up Israel and bringing peace to the Middle-East, is the obvious fulfillment of these prophecies. It came out of the Roman Empire and encompasses the same territory. It is not committed to the destruction of Israel as the Islamists, but desires to swallow it up with a treaty and EU membership. This is now put on hold until the situation changes on the ground, and on the Temple Mount in Jerusalem, and Israel is willing to consecrate the Holy Place. Then they will all be back in the peace mood. After much pain and sorrow, the Final Status Agreement or Peace Treaty will be signed and Israel will likely become part of the EU completing the beast's seventh head. This will be the time of peace and security which comes to an abrupt end beginning the Tribulation period (1 Thess 5:2-3).

The other scenario, being presented by the Islamic Caliphate Theory, requires Israel and the whole Middle-East, including much of Europe, to be dominated by a brutal Islamic regime the likes of ISIS. However, what would this mean for Israel? And what would happen to Christians? You see, not only have they modified biblical history to exclude Rome as an important player, they have also written off the future time of peace and security taught by Daniel and Paul (Dan 9:27, 1Thess 5:2-3).Yes the Antichrist is a man of war, but before he is revealed as the Antichrist he is a man of peace who will amaze the whole world, and sadly even many in the church.

It seems to me that those who accept this Islamic Caliphate theory have written off the West as a major player in the days to come. They see Islam on the rise and ready to take over the world. However, while it is true that Islam has its sights set on world conquest, it would be very foolish to rule out the Western nations that God used to scatter Israel and bring them back again. Islam may be on the warpath against the West but it is a house seriously divided. How many Caliphates are there? How many barbaric factions? How many Jihadists warring against each other? Indeed, about the only thing they agree on is the destruction of Israel. And my friends, that is not going to happen now or ever. Make no mistake about it, no Islamic Caliphate will take over Israel or usher in Daniel's Seventieth Week or the Tribulation Period. This will be a smooth, slick politician who is given authority by the EU to carry out his mission of "Peace and Security."

Corresponding Prophecies of Revelation 13, 17 & 18
There are two beasts that emerge in Revelation Chapter 13. The first is the political system which is the Revived Roman Empire under Antichrist. Then there is a second beast called the False Prophet which represents a religious system that is pictured in Revelation Chapter 17 as a harlot riding the beast.

"And he carried me away in the Spirit into a wilderness; and I saw a woman sitting on a scarlet beast, full of blasphemous names, having seven heads and ten horns. And the woman was clothed in purple and scarlet, and adorned with gold and precious stones and pearls, having in her hand a gold cup full of abominations and of the unclean things of her immorality, and upon her forehead a name was written, a mystery, "BABYLON THE GREAT, THE MOTHER OF HARLOTS AND OF THE ABOMINATIONS OF THE EARTH." And I saw the woman drunk with the blood of the saints, and with the blood of the witnesses of Jesus. And when I saw her, I wondered greatly." Rev 17:3-6 (See chart 12 on page 296)

The apostle John wondered greatly when he saw this woman. But the angel admonished him saying, "Why do you wonder?" It's as though he expected John to know who she was.

The woman is a harlot and yet she represents Babylon where false religion began. The term "harlot" is used biblically to refer to spiritual apostasy and adultery. It is used that way throughout Scripture as the term "virgin" is used of spiritual purity. Thus this woman represents a backslidden religious system - a world religious system full of abominations as it rides atop the political system that gives it prominence. However, we are given more information about the woman and the beast that carries her.

"Here is the mind which has wisdom. The seven heads are seven mountains on which the woman sits, and they are seven kings; five have fallen, one is, the other has not yet come; and when he comes, he must remain a little while. And the beast which was and is not, is himself also an eighth, and is one of the seven, and he goes to destruction. And the ten horns which you saw are ten kings, who have not yet received a kingdom, but they receive authority as kings with the beast for one hour. These have one purpose and they give their power and authority to the beast. These will wage war against the Lamb, and the Lamb will overcome them, because He is Lord of lords and King of kings, and those who are with Him are the called and chosen and faithful. And he said to me, 'The waters which you saw where

the harlot sits, are peoples and multitudes and nations and tongues. And the ten horns which you saw, and the beast, these will hate the harlot and will make her desolate and naked, and will eat her flesh and will burn her up with fire. For God has put it in their hearts to execute His purpose by having a common purpose, and by giving their kingdom to the beast, until the words of God should be fulfilled. And the woman whom you saw is the great city, which reigns over the kings of the earth.'" Rev 17:9-18

We are told that the woman sits on seven hills. This of course is the city of Rome since it was built on seven hills and verse 18 is emphatic that the woman is the "great city which reigns over the kings of the earth." This can only be Rome at the time the book of Revelation was written. Therefore, there is no escaping the fact that the Vatican, a Roman city state in the heart of the EU at the end of the age, will lead the harlot religious system.

The Seven Heads
"Five have fallen, one is, and the other has not yet come. When he comes he must remain a little while (short time). The Beast which was and is not is himself also an eight and is one of the seven and goes to destruction."

We understand from our studies in Daniel that the ten horns are ten kingdoms or nations that empower the individual who represents them with a specific purpose for a short time. But now we understand that this beast has seven heads. The woman sits on seven hills but she rides a beast (political system) with seven heads. If we try to understand the seven heads as kings or Roman Emperors that existed, it does not fit since there were many Emperors after this time. However if we understand that kings may also mean kingdoms, as it does in Daniel 7, the meaning becomes clear. Thus, we conclude that the seven kings of Revelation 17 are seven kingdoms which have and will include Israel. One thing they all have in common is their control of Israel – the land and the people. These are Egypt, Assyria, Babylon, Media/Persia, Greece, Rome and Antichrist's Kingdom (EU). At the time of John, five have come and gone (fallen from power). These are Egypt, Assyria, Babylon, Media/Persia and Greece. One is left - Rome. One is yet to come which remains a little while (EU with Israel - very short – 3 ½ years) and then the eighth which is one of the seven (Antichrist's Kingdom).

The Seventh Head Forming

The seventh head is clearly the EU which is the embodiment of the Revived Roman Empire. However, until the EU incorporates Israel it is not the completed seventh head. The European Neighborhood Policy[17] is the beginning of the process of bringing Israel into the EU with a treaty. Since all of the nations are being aligned in regional unions, Israel will also become part of this alignment and its only option is the EU. Thus the covenant or treaty signed by Israel and the leader of the EU, together with the neighboring countries, will not only be a peace treaty but will also be an alignment of Israel with the EU. This will be the fulfillment of Daniel 9:27. Then the seventh head or kingdom will be complete and it will remain for a *"little while"* (Rev 17:10). When this EU/world leader breaks the covenant three and a half years later he is revealed as the Antichrist (man of lawlessness – 2Thess 2:8) and he will take control of the world and usher in the eight kingdom which is really the seventh that has radically changed its dominion and character (Rev 17:11). (See chart 3 on page 292)

More on the Harlot

It is intriguing that the Vatican continues to be a state in Rome. It continues to dominate Rome. The office of the Roman Catholic Pontiff seems tailored to lead a false religious system that will be aligned with the Beast. It will include all the "mainline" churches and false religions. It will also include the Emerging Church and many Evangelicals and Charismatics. The agenda of saving the planet and Western culture coupled with the Universalist remake of God

---

[17] http://ec.europa.eu/world/enp/index_en.htm

will lure them in. Also, dividing the land of Israel to bring world peace will be a high priority. All those who hold to the truth of Scripture will be hated by all.

Towards the end of the Tribulation, the Antichrist and his ten supporting nations will burn the city of Rome and will attack the religious system headquartered there. The False Prophet will have also abandoned the city by then, since he remains by the Antichrist's side (Rev 17:16-18). This destruction of Rome will likely be the result of a nuclear bomb. This seems obvious from the description in Revelation 18:15-17. Also, consider the vast wealth of the Vatican and understand why the merchants are crying (Rev 18:9). This destruction comes from the hand of God, and it is for all the atrocities committed by the city under the Roman Empire and the Roman Church. Both are guilty of the blood of the saints – Jews and Christians (Rev 17:6). Consider the brutality of the Romans against the Jews and realize that it has not been punished. Also, consider the plans that were hatched in Rome and have a look at the Arch of Titus which mocks the Jews and the Holy Temple. What about the Coliseum itself and the brutality of Rome against Christians? Then add to that all of the Christians who were murdered and tortured by the Catholic Church, throughout the centuries, and one can understand why Rome has a special judgment.

"And in her was found the blood of prophets and of saints and of all who have been slain on the earth." Rev 18:24

Babylon the Great

The name "Babylon the Great" is a mystery according to John because it does not actually refer to Babylon the ancient city, but the city of Rome, the Harlot, and the World Religious System. It also represents the kingdom of Antichrist, which is the embodiment of all the others that have gone before. Indeed, when we consider the statue of Nebuchadnezzar in Daniel 2, we understand that the stone cut out of the mountains (Messiah's kingdom) struck the statue on the feet (Antichrist's kingdom) and destroyed it. Thus, Antichrist's kingdom represents the whole statue of empires that persecuted God's people, and since the head is Babylon, it could be referred to as Babylon. This is borne out by the following verse corresponding to Isaiah 47:7 which refers to Babylon.

"...for she says in her heart, 'I SIT as A QUEEN AND I AM NOT A WIDOW, and will never see mourning.'" Rev 18:7

Now consider this passage concerning Babylon or the Daughter of Babylon:

"Come down and sit in the dust, O virgin daughter of Babylon; sit on the ground without a throne, O daughter of the Chaldeans! For you shall no longer be called tender and delicate.........I was angry with My people, I profaned My heritage and gave them into your hand. You did not show mercy to them, on the aged you made your yoke very heavy. Yet you said, 'I will be a queen forever.' These things you did not consider nor remember the outcome of them." Is 47:1-7

The city of Rome was also referred to by the early church as Babylon (1Pet 5:13). In addition, the harlot religious system is the mother of harlots, because all idolatry and false religion has its origins in the land of Shinar. Therefore, Babylon as the city of Rome, and as the Antichrist Empire, and as the Harlot Religious System, is judged at the end of the Tribulation. But the city of Rome has a specific judgment which is illustrated in Revelation Chapter 18.

Will Ancient Babylon be Rebuilt?

There are some Bible prophecy experts who suggest that the judgment of Revelation 18 is actually intended for the ancient city of Babylon, which is today merely a ruin in Iraq. They speculate that it will be rebuilt and become a great international city once again. However, there is much to suggest that the ancient city of Babylon does not fit the description of the city mentioned in Revelation 17 and 18. For example:

- ➤ It is a center of commerce, enterprise and trade (Rev 18:3, 11-13).
- ➤ It is the city that shed the blood of the martyrs of Jesus (Rev 17:6). Ancient Babylon was in ruins long before Jesus came.
- ➤ It is a city on seven hills (Rev 17:9). Babylon cannot qualify for this, whereas, Rome has always been known as the city on seven hills.
- ➤ Immoral and drunken (Rev 17:2). Rome wins this one also.
- ➤ City that rules over many nations (Rev 17:15-18).
- ➤ Sailors cross the sea to get there (Rev 18:17-18).
- ➤ An entertainment capital (Rev 18:22-23)

Perhaps the greatest reason why ancient Babylon cannot be the city spoken of in Rev 17 and 18 is because it was a ruin at the time of the writing of the book. Also, the only city at the time of the writing that could qualify for Rev 17:18 is the city of Rome!

The Third Door

The third door has to do with the length of the Tribulation period. The Bible indicates that there is a period of seven years at the end of the age which is known as Daniel's Seventieth Week or the Last Shemitah Cycle.[18] It begins with a treaty and a time of peace in the Holy Land and the world. This only lasts for three and a half years until the middle of the Shemitah Cycle when Antichrist is unveiled and war begins. Then the period known as the Great Tribulation begins. Thus the first half is peace and security[19] and the second half is great tribulation. However, most Bible prophecy teachers claim that the whole Shemitah Cycle of seven years is the Tribulation. This presents a mystery. How can there be peace if the Tribulation has begun? How can the events of Revelation Chapter 6 take place in a time of peace and security?

The Third Key

The Tribulation is <u>not</u> seven years long. Jesus Himself said that the Tribulation began in the middle of the Shemitah Cycle which is seven years long. Thus the Tribulation is only three and a half years long and not seven. Calling the whole Shemitah Cycle the Tribulation has caused great confusion with regard to many other aspects of the End-Time scenario. And there is not a single verse or hint in the Bible to support it.

In this chapter, both the Third Key and the Second Key will be used! Congratulations, you are about to discover amazing secrets!

---

[18] The Shemitah is the seventh year when the land was supposed to rest (Lev 25:1-17). The whole seven year period is referred to as the Shemitah Cycle.
[19] 1Thess 5:3

Chapter Four
The Last Shemitah Cycle

Daniel's Seventieth Week is the Last Shemitah Cycle and the backbone of eschatology. Both Jesus and Paul taught from Daniel regarding the end of the age (Mt 24:15, 2 Thess 1:3-4). However, when we study Daniel Chapter 9, it is important to first review the context of Daniel's prayer before we analyze the angel's answer. The answer came in response to his prayer. Therefore, the prayer is essential to understanding the answer. Daniel was praying for the Jewish people, the City of Jerusalem, and the Sanctuary (Temple).

Daniel's Prayer

"O Lord, in accordance with all Your righteous acts, let now Your anger and Your wrath turn away from Your city Jerusalem, Your holy mountain; for because of our sins and the iniquities of our fathers, Jerusalem and Your people have become a reproach to all those around us. So now, our God, listen to the prayer of Your servant and to his supplications, and for Your sake, O Lord, let Your face shine on Your desolate sanctuary." Dan 9:16-17

The Angel's Answer

"Seventy weeks (Lit. SEVENS) have been decreed for your people and your holy city, to finish the transgression, to make an end of sin, to make atonement for iniquity, to bring in everlasting righteousness, to seal up vision and prophecy, and to anoint the most holy place. So you are to know and discern that from the issuing of a decree to restore and rebuild Jerusalem until Messiah the Prince there will be seven weeks and sixty-two weeks; it will be built again, with plaza and moat, even in times of distress. Then after the sixty-two weeks the Messiah will be cut off and have nothing, and the

people of the prince who is to come will destroy the city and the sanctuary. And its end will come with a flood; even to the end there will be war; desolations are determined."Daniel 9:24-26

Seventy Shemitah Cycles

When you look at the calendar on your refrigerator, or wherever you hang it, you take for granted that there are seven days in a week. But have you ever considered the reason? Incidentally, the atheist's calendar looks exactly like yours. There are seven days in his week also. Now you know that there are three hundred and sixty five and a quarter days in a year and that it has to do with the earth's revolution around the sun. You also know that there are approximately thirty days in a month and that it is the result of the moon's revolutions around the earth. But have you considered that there is no reason for a seven day week, other than the fact that God decreed it and commanded the Israelites to observe it as a sign. Amazing isn't it? Yet, what is even more amazing is that each week the good news of the coming Kingdom of God or the Day of the Lord is preached by the Gregorian calendar hanging on your wall. You see, God gave the Shabbat (Sabbath) as a sign. The seventh day was to be set apart as holy - a day of rest. The seventh month was also holy and the seventh year was to be set apart by the Israelites as a year of rest for the land. And since they were an agrarian society this meant a year of rest for them as well. These seven year periods were known as Shemitah periods or cycles. When seven of these Shemitah periods had accumulated, the Israelites were to proclaim the year of Jubilee on the fiftieth year (Lev 25:1-12). So when the angel said "Seventy Sevens," it was not much of a mystery to the Jews. It was seventy of these Shemitah periods based on the Sabbath of the land. Seventy multiplied by seven years!

~~~~~

Seventy Sevens or Shemitah cycles = 7x70 = 490 years

~~~~~

The angel told Daniel that the Jewish people had 490 years decreed for them and the Holy City to accomplish the following:

"....to make an end of sin, to make atonement for iniquity, to bring in everlasting righteousness, to seal up vision and prophecy, and to anoint the most holy place."

These are all themes of Yom Kippur - the Day of Judgment. Therefore, the 490 years are completed on Yom Kippur in the Day of the Lord. This is the Day when Jesus is revealed in Jerusalem!

"So you are to know and discern that from the issuing of a decree to restore and rebuild Jerusalem until Messiah the Prince there will be seven weeks and sixty-two weeks; it will be built again, with plaza and moat, even in times of distress. Then after the sixty-two weeks the Messiah will be cut off and have nothing, and the people of the prince who is to come will destroy the city and the sanctuary. And its end will come with a flood; even to the end there will be war; desolations are determined." Dan 9:25-26

The following are the calculations of Robert Anderson in 1895 which are accepted by the majority.

"From the issuing of a decree to restore and rebuild Jerusalem until Messiah the Prince...."

Notice this is not the decree to rebuild the Temple but the city of Jerusalem issued by Artaxerxes Longimanus "in the month of Nissan, in the twentieth year" (Neh 2:1) - March 14, 445BC

The prophecy states that Jerusalem would be rebuilt within 49 years. And so it was! Then it states that from the issuing of this decree until the Messiah would be rejected (cut off), there would be seven sevens and sixty two sevens - 69 sevens or 483 years. This date was estimated by Mr. Anderson as April 6, 32AD.

$$7 \times 7 \text{ years} + 62 \times 7 \text{years} = 69 \times 7 \text{ years} = 483 \text{ years}$$

Date when Messiah was cut off/rejected (by Israel) = April 6, AD 32 (Palm Sunday)

$$483 \times 360 = \mathbf{173,880} \text{ Days}$$

Then add 24 days from March 14 to April 6, AD 32.

Then add 116 leap days computed by the Royal observatory in Greenwich as having occurred during that time.

$$173,740 + 24 + 116 = \mathbf{173,880}$$

Note the biblical year is 360 days long (see Gen 7:11, 8:3-4 - 5 months = 150 days) – it follows the Lunar calendar.

~~~~~

Whether one agrees with the calculations of Robert Anderson or not, the Messiah was rejected 483 years after the decree to restore and rebuild Jerusalem. Then after the 483 years the Seventy Shemitah Cycle Clock stops because Israel is not in the land and the Holy Place is defiled by Gentiles!

"Then after the sixty-two weeks the Messiah will be cut off and have nothing, and the people of the prince who is to come will destroy the city and the sanctuary and its end will come with a flood; even to the end there will be war; desolations are determined." Dan 9:26

After the 62 weeks, the Messiah was cut off and then the Temple was destroyed some forty years later. So the "after" lasted 40 yrs. Because the last Shemitah Cycle (and all 70) has to do with the Holy Place, it cannot begin until it is consecrated once again. The site of the Holy Place on the Temple Mount must be consecrated as part of the "Final Status" agreement under the so-called "Road Map." Another option is that war will change things on the Temple Mount and Israel will simply decide to consecrate the Holy Place and begin rebuilding the Temple without an agreement. Nevertheless, the revelation given to Daniel goes on to say that "after" the Messiah is rejected, the people of the "prince who is to come" (Antichrist) will destroy the city and the sanctuary. This of course was fulfilled by the Romans in 70 A.D. indicating a connection with Rome, the Roman Empire, and Antichrist. Then the prophecy seems to jump to a period called "the end" and is referred to in verse 27 as "the week." This week is the last Shemitah period set aside for Israel which completes the four hundred and ninety years. This is the period known as "Daniel's Seventieth Week," which likely ends on Yom Kippur, since all that is said to be finished are themes associated with Israel's holiest day of the year.

The large gap in time between the completion of the 483 years and the Last Shemitah Cycle is implied but not defined. It is quite common for the prophetic Scriptures to allow for a large gap in time between the fulfillment of one verse and another. When Jesus stood up in the synagogue in Nazareth and declared that the Scriptures were fulfilled in the hearing of the people, He read only verse one and half of verse two of Isaiah 61, stopping midway in the sentence. He did this because the rest of the passage was to be fulfilled at His second coming. We know from history that the period, referred to as "after the sixty two weeks" in verse 26 of Daniel Chapter 9, was about forty years long (from when Messiah was rejected until Jerusalem was destroyed in 70 A.D). Then since Israel was scattered and no longer in the land, the last seven years were suspended until the time of regathering which the prophets foretold. As already noted in Chapter 1, we are living in the generation of the regathering. Israel is once again in the land and governing the city of Jerusalem. So what is keeping the clock from ticking on the Last Shemitah Cycle? The answer, I believe, is found in the prophecy when we understand that the revelation given to Daniel has to do with the Sanctuary and the "Holy Place."

"So now, our God, listen to the prayer of Thy servant and to his supplications, and for Thy sake, O Lord, let Thy face shine on Thy desolate sanctuary." Daniel 9:17

"Now while I was speaking and praying, and confessing my sin and the sin of my people Israel, and presenting my supplication before the LORD my God in behalf of the holy mountain of my God..." Daniel 9:20

Daniel was crying out to God for his people but, even more specifically, for the Sanctuary and the ruins of Jerusalem. The city of Jerusalem and the Sanctuary were built on the Holy Mountain, Mount Moriah, where Abraham sacrificed the ram in place of Isaac. The Mount, and more specifically the Temple, was and still is, at the heart of Judaism. Without the Temple, the Jews could not keep the feasts or offer the sacrifices proscribed in the Law of Moses. Its destruction was the ultimate sign of God's judgment and its rebuilding was the sign of God's restoration of His people and the Messianic era. No wonder that Daniel is interceding for the Sanctuary, the Holy Place. And the response from the angel was specifically in answer to this prayer regarding the Holy Place and the coming of Messiah.

When Messiah was cut off and rejected, the Jewish people were scattered and the City and Sanctuary again destroyed. However, God did not cease to work with and on behalf of Israel as we see clearly by His dealings down through the centuries. The incredible miracle of the rebirth of the nation in 1948 and the supernatural deliverances in the subsequent wars make this clear. What did stop was the prophetic clock with regard to the Sanctuary or the Temple Mount. The events that are predicted to take place in the Last Shemitah Cycle (Daniel's Seventieth Week) all have to do with the Holy Place. The Holy Place is in Jewish hands today but is not yet consecrated. No Jew is allowed to pray on the Temple Mount, even though it is in Jewish hands and the supreme court of the country says that Jews must be allowed to pray there. This illustrates clearly that the Seventieth Week or Last Shemitah Cycle has not yet begun. The angel said that it would begin with the making of a covenant and that it would have in it provision for worship in the Holy Place and the reinstitution of sacrifices. This would be perceived as the

Millennium by the Jews and the individual who makes this covenant with them would be received as the Messiah.

Israel is, at the moment, unwilling to consecrate the Holy Place and begin worship there. This is due to the fact that the Muslim holy places are on the Temple Mount and Israel is unwilling to provoke another war. However, it may take another war to change this situation. In any event, the peace treaty or covenant they will sign with Antichrist will resolve this dispute and allow Israel to worship on the Temple Mount again. Then the last seven years of the age will begin!

The Last Shemitah Cycle

"And he will make a firm covenant with the many for one week, but in the middle of the week he will put a stop to sacrifice and grain offering; and on the wing of abominations will come one who makes desolate, even until a complete destruction, one that is decreed, is poured out on the one who makes desolate." Dan 9:27

There are seven years or one week of years left in the prophecy known as Daniel's Seventieth Week or the Last Shemitah Cycle and it begins with a covenant or peace treaty! The prophecy clock starts again with the initiation of a treaty between the apostate Jewish leaders and a world leader who becomes the Antichrist. This treaty directly involves the Temple Mount. It also includes EU membership! Then in the middle of this seven year period this EU leader breaks the treaty and sets up the Abomination of Desolation on the Temple Mount.

The Antichrist makes or confirms a covenant with the "many." The "many" is a term used for apostate Jewish leaders who have become humanistic and have renounced the Torah. We deduct this from the history of the Jews under Antiochus Epiphanes who was the prototype of Antichrist and the one referred to in Daniel Chapter 11 (see verse 31), which seems to shift from the history of this man to a parallel history of Antichrist at the end of the age. Jesus makes reference to this event under Antiochus known as the Abomination of Desolation and repeated again by Antichrist (Mt 24:15).

How Long is the Tribulation?

The peace treaty divides Jerusalem and brings "peace" to the region for three and a half years. The Antichrist is revealed with the Abomination of Desolation. This event commences the Tribulation, which lasts for the remaining three and a half years. Therefore, the Tribulation is three and a half years long. This fact is confirmed by Jesus and Paul in the following verses.

"Therefore when you see the Abomination of Desolation which was spoken of through Daniel the prophet, standing in the holy place (let the reader understand), then those who are in Judea must flee to the mountains......For then there will be a great tribulation, such as has not occurred since the beginning of the world until now, nor ever will." Mt 24:15,21

"For you yourselves know full well that the day of the Lord will come just like a thief in the night. While they are saying, 'Peace and safety!' then destruction will come upon them suddenly like labor pains upon a woman with child, and they will not escape."1 Thess 5:1-3

Jesus said that when you see the Abomination of Desolation then there will be a Great Tribulation. When you see then there will be - it is very clear! Paul said that the Tribulation would come suddenly during a period of Peace and Security! And we know from Daniel 9:27 that the first three and a half years of the Last Shemitah Cycle will bring peace and security because it allows for Jewish worship on the Temple Mount!

Why Do Many Say the Tribulation is 7 Years Long?

When Christopher Columbus discovered America, he thought he had arrived in India. Based on the understanding that he had at the time, his assumptions were reasonable. Yet, he had not reached India at all but a new and unknown world. And as a result of his wrong conclusions, Native Americans are still called Indians although they are not and never have been Indian. In a similar way, many Bible teachers, while discovering truth in the prophetic Scriptures, after centuries of ignorance, concluded that the Tribulation is seven years long. Like Columbus, who was unwilling to consider an alternative, they build elaborate theories and end-time scenarios on this assumption. And though many of the same teachers know that the Tribulation is in fact three and a half years long, their insistence on referring to the entire seven year period of the Last Shemitah Cycle as "The Tribulation," presents major problems for students of eschatology. I believe that this miscalculation is a result of the lack of understanding of the Jewish roots of the Bible (both Old and New Testaments). Daniel was a Jew, and the Last Shemitah Cycle is a period of time set apart for the Jewish people. It is their Shemitah. To divorce it from this context is a serious mistake. The Great Tribulation is the time of "Jacob's Distress" and not the time of American, European, African, or Asian distress. There will indeed be horrific distress for all the earth during this time, but the epicenter of that distress will be in Israel.

"For thus says the LORD, 'I have heard a sound of terror, of dread, and there is no peace. Ask now, and see if a male can give birth. Why do I see every man with his hands on his loins, as a woman in childbirth? And why have all faces turned pale? Alas! For that day is great, there is none like it; and it is the time of Jacob's distress, but he will be saved from it.'" Jer 30:5-7

~~~~~

The Seventieth Week or Last Shemitah Cycle is broken into 2 halves!

1st Half - Peace & Security - 1 Thess 5:3

2nd Half - Great Tribulation - 2 Thess 2:3-4

1st Half also known as "The Apostasy"

2nd Half also known as "The Day of the Lord"

~~~~~

Take a look at chart 7 on page 294. Can you see clearly that the Tribulation is three and a half years long? There is a significant body of Scripture to support this and none to support a seven year long Tribulation. The Tribulation begins with the Abomination (Abom) and ends with Jesus appearing. The "Abom" begins the war that ends with all the nations coming against Jerusalem. It is the Armageddon Campaign. Many Scriptures clearly identify the Tribulation as the Day of the Lord (See Chapter 5).

Covenant with Sheol

Daniel 9:27 says that the Antichrist will make a covenant with the Jewish leaders for seven years. This is undoubtedly the so called "Peace Treaty" that will be brokered with the EU. Today the whole world is preoccupied with making this agreement. The document that the international community considers to be the foundation for this agreement is called the "Road Map." At the core of the "Road Map" which was supposed to have been implemented years ago, is the "Final Status of Jerusalem." This "Final Status Agreement" would require a solution to the situation on the Temple Mount. The aspirations of religious Jews regarding the Holy Place would have to be satisfied for such an agreement to be signed.

" *Parties reach final and comprehensive permanent status agreement that ends the Israel - Palestinian conflict in 2005, through a settlement negotiated between the parties based on UNSCR 242, 338, and 1397, that ends the occupation that began in 1967, and includes an agreed, just, fair,* and realistic solution to the refugee issue, and a negotiated resolution on the status of Jerusalem that takes into account the political and religious concerns of both sides, and protects the religious interests of Jews, Christians, and Muslims worldwide, and fulfills the vision of two states, Israel and sovereign, independent, democratic and viable Palestine, living side-by-side in peace and security"[20]

Isaiah speaks of Israel's covenant with Antichrist as their "Covenant with Sheol."

"Therefore, hear the word of the LORD, O scoffers, who rule this people who are in Jerusalem, because you have said, 'We have made a covenant with death, and with Sheol we have made a pact the overwhelming scourge will not reach us when it passes by, for we have made falsehood our refuge and we have concealed ourselves with deception.' ......Your covenant with death will be canceled, and your pact with Sheol will not stand; when the overwhelming scourge passes through, then you become its trampling place. As often as it passes through, it will seize you; for morning after morning it will pass through, anytime during the day or night, and it will be sheer terror to understand what it means. The bed is too short on which to stretch out, and the blanket is too small to wrap oneself in. For the LORD will rise up as at Mount Perazim, He will be stirred up as in the valley of Gibeon, to do His task, His unusual task, and to work His work, His extraordinary work. And now do not carry on as scoffers, or your fetters will be made stronger; for I have heard from the Lord GOD of hosts of decisive destruction on all the earth." Is 28:16-22

As is typical with the words of the prophets, this passage is about the current situation at the time of its writing and then it jumps to the scenario at the end of the age. We can tell this by the language used. For example; the prophet talks about a destruction he has heard which affects all the earth. The leaders of Israel today are not listening to God any more than they were then. They are referred

---

[20] "A performance-based road map to a permanent two-state solution to the Israeli-Palestinian conflict."

to as "scoffers." They make a "covenant with Sheol" or "death" which is supposed to protect them from the Gentile armies (floods are a reference to armies, Dan 9:26, 11:10, Rev 12:15). The covenant or pact with Sheol will not stand. The Lord will go forth and fight as at Perazim (1Chron 14:11) and Gibeon (Josh 10:7-15).

The world's financial and political elite have adopted the phrase "Peace and Security" as their benevolent mantra and excuse for all that they do! They have concluded that until they can solve the problems in the Middle-East between Israel and its Anti-Semitic neighbors, they will not reach their goal. Thus they are devoted to the implementation of the agenda of the Road Map."

Who is the Restrainer?

"And you know what restrains him now, so that in his time he may be revealed. For the mystery of lawlessness is already at work; only he who now restrains will do so until he is taken out of the way. And then that lawless one will be revealed whom the Lord will slay with the breath of His mouth and bring to an end by the appearance of His coming....." 2Thess 2:6-8

The issue of who is restraining Antichrist has been very baffling to Bible scholars. The majority of those who hold to the pre-week view[21] believe that it is either the church or the Holy Spirit that is being referred to. However, neither of these answers is acceptable. Even though the rapture of the Bride of Christ occurs at this time, the greatest harvest of Christians will come to the Lord during the Tribulation. It will be a great multitude from every tribe and tongue that will be filled with the Spirit and do great exploits. If the church were the one to restrain the Antichrist, then this great multitude should certainly qualify as a significant expression of the church. Also, if the Holy Spirit is removed from the earth at the Rapture, as many Pre-Weekers assert, then how does this great multitude come to know Messiah? Also, who causes the Spirit of grace and

---

[21] Those who believe the Rapture comes before the Seventieth Week or Last Shemitah Cycle

supplication to be poured out on the Jews or empowers the "Two Witnesses," to do the great works that they do? Those who suggest that the restrainer is the church or the Holy Spirit need to examine these issues more carefully. Another theory that has been suggested is that the restrainer is the devil himself who is restraining lawlessness. When he is cast out of the heavens during the middle of the week, he supposedly unrestrains himself. None of these answers make any sense. Therefore the question remains, who is the restrainer?

The answer to this question about the restrainer is not a mystery. It has escaped us for so many years because the church, having lost its Jewish roots, failed to understand that Paul was teaching from the eleventh 11th and 12th chapters of Daniel. He didn't mention the restrainer's name because he expected the Thessalonians to understand, just as Jesus expected his hearers to understand. He said, "Don't you remember that while I was still with you I was telling you these things?" What was he telling them? He was telling them about the Antichrist and the Abomination of Desolation from Daniel Chapter 11. The context was the Great Tribulation or the time of Israel's distress. He told them that the Antichrist or "man of lawlessness" could <u>not</u> be revealed until that time because he was being restrained. Logically, he took them to Chapter 12 and explained who the restrainer was from verse 1, and according to Daniel 12:1 the restrainer of satan and the Antichrist is Michael the Archangel.

The Fourth Door

The fourth door has to do with the timing of events, particularly the Rapture. Theories regarding timing have generated enormous confusion in the church. Christians are divided into different camps staunchly defending their positions. Some say the Rapture can happen any time. Others say it will happen after the Tribulation. More say it is Mid-Tribulation and still others say it is closer to the end. And the rest say they don't know. Add to that all of the false dates that have been set based on crazy hypotheses and you see the problem. Obviously there is a mystery here that has not been successfully unraveled. The key to the fourth door has not been found. If we find a key then we will find the wall and open the door. So does the Bible really tell us when these events occur? The answer is absolutely yes!

The Fourth Key

Understanding the Day of the Lord is the secret to the timing of events.

The understanding of the Day of the Lord, a theme that runs throughout the Bible, has been lost or corrupted by the church so that it cannot properly interpret the timing of events since they depend on this theme. The next chapter will unfold this theme and make it abundantly clear. Then the following chapter will unlock the timing using this key! Pay careful attention as we walk on through and don't miss it! Always remember, however, that you can go back and have another look!

Chapter Five
The Day of the Lord

The Day of the Lord is a main theme of Scripture from Genesis to Revelation, but the church, for the most part, knows little or nothing about it. Yet the teaching with regard to the Day of the Lord, as prophesied by the prophets of Israel and unfolded by the Messiah and the New Testament Apostles, is at the heart of understanding the end of the age scenario. In fact, it is the "end time" scenario. Eschatology, or the study of the last days, is the study of the Day of the Lord. Unfortunately, the church, missing its Jewish roots, lost this understanding. The result was an emphasis, at least among pre-millennialists, on the "Tribulation" period and the timing of the Rapture. However, without an understanding of the Day of the Lord, little sense can be made of the eschatological Scriptures. I believe this to be the primary reason why there is so much confusion with regard to the Rapture and the coming of the Lord. The Day of the Lord is the key to knowing when the Lord returns and when the Rapture will take place.

The Sabbath Rest – Millennium

"And the LORD spoke to Moses, saying, But as for you, speak to the sons of Israel, saying, 'You shall surely observe My Sabbaths; for this is a sign between Me and you throughout your generations, that you may know that I am the LORD who sanctifies you.'" Ex 31:13

God gave the Sabbath to Israel as a sign. The seventh day was to be set apart as holy, a day of rest. The seventh month was also holy and the seventh year was to be set apart by the Israelites as a year of rest for the land. In addition, when seven of these Shemitah periods had accumulated, the Israelites were to proclaim the year of Jubilee on the fiftieth year. The Jubilee was a special time of deliverance and freedom for the people. It was a time of celebration - a special time to remember God's goodness and to show kindness to others. It was a rehearsal for the Day of the Lord, the Day of Rest, just like the weekly Sabbath, the monthly Sabbath, and the yearly Sabbath. They each proclaim the Day of the Lord, the Kingdom of Messiah, the Unique Day of God's favor and rest, which is the Seventh Millennium. This was the understanding of the Jewish prophets and it has been taught down through the ages by the Jewish rabbis and also by the writers of the New Testament. Consider the following quotes from the Babylonian Talmud.

"The Tanna rebe Eliyyahu teaches: 'The world is to exist six thousand years. In the first two thousand there was desolation; two thousand years the Torah flourished; and the next two thousand years is the Messianic era...' [22]

"R. Kattina said: 'Six thousand years shall the world exist, and one (thousand, the seventh), it shall be desolate, as it is written, And the Lord alone shall be exalted in that day. Abaye said: it will be desolate two (thousand), as it is said, After two days will he will revive us: in the third day, he will raise us up, and we shall live in his sight.'" [23]

"It has been taught in accordance with R. Kattina: 'Just as the seventh year is one year of release in seven, so is the world: one thousand years out of seven shall be fallow, as it is written, And the Lord alone shall be exalted in that day, and it is further said, a Psalm and song for the Sabbath day, meaning the day is altogether Sabbath - and it is also said, For a thousand years in thy sight are but as yesterday when it is past."[24]

Where did the Jewish rabbis get this understanding? It appears they got it from Scripture, from the writings of Moses and others. Consider the following:

---

[22] *Talmud Tractate Sanhedrin 97a, 200 BCE*
[23] Ibid.
[24] Ibid.

"And the LORD God commanded the man, saying, 'From any tree of the garden you may eat freely; but from the tree of the knowledge of good and evil you shall not eat, for in the day that you eat from it you shall surely die.'" Gen 2:16-17

In this passage of Genesis, the rabbis understood Moses (Moses wrote Genesis) to mean that a day was 1000 years, and that Adam died on the day that he ate from the tree of the knowledge of good and evil just like God had said. Adam died when he was 930 years old and never reached 1000 years or the end of the first day. No one else reached it either, including Methuselah who came the closest. Another confirmation that Moses taught this is in Psalm 90, which of course was also written by Moses.

"For a thousand years in Thy sight are like yesterday when it passes by, or as a watch in the night." Psalms 90:4

Another passage of Scripture that led the rabbis to the same conclusion that a day (prophetically speaking) was one thousand years is Malachi Chapter 4.

"But for you who fear My name the sun of righteousness will rise with healing in its wings; and you will go forth and skip about like calves from the stall." Mal 4:2

They understood this verse to be a reference to the Messiah coming on day four or the fourth millennium. Since the sun was created on the fourth day they interpreted "the sun of righteousness" to be a reference to the Messiah coming on the fourth millennium bringing deliverance to Israel. Were they right? Yes! Messiah did come at the very end of the fourth day or millennium. The wings referred to were the "Tzi-Tzit" or tassels of his garments (Mt 9:20).

"Come, let us return to the LORD. For He has torn us, but He will heal us; He has wounded us, but He will bandage us. He will revive us after two

days; He will raise us up on the third day that we may live before Him."
Hosea 6:1

The rabbis understood this passage to refer to the Messianic era. The Jewish people would be wounded for two days, but on the third day of Messiah, they would be healed. Two thousand years they would suffer, and on the third millennium, the Kingdom would come. Jesus Himself seems to have verified this by the following statements:

"And He said to them, 'Go and tell that fox, 'Behold, I cast out demons and perform cures today and tomorrow, and the third day I reach My goal.' Nevertheless I must journey on today and tomorrow and the next day; for it cannot be that a prophet should perish outside of Jerusalem." Luke 13:32

Careful examination of the text tells us that Jesus did not reach His goal on the third day after this statement. He was not referring to twenty-four hour periods at all, but rather, the "Third Day" or Third Millennium. Jesus says that He will perform cures and cast out demons for two millennia and then He will reach His goal - the Kingdom of God. One would be hard pressed to interpret this passage any other way.

"Jesus answered and said to them, "Destroy this temple, and in three days I will raise it up. The Jews therefore said, 'It took forty-six years to build this temple, and will You raise it up in three days?' But He was speaking of the temple of His body." John 2:19-21

The Hebrew prophets often used common, well-known idioms or figures of speech in their prophetic writings. Also, there are many examples of prophecies that have more than one meaning. Jesus, being a Jew, and of course, the premier Jewish Prophet, was no exception. The rabbis understood this way of speaking and always studied the Scriptures for the deeper meaning. John tells us here that Jesus was speaking of the temple of His body. This is one meaning. However, the second meaning is that Jesus was stating that the Temple in Jerusalem would be destroyed and would lay desolate for two days (two millennia) and that He would rebuild it on the third day (third millennium). This understanding of one day being a thousand years and the Day of the Lord being a thousand years long is also confirmed by other New Testament writers.

"But do not let this one fact escape your notice, beloved, that with the Lord one day is as a thousand years, and a thousand years as one day (or day one)." *2 Pet 3:8*

In this passage, Peter emphatically states that the Day of the Lord is one thousand years long and that, with reference to the prophetic Scriptures regarding the end of the age, the Lord is counting days in thousands of years. Many conclude that Peter is here saying that God does not keep track of time and does not care how long it takes to do something. However, no first century Jew would ever say such a thing. God had taught them that the right day and the right time for each event was of the utmost importance. Each feast day had to be celebrated and each sacrifice had to be offered at exactly the right time. Jesus Himself, in fulfilling over three hundred Messianic prophecies, had perfect timing in everything. Peter would never have made such a statement. What he is saying is merely reiterating what was already prophesied by the Hebrew prophets and interpreted by the rabbis including Messiah Himself. With regard to the coming of the Day of God and the interpretation of prophetic Scripture, we must not let this "fact" (implied in the Greek) escape our notice that one day with the Lord is equal to one thousand years.

John the Apostle, in the last book of the Bible, again confirms that the Day of the Lord or the Kingdom of Messiah is to last for one thousand years (Rev 20:1-6). Also in John's gospel, we find many references to the Seventh Day or the Day of the Lord.

"No one can come to Me, unless the Father who sent Me draws him; and I will raise him up on the last day." John 6:44

"He who rejects Me, and does not receive My sayings, has one who judges him; the word I spoke is what will judge him at the last day." John 12:48

"Martha said to Him, 'I know that he will rise again in the resurrection on the last day.'" John 11:24

The "Last Day" was not a reference to the last twenty-four hour period at the end of the age. It is clear from these passages that it was the Day when the righteous would be resurrected and the wicked judged. No student of eschatology would suggest that these events take place within a twenty-four hour period. Neither can we suggest that it is a reference to an unknown or insignificant amount of time. The theme of the "Last Day" was a common one to the first century Jews as evidenced by Martha's statement to Jesus and Jesus' repeated mention of the "Last Day." There was apparently no need to explain it since everybody was expected to understand. The "Last Day" was of course "the Day of the Lord" - the Seventh Day - the Kingdom of Messiah - the Millennial Reign.

The writer of Hebrews, although not mentioning any specific time period, echoes the familiar theme of the Day of God or the Seventh Millennium Sabbath Rest in the following passage:

"For indeed we have had good news preached to us, just as they also; but the word they heard did not profit them, because it was not united by faith in those who heard. For we who have believed enter that rest, just as He has said, 'As I swore in My wrath, they shall not enter My rest,' although His works were finished from the foundation of the world. For He has thus said somewhere concerning the seventh day, 'And God rested on the seventh day from all His works'; and again in this passage, 'They shall not enter My rest.' Since therefore it remains for some to enter it, and those who formerly had good news preached to them failed to enter because of disobedience, He

again fixes a certain day, 'Today,' saying through David after so long a time just as has been said before, 'Today if you hear His voice, do not harden your hearts.' For if Joshua had given them rest, He would not have spoken of another day after that. There remains therefore a Sabbath rest for the people of God. For the one who has entered His rest has himself also rested from his works, as God did from His." Heb 4:2-10

Premillennialism – the Apostolic Position

Another powerful testimony to this fact of the Day of the Lord being 1000 years is the understanding of the early church fathers! It seems clear that Premillennialism[25] was passed on from the apostles.

"The most striking point in the eschatology of the ante-Nicene age is the prominent chiliasm, or millenarianism, that is the belief of a visible reign of Christ in glory on earth with the risen saints for a thousand years, before the general resurrection and judgment." (Philip Schaff, History of the Christian Church, 2:614).

Epistle of Barnabas (Late First Century)

"And God made in six days the works of His hands, and made an end on the seventh day, and rested on it, and sanctified it. Attend, my children, to the meaning of this expression, 'He finished in six days.' This implieth that the Lord will finish all things in six thousand years, for a day is with Him a thousand years. And He Himself testifieth, saying, 'Behold, today will be as a thousand years.' Therefore, my children, in six days, that is, in six thousand years, all things will be finished. 'And He rested on the seventh day.' This meaneth: when His Son, coming [again], shall destroy the time of the wicked man, and judge the ungodly, and change the-sun, and the moon, and the stars, then shall He truly rest on the seventh day." [Epistle of Barnabas, XV]

---

[25] Premillennialism is the belief that Jesus comes back before the Millennium period.

Justin Marytr (AD 110-165)

"But I and others, who are right-minded Christians on all points, are assured that there will be a resurrection of the dead, and a thousand years in Jerusalem, which will then be built, adorned, and enlarged as the prophets Ezekiel and Isaiah and others declare" (Dialogue with Trypho, Ch. 80).

Irenaeus (AD. 120-202)

"For in as many days as this world was made, in so many thousand years shall it be concluded. And for this reason the Scripture says: "Thus the heaven and the earth were finished, and all their adornment. And God brought to a conclusion upon the sixth day the works that He had made; and God rested upon the seventh day from all His works." This is an account of the things formerly created, as also it is a prophecy of what is to come. For the day of the Lord is as a thousand years; and in six days created things were completed: it is evident, therefore, that they will come to an end at the sixth thousand year." [Against Heresies V. XXVIII, 3]

Methodius (AD. 260-312)

"For a thousand years in Thy sight are but as yesterday: seeing that is past as a watch in the night."For when a thousand years are reckoned as one day in the sight of God, and from the creation of the world to His rest is six days, so also to our time, six days are defined, as those say who are clever arithmeticians. Therefore, they say that an age of six thousand years extends from Adam to our time. For they say that the judgment will come on the seventh day, that is in the seventh thousand years." [Extracts From The Work on Things Created. IX]

The Two Parts of the Day of the Lord

The Day of the Lord refers to a time period which the church has mistakenly broken into two parts. Some believe the Day of the Lord to be a time of judgment and wrath only, while others see it as a time of peace and rest for the earth under the benevolent rule of Messiah. Both of these positions are used to defend different theories with regard to the Rapture. Yet, both of these views are wrong. The Day of the Lord is a time of wrath and judgment and a time of rest and peace in the Messianic kingdom. Both the Millennial Kingdom and the Great Tribulation are referred to by the prophets as the Day of the Lord. The following are verses that refer to the Millennial Reign and the Tribulation as the Day of the Lord.[26] (For an illustration see chart 6 on page 293)

(**Millennium**) *"In that day the Branch of the LORD will be beautiful and glorious, and the fruit of the earth will be the pride and the adornment of the survivors of Israel. And it will come about that he who is left in Zion and remains in Jerusalem will be called holy-- everyone who is recorded for life in Jerusalem.* (**The Tribulation**) *When the Lord has washed away the filth of the daughters of Zion, and purged the bloodshed of Jerusalem from her midst, by the spirit of judgment and the spirit of burning,* (**Millennium**) *then the LORD will create over the whole area of Mount Zion and over her assemblies a cloud by day, even smoke, and the brightness of a flaming fire by night; for over all the glory will be a canopy. And there will be a shelter to give shade from the heat by day, and refuge and protection from the storm and the rain." Isaiah 4:2-6*

(**The Tribulation**) *"The earth is broken asunder, the earth is split through, the earth is shaken violently. The earth reels to and fro like a drunkard, and it totters like a shack, for its transgression is heavy upon it, and it will fall, never to rise again. So it will happen in that day, that the LORD will punish the host of heaven, on high, and the kings of the earth, on earth. And they will be gathered together like prisoners in the dungeon, and will be confined in prison; and after many days they will be punished.* (**The Millennium**) *Then the moon will be abashed and the sun ashamed, for the LORD of hosts will reign on Mount Zion and in Jerusalem, and His glory will be before His elders." Isaiah 24:19-23*

(**The Millennium**) *"Now it will come about that in the last days the mountain of the house of the LORD will be established as the chief of the mountains, and will be raised above the hills; and all the nations will stream*

---

[26] These are but a sampling of verses concerning the Day of the Lord which is a major theme of the prophets.

to it. And many peoples will come and say, "Come, let us go up to the mountain of the LORD, to the house of the God of Jacob; that He may teach us concerning His ways and that we may walk in His paths." For the law will go forth from Zion and the word of the LORD from Jerusalem. And He will judge between the nations, and will render decisions for many peoples; and they will hammer their swords into plowshares and their spears into pruning hooks nation will not lift up sword against nation, and never again will they learn war." Is 2:2-4*

(**The Tribulation**) *"Enter the rock and hide in the dust from the terror of the LORD and from the splendor of His majesty. The proud look of man will be abased and the loftiness of man will be humbled, and the LORD alone will be exalted in that day. For the LORD of hosts will have a day of reckoning against everyone who is proud and lofty and against everyone who is lifted up, that he may be abased. And it will be against all the cedars of Lebanon that are lofty and lifted up, against all the oaks of Bashan, against all the lofty mountains, against all the hills that are lifted up, against every high tower, against every fortified wall, against all the ships of Tarshish and against all the beautiful craft. The pride of man will be humbled and the loftiness of men will be abased; and the LORD alone will be exalted in that day, but the idols will completely vanish. Men will go into caves of the rocks and into holes of the ground before the terror of the LORD and the splendor of His majesty, when He arises to make the earth tremble. In that day men will cast away to the moles and the bats their idols of silver and their idols of gold, which they made for themselves to worship, in order to go into the caverns of the rocks and the clefts of the cliffs before the terror of the LORD and the splendor of His majesty, when He arises to make the earth tremble." Is 2:12-21*

(**The Millennium**) *"Thus says the Lord GOD, 'When I gather the house of Israel from the peoples among whom they are scattered, and will manifest My holiness in them in the sight of the nations, then they will live in their land which I gave to My servant Jacob. They will live in it securely; and they will build houses, plant vineyards and live securely* (**The Tribulation**) *when I execute judgments upon all who scorn them round* *about them. Then they will know that I am the LORD their God.'" Ezek 28:25-26*

(**The Millennium**) *"Shout for joy, O daughter of Zion! Shout in triumph, O Israel! Rejoice and exult with all your heart, O daughter of Jerusalem! The LORD has taken away His judgments against you,* (**The Tribulation**) *He has cleared away your enemies. The King of Israel, the LORD, is in your midst; you will fear disaster no more.* (**The Millennium**) *In that day it will be said to Jerusalem: "Do not be afraid, O Zion; do not let your hands fall limp. The LORD your God is in your midst, a victorious warrior. He will exult over you with joy, He will be quiet in His love, He will rejoice over you with shouts of joy. I will gather those who grieve about the appointed feasts -- they came from you, O Zion; the reproach of exile is a burden on them. Behold, I am going to deal at that time with all your oppressors, I will save the lame and gather the outcast, and I will turn their shame into praise and renown in all the earth. At that time I will bring you in, even at the time when I gather you together; indeed, I will give you renown and praise among all the peoples of the earth, when I restore your fortunes before your eyes, Says the LORD." Zeph 3:14-20*

(**The Tribulation**) *"The sun will be turned into darkness, and the moon into blood, before* (**The Millennium**) *the great and awesome day of the LORD comes.* (**The Tribulation**) *And it will come about that whoever calls on the name of the LORD will be delivered; for on Mount Zion and in Jerusalem there will be those who escape, as the LORD has said, even among the survivors whom the LORD calls." Joel 2:31-32*

(**The Millennium**) *"And the wolf will dwell with the lamb, and the leopard will lie down with the young goat, and the calf and the young lion and the fatling together; and a little boy will lead them. Also the cow and the bear will graze, their young will lie down together, and the lion will eat straw like the ox. The nursing child will play by the hole of the cobra, and the weaned child will put his hand on the viper's den. They will not hurt or destroy in all My holy mountain, for the earth will be full of the knowledge of the LORD As the waters cover the sea. Then in that day the nations will* resort to the root of Jesse, Who will stand as a signal for the peoples; and His resting place will be glorious. Then it will happen on that day that the Lord will again recover the second time with His hand the remnant of His people, who will remain, from Assyria, Egypt, Pathros, Cush, Elam, Shinar, Hamath, and from the islands of the sea. And He will lift up a standard for the nations and assemble the banished ones of Israel, and will gather the dispersed of Judah from the four corners of the earth." Isa 11:6-12

(**The Millennium**) "For behold, I create new heavens and a new earth; and the former things will not be remembered or come to mind. But be glad and rejoice forever in what I create; for behold, I create Jerusalem for rejoicing and her people for gladness. I will also rejoice in Jerusalem and be glad in My people; and there will no longer be heard in her the voice of weeping and the sound of crying. No longer will there be in it an infant who lives but a few days, or an old man who does not live out his days; for the youth will die at the age of one hundred and the one who does not reach the age of one hundred will be thought accursed. They will build houses and inhabit them; they will also plant vineyards and eat their fruit. They will not build and another inhabit, they will not plant and another eat; for as the lifetime of a tree, so will be the days of My people, and My chosen ones will wear out the work of their hands. They will not labor in vain, or bear children for calamity; for they are the offspring of those blessed by the LORD, and their descendants with them. It will also come to pass that before they call, I will answer; and while they are still speaking, I will hear. The wolf and the lamb will graze together, and the lion will eat straw like the ox; and dust will be the serpent's food. They will do no evil or harm in all My holy mountain," says the LORD." Is 65: 17-25

(**The Tribulation**) "Enter the rock and hide in the dust from the terror of the LORD and from the splendor of His majesty. The proud look of man will be abased and the loftiness of man will be humbled, and the LORD alone will be exalted in that day. For the LORD of hosts will have a day of reckoning against everyone who is proud and lofty and against everyone who is lifted up, that he may be abased. And it will be against all the cedars of Lebanon that are lofty and lifted up, against all the oaks of Bashan, against all the lofty mountains, against all the hills that are lifted up, against every high tower, against every fortified wall, against all the ships of Tarshish and against all the beautiful craft. The pride of man will be humbled and the loftiness of men will be abased; and the LORD alone will be exalted in that day, but the idols will completely vanish. Men will go into caves of the rocks and into holes of the ground before the terror of the LORD and the splendor of His majesty, when He arises to make the earth tremble. In that day men will cast away to the moles and the bats their idols of silver and their idols of gold, which they made for themselves to worship, in order to go into the caverns of the rocks and the clefts of the cliffs before the terror of the LORD and the splendor of His majesty, when He arises to make the earth tremble." Is 2:10-21

(**The Tribulation**) "The earth is broken asunder, the earth is split through, the earth is shaken violently. The earth reels to and fro like a drunkard and it totters like a shack, for its transgression is heavy upon it, and it will fall, never to rise again. So it will happen in that day, that the LORD will punish the host of heaven on high, and the kings of the earth on earth. ²They will be gathered together like prisoners in the dungeon, and will be confined in prison; and after many days they will be punished." Is 24:19-22

(**The Tribulation**) "Wail, for the day of the LORD is near! It will come as destruction from the Almighty. Therefore all hands will fall limp, and every man's heart will melt. They will be terrified, pains and anguish will take hold of them; they will writhe like a woman in labor, they will look at one another in astonishment, their faces aflame. Behold, the day of the LORD is coming, cruel, with fury and burning anger, to make the land a desolation; and He will exterminate its sinners from it. For the stars of heaven and their constellations will not flash forth their light; the sun will be dark when it rises and the moon will not shed its light. Thus I will punish the world for its evil and the wicked for their iniquity; I will also put an end to the arrogance of the proud and abase the haughtiness of the ruthless. I will make mortal man scarcer than pure gold and mankind than the gold of Ophir. Therefore I will make the heavens tremble, and the earth will be shaken from its place at the fury of the LORD of hosts In the day of His burning anger." Isa 13:6-13

(**The Tribulation**) "Draw near, O nations, to hear; and listen, O peoples! Let the earth and all it contains hear, and the world and all that springs from it. For the LORD'S indignation is against all the nations, and His wrath against all their armies; He has utterly destroyed them, He has given them over to slaughter. So their slain will be thrown out, and their corpses will give off their stench, and the mountains will be drenched with their blood. And all the host of heaven will wear away, and the sky will be rolled up like a scroll; all their hosts will also wither away as a leaf withers from the vine, or as one withers from the fig tree. For My sword is satiated in heaven, behold it shall descend for judgment upon Edom and upon the people whom I have devoted to destruction. The sword of the LORD is filled with blood, it is sated with fat, with the blood of lambs and goats, with the fat of the kidneys of rams. For the LORD has a sacrifice in Bozrah and a great slaughter in the land of Edom. Wild oxen will also fall with them and young bulls with strong ones; thus their land will be soaked with blood, and their dust become greasy with fat. For the LORD has a day of vengeance, a year of recompense for the cause of Zion. Its streams will be turned into pitch, and its loose earth into brimstone, and its land will become burning pitch. It will not be quenched night or day; its smoke will go up forever." Isa 34:1-10

(**The Millennium & The Tribulation**) "To proclaim the favorable year of the LORD and the day of vengeance of our God..." Isa 61:2

(**The Tribulation**) "For the day of vengeance was in My heart, and My year of redemption has come. I looked, and there was no one to help, and I was astonished and there was no one to uphold; so My own arm brought salvation to Me, and My wrath upheld Me. I trod down the peoples in My anger and made them drunk in My wrath, and I poured out their lifeblood on the earth." Isa 63:4-6

(**The Tribulation**) *"Blow a trumpet in Zion, and sound an alarm on My holy mountain! Let all the inhabitants of the land tremble, For the day of the LORD is coming; Surely it is near, A day of darkness and gloom, A day of clouds and thick darkness." Joel 2:1-2*

(**The Tribulation**) *"For behold, in those days and at that time, when I restore the fortunes of Judah and Jerusalem, I will gather all the nations and bring them down to the valley of Jehoshaphat. Then I will enter into judgment with them there on behalf of My people and My inheritance, Israel, whom they have scattered among the nations; and they have divided up My land." Joel 3:1-2*

(**The Tribulation**) *"Near is the great day of the LORD, near and coming very quickly; listen, the day of the LORD! In it the warrior cries out bitterly. A day of wrath is that day, a day of trouble and distress, a day of destruction and desolation, a day of darkness and gloom, a day of clouds and thick darkness, a day of trumpet and battle cry against the fortified cities and the high corner towers. I will bring distress on men so that they will walk like the blind, because they have sinned against the LORD; and their blood will be poured out like dust and their flesh like dung. Neither their silver nor their gold will be able to deliver them on the day of the LORD'S wrath; and all the earth will be devoured in the fire of His jealousy, for He will make a complete end, indeed a terrifying one, of all the inhabitants of the earth." Zeph 1:14-18*

Is Joel 2:32 a Contradiction?

Joel states clearly that the Day of the Lord comes after the Time of Wrath and Destruction.

"The sun will be turned into darkness, and the moon into blood, before the great and awesome day of the LORD comes. And it will come about that whoever calls on the name of the LORD will be delivered; for on Mount Zion and in Jerusalem there will be those who escape, as the LORD has said, even among the survivors whom the LORD calls." Joel 2:31-32

We know from many other Scriptures that the sun turning to darkness and the moon to blood occur at the end of the time of Wrath or the Tribulation. Is there a contradiction here? Not when we understand the prophet's perspective of the Millennium as the Day of the Lord proper and the Tribulation as merely the cleansing of the earth in preparation for it. The Tribulation is the beginning of the Day of the Lord and also known as the Day of the Lord. When the prophet looked into the distant future the events ran together, as we would expect, since three and a half years is but a small fraction of one thousand years. Joel saw the Lord intervening with great judgment and establishing His reign or Day. The cosmic signs in the Sun and Moon are cataclysmic events that will happen before the Millennium. However they are also part of the Day of the Lord. Joel himself makes this clear in the same chapter where he calls the Day of the Lord a time of great darkness which is definitely not the Millennium.

For the day of the LORD is coming; surely it is near, a day of darkness and gloom, a day of clouds and thick darkness. Joel 2:1-2

This is a perfect example of why we must not take verses out of their context. The context of all of Joel Chapter 2, and the whole book for that matter, is the Day of the Lord.

Premillennialists, who say that the Day of the Lord is the "Time of Wrath" only, are contradicting the words of Joel. Notice the "before" which is a reference to before the Millennium. However, those who would use this verse to say that the Tribulation is not the Day of the Lord are contradicting all the verses we have just listed, including Joel, not to mention many in the New Testament as well.

The Eve of Shabbat (Sabbath)

To understand this supposed contradiction between the Day of the Lord Millennium and the Day of the Lord Tribulation we must access the thinking of the Jewish prophets and rabbis including those who wrote the New Testament. Just before the Sabbath there would be great activity in each household as the house was being cleansed of leaven and prepared for the Sabbath. Religious Jews still do this today. Since the Sabbath starts at sundown, it would not always be at the same time. The diminishing light of the sun would be the signal that the Sabbath was here. But when would the Sabbath officially begin? Should the sun disappear at six o'clock would it be considered the Sabbath at five minutes to six or ten minutes to six? If you asked a Jewish family at five thirty that same evening what day it was, they would very likely say it was the Shabbat. In the same way, if we consider that the Sabbath Rest of God (The Millennium or Seventh Day) is one thousand years long preceded by six days of one thousand years each, then three and a half years before the Seventh Day (or Millennium) would be about five minutes to six. In the minds of the prophets and New Testament writers, the Great Tribulation is the eve of the Sabbath. It is the cleansing of the earth prior to the Day of the Lord. Therefore, it is not difficult to see why they referred to both as the Day of the Lord since in their minds, when the cleansing of the earth begins, the Millennial reign of Messiah will have begun.

Birth Pains

The "Birth Pains" mentioned by Paul in 1 Thess 5 are the same ones referred to by Jesus. They are "The Birth Pains of The Messiah." They got their understanding from the Hebrew prophets and undoubtedly Jesus and Paul were merely making reference to this well-known teaching. Consider the following verses:

"Ask now, and see, if a male can give birth. Why do I see every man with his hands on his loins, as a woman in childbirth? And why have all faces turned pale? Alas! for that day is great, there is none like it; and it is the time of Jacob's distress, but he will be saved from it." Jer 30:6-7

"For nation will rise against nation, and kingdom against kingdom, and in various places there will be famines and earthquakes. But all these things are merely the beginning of birth pangs." Mt 24:7-8

Notice Jesus said these are only the beginning of birth pains. They are like false labor. The real birth pains begin in verse 15 (Mt 24:15).

The Day of the Lord in the New Testament
We have cited many Scriptures that refer to the Day of the Lord as the time of judgment or tribulation. With this, the teaching of the New Testament agrees.

"For you yourselves know full well that the day of the Lord will come just like a thief in the night while they are saying, 'Peace and safety!' then destruction will come upon them suddenly like birth pangs upon a woman with child; and they shall not escape." 1 Thess 5:2-3

"Now we request you, brethren, with regard to the coming of our Lord Jesus Christ, and our gathering together to Him, that you may not be quickly shaken from your composure or be disturbed either by a spirit or a message or a letter as if from us, to the effect that the day of the Lord has come. Let no one in any way deceive you, for it (the Day of the Lord) *will not come unless the apostasy comes first, and the man of lawlessness is revealed, the son of destruction, who opposes and exalts himself above every so-called god or object of worship, so that he takes his seat in the temple of God, displaying himself as being God." 2 Thess 2:1-4*

The Tribulation is the Day of The Lord
Since we know that, the Day of the Lord begins with the Tribulation, and we know that the Tribulation begins with the Abomination of Desolation, it is clear that the Day of the Lord begins with the Abomination of Desolation or the ABOM for short.

"Therefore when you see the ABOMINATION OF DESOLATION which was spoken of through Daniel the prophet, standing in the holy place (let the reader understand), then those who are in Judea must flee to the mountains. Whoever is on the housetop must not go down to get the things out that are in his house. Whoever is in the field must not turn back to get his cloak. But woe to those who are pregnant and to those who are nursing babies in those days! But pray that your flight will not be in the winter, or on a Sabbath. For then there will be a great tribulation, such as has not occurred since the beginning of the world until now, nor ever will." Mt 24:15-21

"For you yourselves know full well that the day of the Lord will come just like a thief in the night. While they are saying, 'Peace and safety!' then destruction will come upon them suddenly like labor pains upon a woman with child, and they will not escape." 1 Thess 5:2-3

"Now we request you, brethren, with regard to the coming of our Lord Jesus Christ and our gathering together to Him, that you not be quickly shaken from your composure or be disturbed either by a spirit or a message or a letter as if from us, to the effect that the day of the Lord has come." 2 Thess 2:1-13

"...each man's work will become evident; for the day will show it because it is to be revealed with fire, and the fire itself will test the quality of each man's work." 1 Cor 3:13

"I have decided to deliver such a one to Satan for the destruction of his flesh, so that his spirit may be saved in the day of the Lord Jesus." 1 Cor 5:5
"For I am confident of this very thing, that He who began a good work in you will perfect it until the day of Christ Jesus." Phil 1:6

"...so that you may approve the things that are excellent, in order to be sincere and blameless until the day of Christ..." Phil 1:10

"...holding fast the word of life, so that in the day of Christ I will have reason to glory because I did not run in vain nor toil in vain." Phil 2:16

"...not forsaking our own assembling together, as is the habit of some, but encouraging one another; and all the more as you see the day drawing near." Heb 10:25

"But the day of the Lord will come like a thief, in which the heavens will pass away with a roar and the elements will be destroyed with intense heat, and the earth and its works will be burned up." 2 Peter 3:10

Also the book of Revelation is about the Day of the Lord (Rev 1:10).

The Day of Vengeance of Our God
When Jesus stood up in the synagogue in Nazareth and quoted these words, he left out the second part of verse 2.

"And the book of the prophet Isaiah was handed to Him. And He opened the book and found the place where it was written, 'THE SPIRIT OF THE LORD IS UPON ME, BECAUSE HE ANOINTED ME TO PREACH THE GOSPEL TO THE POOR. HE HAS SENT ME TO PROCLAIM RELEASE TO THE CAPTIVES, AND RECOVERY OF SIGHT TO THE BLIND, TO SET FREE THOSE WHO ARE OPPRESSED, TO PROCLAIM THE FAVORABLE YEAR OF THE LORD.' And He closed the book, gave it back to the attendant and sat down; and the eyes of all in the synagogue were fixed on Him. And He began to say to them, "Today this Scripture has been fulfilled in your hearing." Luke 4:17-21

Jesus' ministry lasted for three and a half years. The number seven is the complete number, but three and a half is not. God does not do His work in three and a half but always in seven. Thus, Jesus left out the "day of vengeance of our God" because that is the second half of His earthy ministry when He comes to deal out retribution upon His enemies. This is the Day of the Lord – the Day of Vengeance of our God. It is also three and a half years long and will complete Jesus' preparation of the earth before His reign.

Can We Hasten the Day?

"But the day of the Lord will come like a thief, in which the heavens will pass away with a roar and the elements will be destroyed with intense heat, and the earth and its works will be burned up. Since all these things are to be destroyed in this way, what sort of people ought you to be in holy conduct and godliness, <u>looking for and hastening</u> ("speudontas"— earnestly desiring as in ASV) the coming of the day of God, because of which the heavens will be destroyed by burning, and the elements will melt with intense heat! But according to His promise we are looking for new heavens and a new earth, in which righteousness dwells. 2 Peter 3:10-13

The above underlined verse seems to suggest that we can actually hasten or speed up the coming of the Day of the Lord. If that is true, then I suppose it is also possible to slow it down. And if we can do that, then it all depends on us when Jesus comes, which is what many preachers believe. However, as with every other verse, it must be kept in its context and the context here is the Day of the Lord. He says that it will come "like a thief" which is a repeat of Jesus' words. It was Peter, who when he heard this "thief" illustration, asked Jesus who He was referring to (Luke 12:41). He knows it is a warning and reiterates it as such. Peter is rebuking those who mock end-time predictions and repeats Jesus' warning that we must be careful not to let the Day come on us as a thief. After discussing the judgment of the end-times on the wicked and the deliverance of the righteous, he encourages us to strive for holy living and conduct. He tells us to "look for" or "look forward to" that Day. He then adds the Greek word *"speudontas"*, which can be translated "hastening" or "earnestly desiring" as it is in the ASV.[27] It is likely that "earnestly desiring" is in fact the correct translation rather than hastening. If it is translated as "earnestly desiring," then it sounds like this: "Looking forward to and earnestly desiring the Day of God." Jesus did teach us to pray for the kingdom to come and that it is something we should be longing for rather than putting off.

---

[27] American Standard Version

Perhaps Peter believed that our looking forward to and longing for that Day would hasten its coming, although this is unlikely. Nevertheless, we certainly cannot conclude that not looking forward to it or living in an unholy manner will slow it down. Perhaps the Lord is provoked by bridal love or the increased wickedness of men to speed up the time and both deliver and judge. But if there is any speeding up mentioned on account of holy conduct and bridal passion, there is certainly no slowing down mentioned on account of apathy and indifference. Indeed, sins such as these speed up judgment rather than slow it down (Rev 3:3). Besides, the Scripture indicates that the Father has already fixed the day.

"Therefore having overlooked the times of ignorance, God is now declaring to men that all people everywhere should repent, because He has fixed a day in which He will judge the world in righteousness through a Man whom He has appointed, having furnished proof to all men by raising Him from the dead." Acts 17:30-31

This verse tells us clearly that the Day of God is a fixed period of time, which is clearly set by the Father. This means that it cannot be altered and is preceded by certain clear signs, which we are supposed to understand. It is unlikely that Peter was telling us we could make it come faster. He was probably encouraging anticipation and longing in our hearts, and as he put it in Chapter 1 of the same epistle, "until the Day dawns and the morning star arises in your hearts." If he was hinting at any flexibility in the timing of Jesus return, God already has allowed for it. When Jesus said that the tribulation period had been cut short, He had already cut it short in His word. The Scriptures, which cannot be wrong, have already stated the shortened amount of time, which is three and a half years.

The Fifth Door

The fifth door has to do with the Bride of Christ and the Rapture. It is not only about the timing of the Rapture but what it is and who is it for. There are multitudes who claim to be Christians who do not really follow the Lord or walk in holiness. Are they part of the Bride? Will they be raptured? Does the Bride really make herself ready? Does she have to become without spot or wrinkle or is she already that way? Are there two churches or just one? Does she have to go through the Tribulation to be made ready or can she be ready without it? Does the timing of the Rapture depend on her readiness? As we look around the church we hardly see readiness. Indeed it is quite the opposite. And why do we see in the Scriptures Christians that escape[28] the coming days and others left behind?[29] There is a mystery here that has caused confusion and even apathy. Is there an answer? Is there a lost key that unlocks a hidden door? The answer is yes!

The Fifth Key

The Bride is a Remnant of Believers

The Rapture is a rescue of a remnant of believers who are walking in devotion to Christ as a bride eagerly awaiting His return. The majority of those who claim to belong to Him are lukewarm in their devotion and will go through the Tribulation period, at the end of which a great harvest from the nations will be gathered in. In this next chapter the Fifth Key will be found and with it we will open the Fifth Door. Then the following chapter will unveil the mystery of the First Fruits. Oh by the way, don't forget to pick up the Fourth

---

[28] Luke 21:36
[29] Rev 7:14

Key also in this next chapter. Take your time. Examine everything carefully. You don't want to miss anything!

Chapter Six
The Rapture of the Bride

The word "rapture" comes from the Latin word "*rapturo*." This word was used by the Latin translators of the Bible for the Greek word "*harpazo*" used in 1 Thessalonians 4:17. This word means to be "caught up" or "seized." For many years, I thought that the Rapture was only mentioned in a couple of passages, but I have since discovered that it is a major theme of the New Testament. There has been much debate throughout the years regarding the timing of the Rapture. However today, among Charismatics and Pentecostals, the Rapture has fallen out of vogue and is usually scoffed at and its proponents ridiculed as "escapists" or something like that. Indeed, the Western Church seems to find the whole subject of eschatology and the soon coming of Christ distasteful and even irrelevant. To them all that matters now is transforming culture and infiltrating political systems so that they can "be the head and not the tail." However, the Lord held out a promise of deliverance to those who are eagerly awaiting Him (Heb 9:28). He is coming soon to take them to Himself that where He is they will be also (John 14:3). He repeatedly warned His disciples to be on the alert and never has this warning been more meaningful than it is today!

"Now there is in store for me the crown of righteousness, which the Lord, the righteous Judge, will award to me on that day - and not only to me, but also to all who have longed for his appearing." 2 Timothy 4:8 NIV

"…so Christ also, having been offered once to bear the sins of many, will appear a second time for salvation (deliverance) without reference to sin, to those who eagerly await Him." Hebrews 9:28

The Greek word *"soteria"* translated "salvation" in the New Testament also means "deliverance." This fact has been obscured since the word "salvation" has been used so much in a religious sense, of our salvation from sin. Thus when we substitute the word deliverance in these passages we often get a clearer meaning of what is being said.

The above passages make it clear that Christ will come and bring deliverance (salvation) to those who are longing for and eagerly awaiting Him. The clear implication is that this deliverance is not for those who are disinterested or who find the timing of His coming irrelevant. These believers who are not living in anticipation of His soon return will likely go through the Tribulation of the Day of the Lord.

The Bridegroom is Coming

In recent years we have come to understand that Jesus is following the ancient wedding ritual with His ketubah (covenant) and the bride price of His precious blood. He has also given us the bridal gift of the Holy Spirit to get us ready for the wedding. He promised to come again and receive us to Himself that where He is we may be also. It is the heart of the Bridgroom and the Bride to be together. And this is the whole point of the wedding shophar of 1 Thess 4:17, to meet Him in the air and to always be with Him.

"Then we who are alive and remain will be caught up (raptured) together with them in the clouds to meet the Lord in the air, and so we shall always be with the Lord." 1 Thess 4:17

The Post-Trib folks do not get this aspect of our relationship with Christ. We are not just bethrothed to Christ symbolically, we are literally His Bride. We are literally getting married. Jesus literally gave Himself up for His Bride so that He could present her to Himself in all her glory. This is not some add on, or "by the way," to Jesus returning and ruling. No, it's a great mystery! The wedding is a central part of God's End-Time plan that is not just about authority and ruling, but about intimacy. Paul tells us to comfort one another with the hope of the Rapture.

"FOR THIS REASON A MAN SHALL LEAVE HIS FATHER AND MOTHER AND SHALL BE JOINED TO HIS WIFE, AND THE TWO SHALL BECOME ONE FLESH. This mystery is great; but I am speaking with reference to Christ and the church." Eph 5:31-32

Wrath of God or Wrath of Satan?

"For God has not destined us for wrath but for obtaining salvation (deliverance) through our Lord Jesus Christ." 1 Thess 5:9

For many years I believed that the Bride would go through all of the Tribulation. Since I was convinced that the "parousia"[30] was a single event, I felt there was no other option. When confronted with this verse (1Thess 5:9), I concluded, as did many others, that it was referring to the wrath of God only. When the "Pre-Wrath" view was made popular by Marvin Rosenthal, I switched to that position. However, I now believe both of these views are missing the point of this passage. What is said is that God has not destined us for wrath, period. There is no basis on which to differentiate between the wrath of God and the wrath of satan. Whether the wrath is coming directly from heaven or through satan is of no real consequence. The result is equally terrifying for those who experience it. Drawing such a distinction between the wrath of God and the wrath of satan is also out of step with the whole of Scripture. God has always used the devil to sift and test mankind and the Tribulation period is no exception. For example, when God punished the nation of Israel for her sins, He chose to use the Gentile nations such as Babylon and Assyria declaring that they were pouring out His wrath (2Kings 17:18, Ezek 5:13, 21:31). Also, Moses clearly taught that the curses that would come upon

---

[30] Explained in Chapter 8

the people from many different sources, because of their disobedience against God, were the result of His wrath (Deut 28).

To speak of the wrath of satan being unleashed upon mankind as though it were not the wrath of God unleashed, would be inconsistent with the rest of Scripture. The Tribulation period itself is known as the Day of Wrath and Indignation (1Thess 5:2-3, Jer 30:6-7, Zeph 1:14, Is 26:17-21). It is all referred to as the Day of the Lord. There are, however, degrees of intensity in the wrath that is poured out. Those who receive of the wrath of satan, should they turn to God, can yet be saved, while those who reject God and align themselves with the devil, have no hope of salvation and will receive specific punishment directly from Messiah. But to say that the wrath of satan unleashed is not part of the wrath of God on mankind is inaccurate. Besides, as far as the Bride of Christ is concerned, such a distinction would be completely irrelevant. God has not destined her for wrath of any kind, but for salvation (deliverance) and union with the Messiah.

Most Bible teachers acknowledge that the notion of Messiah beating up His Bride is ludicrous. What bridegroom would do such a thing? Yet, why would the Messiah allow His Bride to be beaten up by the devil? Imagine a bridegroom saying to his bride before their wedding: "Honey I promise I will never beat you up or mistreat you in any way. You can be certain of that. I love you. However, I have arranged for the worst thug in town to beat you up before our marriage just to make sure you are ready to marry me."

Chart 8 on page 294 shows three views of the Rapture. The Pre-Week view, commonly referred to as the Pre-Trib view. The Post-Trib view which is really not a rapture from anything but merely a lifting up in the air only to come back down. Then there is the Mid-Week view, which is mistakenly called a Mid-Trib view. But it is not a Mid-Trib view since the Tribulation is only three and a half years long and not seven. Thus it is the Pre-Trib Mid-Week or

Mid-Shemitah Cycle view, as we will see, that is clearly taught in Scipture!

What About Persecution – Bring it On?

According to Jesus, the Day of the Lord or the Tribulation is a time of distress such as has never occurred in the history of man and never will again. If we combine all of the wars and natural disasters throughout history, we scarcely scratch the surface of the human suffering that will occur during the Tribulation period. In fact, Jesus said that if God had not cut this time short to three and a half years, no flesh would survive. Consider the fact that there are about seven billion people on the planet today and you understand how many will die of famine, disease, earthquakes, tsunamis, pestilence, chemical warfare, intense heat, hailstones, nuclear warfare, and God knows what else. Perhaps as many as five billion people will die, and that is probably a low estimate. Now imagine all that happening in just three and a half years. In 2001, three thousand people died in New York from the collapse of the Twin Towers and the nation is still shaken by it. Many people in the world are still suffering from the 2004 tsunami that struck the Indian Ocean killing three hundred thousand. And who can forget what happened to New Orleans in 2005? People are still displaced from that disaster. But what will it be like when asteroids a mile or two wide fall out of the sky, mountains and islands move out of their places and massive earthquakes strike all the major cities? What will it really be like when the plagues of Revelation are released? What about the persecution and torture of believers and their families who will not fall in line with the will of the global government? Jesus warned us about those days that would come suddenly upon the earth and so did all the prophets and the apostles. This is a time of great testing and sifting of mankind so that only those worthy of the Millennial Kingdom will survive.[31]

---

[31] Luke 20:35

When we consider the suffering of the Great Tribulation, it is hard to imagine how Post-Trib believers paint a picture of the church protected during this time in "Goshen cities" and the like. One author says that the Tribulation will "be a great day for those who respond. They will experience the greatest revival in history." Well, praise God for the great revival and harvest, but I can think of something much more exciting – like being with Jesus. Besides, where does the Scripture admonish us to look forward to going through the Tribulation? It doesn't. Indeed, it's quite the opposite. Jesus told us that it would come suddenly like a trap on the whole world. There will be no cities of refuge or places where the Tribulation will not reach. It will affect all people everywhere. Then He told us to be on the alert, watching and praying and walking in intimacy with Him (implied) that we may be able to escape all these things and stand before the Son of Man.[32] Post-Tribbers argue that He didn't mean escape but to have strength to go through the Tribulation. However, it's pretty hard to change *"ekpheugo"* which means "to flee out of," "flee away," or "escape," into "hang in there." Nevertheless, when you consider that the result of this *"ekpheugo"* is standing before the Son of Man who is in the heavens during this time, it is undeniably a reference to the Rapture.

Another argument that is often presented by those of the Post-Trib Rapture view is that since persecution has always been the lot of Christians, why then would God take us out of the Tribulation? Why would we be treated any different than all those other believers throughout the centuries? They argue instead for God's protection on the church in the midst of persecution saying, "The saints will not receive God's judgments" and "We need not fear that we will compromise under pressure of persecution." Well, I certainly believe that God is able to protect believers. However, though there will be miraculous interventions, there is no promise

---

[32] Luke 21:34-36

that Christians will be protected from suffering in the Tribulation or any other time. Of course the reason they now say that the church will not suffer God's judgments is because the Scripture is clear that "God has not destined us for wrath."[33] This is a modified Post-Trib view. Of course, Paul was referring to the Tribulation as the time of wrath. But this is an attempt to separate God's judgments from satan's wrath, in order to comply with Scripture. Yet, it presents the devil's unrestrained day of terror as somehow more tolerable than God's judgments. When I hear this argument presented, I can only think of King David who said he would rather fall into the judgment of God than that of men.[34]

Of course, it is true that Christians have always been persecuted. The early church was promised by Jesus Himself that they would be hated by all and killed for their faith.[35] Yet they were the ones who told us that "The Tribulation" was coming. Also, throughout history Christians have been persecuted, and today in many countries believers are suffering persecution and death for their commitment to Christ. And though there are many stories of heroism and dramatic deliverances, by and large they are not being protected or spared. But despite all this, Jesus was specific when He said that the Tribulation would be unlike any other time in history. It is not called "The Tribulation" for no reason. Thus comparing it to the tribulation endured today, or in the first few centuries, is not valid. When we consider the brutality against Christians by Nero, this is a sober warning. Also, if God is going to protect Christians in the Tribulation, why did He not protect the early believers or why does He not give the Chinese believers at least one city of refuge?

---

[33] 1Thess 5:9
[34] 2Sam 24:14
[35] Luke 21:12 "But before all these things they will lay their hands on you…"

Purifying the Church?

There is no doubt that the Tribulation period is a sifting and refining process. It is the Time of Jacob's Distress when there is a final purging in Israel culminating in the deliverance of a remnant. Those who hold to a Post-Trib view of the Rapture cite this as the reason why the church must endure it. However, this view of the Bride of Christ having to get purged by wrath is foreign to the New Testament. As already stated it is inconsistent with the whole analogy of a bride and groom whose relationship is one of love and choice. The Groom loves the Bride and gave Himself up for her (Eph 5) while the Bride is passionately in love with the Groom longing for His appearing (Heb 9:28). The purging is not for those who have chosen to follow Christ but those who have not, or those who say they have but do not live in a manner pleasing to Him. The New Testament teaches us that believers are expected to live lives that are above reproach and worthy of the Messiah. Only those will be taken to Him in the Rapture. The following are some Scriptures that make this fact clear:

"For the grace of God has appeared, bringing salvation to all men, instructing us to deny ungodliness and worldly desires and to live sensibly, righteously and godly in the present age, looking for the blessed hope and the appearing of the glory of our great God and Savior, (deliverer) Christ Jesus; who gave Himself for us, that He might redeem us from every lawless deed and purify for Himself a people for His own possession, zealous for good deeds." Titus 2:11-14

"...just as He chose us in Him before the foundation of the world, that we should be holy and blameless before Him." Eph 1:4

"Now may the God of peace Himself sanctify you entirely; and may your spirit and soul and body be preserved complete, without blame at the coming of our Lord Jesus Christ."" 1 Thess 5:23

Therefore, beloved, since you look for these things, be diligent to be found by Him in peace, spotless and blameless..." 2Pet 3:14

"...that you keep the commandment without stain or reproach until the appearing of our Lord Jesus Christ..." 1Tim 6:14

"....yet He has now reconciled you in His fleshly body through death, in order to present you before Him holy and blameless and beyond reproach-- if indeed you continue in the faith firmly established and steadfast, and not moved away from the hope of the gospel that you have heard, which was proclaimed in all creation under heaven, and of which I, Paul, was made a minister." Col 1:22-23

The hope of the gospel is to be presented before Him! Those who reject the Rapture say that the church has to go through the Tribulation to become pure and spotless, or to become strong and unified, or to become the "End-Time Apostolic Church," or something along that line. Indeed, for many Post-Tribbers this is the capstone of their eschatology and one which invokes no small amount of passion and debate. However, is this a biblical view of the church? Was this the understanding of the early believers? Did they believe they had to go through tribulation in order to be made pure? Did they need tribulation to be in unity and ready for Christ? They were washed in the Blood, filled with the Spirit and bethrothed to Christ and so are we. But is that enough? Is the fire of tribulation necessary to make us truly pure or truly one? Is it the Blood, the Spirit and the Tribulation that bear witness?[36] Or is santification now by the Spirit and tribulation?[37] Are we to believe that the all out terror of satan is going to accomplish something that the cross and the power of the Holy Spirit could not? Am I exaggerating here? Are Post-Tribbers really saying this? I hope not! But the standard line among Post-Tribbers is that the Bride of Christ is prepared in the context of the judgment and wrath of the

---

[36] 1John 5:8
[37] 2Thess 2:13

Tribulation. They often look to Daniel's words when he says that the saints will be purified and purged during this time.[38] However, the saints Daniel spoken of were Jews since he knew of no others. We know that the Jews are being purged, purified and refined during the Tribulation so that they can come to Christ and enter into their long-awaited Davidic kingdom. Indeed, all who go through the Tribulation go through it for that purpose, since that is the reason it comes upon men - to test and sift their hearts. And it is for the same reason that the Lukewarm church will also go through the Tribulation, because they have not availed themselves of the cleansing Blood or the work of the Holy Spirit. They have been happy to have a little bit of God rather than pursuing the fullness of His Presence.[39] They have been preoccupied with their own agenda rather than the person of Christ Himself. They have been consumed by a Martha spirit of busyness and works rather than the Mary spirit of love and intimacy. Indeed, Jesus warned the last days church about lukewarmness and promised to reward the overcomers.[40] These are the two churches mentioned in the beginning of Revelation, the Lukewarm church and the Overcoming Church. The Philadelphian Church is representative of the Overcoming Church and Jesus promised to keep them from the Tribulation. He did not say He would keep or guard *("tereo")* them as Post-Tribbers suggest. He said he would keep them out of *("ek")* or from the hour of trial.

As we have seen, some say suffering and even martyrdom are necessary for the Bride of Christ to endure if she is going to reign with Him. It is true that Paul encouraged the Romans that they would reign with Him if they suffered with Him.[41] However, he was not saying that suffering was part of the santification process and was necessary for the Bride to endure in order to be presented

---

[38] Dan 7:27, 12:10
[39] Eph 3:19
[40] Rev 2 & 3
[41] Rom 8:17

to Christ. On the contrary, he was affirming them throughout the chapter as co-heirs with Christ and adopted sons of the Father because of the presence of the Holy Spirit in them. What he did say was that they could not turn away from the persecution that came with following Christ and still expect to reign with Him. They had to be willing to suffer if that was necessary to stay true to Him. This is the same thing that both Peter and James said to the church. They encouraged the brethren that if they must suffer for a little while it would only prove the genuineness of their faith and cause them to have more endurance and maturity.[42] This is quite different from the idea that they needed to go through tribulation and persecution in order to be made pure or righteous. Also, when we consider the overcomers in Revelation 12, it is easy to assume that they have been martyred and this is the reason they overcame satan. However, they are not martyred but are caught up to God. What the text says is that, "They overcame by the Blood of the Lamb and the word of their testimony and because they did not love their lives <u>even</u> to death." It does not say that they were killed but that they didn't care. They loved Jesus so much that they would have gladly died for Him.

The idea that the church is purified by the Tribulation, besides the theological can of worms it opens, is contradictory to the whole concept of a victorious church releasing the judgments of the Tribulation as is taught by some Post-Tribbers. It is actually a confession that this Tribulation church is lukewarm. Where is this great "End-Time Apostolic Church," united in focus and prayer and releasing "smart missiles" on satan? And how can it be such a church when it still needs satan's wrath to make it pure? How very contradictory is this? Where did it come from and how can those who know the cleansing Blood and the power of the Holy Spirit accept it? How can a Bride be prepared by the enemy of the Groom? Surely bridal preparation is more about love and intimacy than

---

[42] 1Pet 1:6-7, James 1:2-4, Rom 5:3-5

hardship and suffering? What bridal paradigm is this and where can it be found either in ancient or modern times? Surely it is the Holy Spirit who has come to prepare the Bride of Christ for her wedding and she is not waiting for some satanic counterfeit messiah to get the job done. Furthermore, why would Jesus tell us to be ready if He knew that it was impossible without us going through the Tribulation? Indeed, He warns us to be ready because of the Tribulation. All of the warnings given by Jesus carry the theme of being ready to go with Him and not being left behind. Consider the parable of the virgins which is part of the Olivet Discourse. All the virgins (believers) are pictured as waiting for the Bridegroom, yet five are foolish and five are prudent. Five were ready when He came and five were not. Five were allowed into the wedding feast and five were not. If being ready for the Bridegroom to come for us was not the most important thing, why would Jesus have focused on it so? Instead He could have said something like, "Just carry on with the work I gave you, that's all that matters" or as the scoffers say, "Don't worry, it will all pan out in the end."

Timing of the Rapture

"But we do not want you to be uninformed, brethren, about those who are asleep, so that you will not grieve as do the rest who have no hope. For if we believe that Jesus died and rose again, even so God will bring with Him those who have fallen asleep in Jesus. For this we say to you by the word of the Lord, that we who are alive and remain until the coming of the Lord, will not precede those who have fallen asleep. For the Lord Himself will descend from heaven with a shout, with the voice of the archangel and with the trumpet of God, and the dead in Christ will rise first. Then we who are alive and remain will be caught up together with them in the clouds to meet the Lord in the air, and so we shall always be with the Lord. Therefore comfort one another with these words (Remember there is no chapter and verse in the original). Now as to the times and the epochs, brethren, you have no need of anything to be written to you. For you yourselves know full well that the day of the Lord will come just like a thief in the night. While they are saying, "Peace and safety!" then destruction will come upon them suddenly like

labor pains upon a woman with child, and they will not escape. 1 Thess 4:13-18, 5:1-3

When we read this passage as Paul wrote it, without the chapter and verse notations, we see clearly that the Rapture of 4:17 is linked together with the Day of the Lord of 5:2. After speaking about the Rapture, which was his main focus, and telling them to comfort each other with these words, he says that they don't need to be told about dates and times because they know full well that the Day of the Lord will come like a thief in the night. If the Day of the Lord and the Rapture were not simultaneous, why would Paul not change the subject in the passage? Instead he used the terms interchangeably indicating that they were the same. In other words the Rapture will come when the Day of the Lord comes and it will come like a thief in the night. Incidentally the Rapture is also spoken of as coming like a thief in the night (Mt 24:42-43).

Then Paul clearly tells us what begins the Day of the Lord:

"While they are saying, 'Peace and safety!' then destruction will come upon them suddenly like labor pains upon a woman with child, and they will not escape."

This is the middle of the Last Shemitah Cycle, during a time of Peace and Security, when Antichrist breaks his covenant and sets up what is known as the Abomination that causes Desolation or Destruction. Then Paul goes on with the link between the Day of the Lord and the Rapture.

"But you, brethren, are not in darkness, that the day would overtake you like a thief; (the Day of the Lord) for you are all sons of light and sons of day. We are not of night nor of darkness; so then let us not sleep as others do, but let us be alert and sober. For those who sleep do their sleeping at night, and those who get drunk get drunk at night. But since we are of the day, let us be sober, having put on the breastplate of faith and love, and as a helmet, the

hope of salvation (deliverance). For God has not destined us for wrath, (the Day of the Lord Wrath) but for obtaining salvation (deliverance) through (by his coming) our Lord Jesus Christ, who died for us, so that whether we are awake or asleep, we will live together with Him. Therefore encourage one another and build up one another, just as you also are doing." 1 Thess 5:4-11

The Rapture and the Day of the Lord Are Simultaneous

"Now we request you, brethren, with regard to the coming of our Lord Jesus Christ and our gathering together to Him, that you not be quickly shaken from your composure or be disturbed either by a spirit or a message or a letter as if from us, to the effect that the day of the Lord has come." 2 Thess 2:1-2

This sentence is even clearer than that in 1 Thess 5. Just the plain rules of grammar when applied make it impossible to miss. The Rapture and the Day of the Lord are the same subject in the same sentence. Paul says that with regard to the coming of the Lord and "our gathering together to Him" (which is the Rapture) that they should not receive any report that says the Day of the Lord has already come. There can be no mistake here — the Rapture and the Day of the Lord are simultaneous events!

The Apostasy Must Come First

"Let no one in any way deceive you, for it (the Day of the Lord & Rapture) will not come unless the apostasy comes first, and the man of lawlessness is revealed, the son of destruction, who opposes and exalts himself above every so-called god or object of worship, so that he takes his seat in the temple of God, displaying himself as being God" (This is the ABOM). 2 Thess 2:3-4

The Rapture and the Day of the Lord cannot come until the Apostasy, which is the Covenant with Antichrist, comes first and the man of lawlessness is revealed. This is known as the Abomination of Desolation or the "ABOM" as we call it. So again, as in 1 Thess 5:3, the Rapture is presented as happening after the Antichrist is revealed with the Abom in the middle of the Seventieth Week. In fact, Paul categorically states that the Rapture and the Day of the Lord, which are simultaneous events, cannot happen until the middle of the Last Shemitah Cycle and the Abom occurs. Thus it is absolutely impossible for the Rapture to happen prior to the Abom, which rules out a Pre-Week Rapture.

Proponents of the Post-Trib Rapture find comfort and confidence in these verses since they rule out a Pre-Week Rapture. However, they also rule out a Post-Trib Rapture since the Rapture is presented as happening in the middle of the Week along with the Abomination of Desolation and the Day of the Lord.

Paul goes on to talk about what or who is restraining the Antichrist from being revealed until that time and reiterates how the Rapture (deliverance) has been ordained for those who are walking with the Lord in a sanctified life!

"Do you not remember that while I was still with you, I was telling you these things? And you know what restrains him now, so that in his time he will be revealed. For the mystery of lawlessness is already at work; only he who now restrains will do so until he is taken out of the way. Then that lawless one will be revealed whom the Lord will slay with the breath of His mouth and bring to an end by the appearance of His coming; that is, the one whose coming is in accord with the activity of Satan, with all power and signs and false wonders, and with all the deception of wickedness for those who perish, because they did not receive the love of the truth so as to be saved. For this reason God will send upon them a deluding influence so that they will believe what is false, in order that they all may be judged who did not believe the truth, but took pleasure in wickedness. But we should always give thanks to God for you, brethren beloved by the Lord, because God has chosen you from the beginning for salvation (deliverance) through sanctification by the Spirit and faith in the truth. 2Thess 2:1-13

The fact that the Day of the Lord Tribulation begins with the Abom in the middle of the Week, was also clearly confirmed by Jesus in the Olivet Discourse of Mt 24 and Mark 13.

"Therefore when you see the ABOMINATION OF DESOLATION which was spoken of through Daniel the prophet, standing in the holy place (let the reader understand), then those who are in Judea must flee to the mountains. Whoever is on the housetop must not go down to get the things out that are in his house. Whoever is in the field must not turn back to get his cloak. But woe to those who are pregnant and to those who are nursing babies in those days! But pray that your flight will not be in the winter, or on a Sabbath. For then there will be a great tribulation, such as has not occurred since the beginning of the world until now, nor ever will. Unless those days had been cut short, no life would have been saved; but for the sake of the elect those days will be cut short. Matt 24:15-22

"But when you see the ABOMINATION OF DESOLATION standing where it should not be (let the reader understand), then those who are in Judea must flee to the mountains. The one who is on the housetop must not go down, or go in to get anything out of his house; and the one who is in the field must not turn back to get his coat. But woe to those who are pregnant and to those who are nursing babies in those days! But pray that it may not happen in the winter. For those days will be a time of tribulation such as has not occurred since the beginning of the creation which God created until now, and never will." Mark 13:14-19

Is The Coming of The Lord a Single Event?

The answer to this question is of crucial importance. If it is a single event, then only a Post-Trib view of the Rapture is possible. This was my conclusion for many years and it caused me to dismiss all other scenarios without even studying them. However, I no longer find this view to be in harmony with Scripture.

There are two Greek words used for Jesus' coming in the New Testament. They are *"parousia"* (presence) and *"erchomai"* (coming).

Erchomai is always used of Jesus literally appearing and entering Earth through the clouds. It is a literal appearing on His way to Earth. Parousia is the word which is used concerning the whole time period of the Day of the Lord, when He is present but not necessarily revealed.[43] This word literally means "presence." Vines Expository Dictionary of New Testament Words has this to say:

"PAROUSIA, lit, a presence, para, with, and ousia, being, denotes both an arrival and a consequent presence with. For instance, in a papyrus letter a lady speaks of the necessity of her parousia in a place in order to attend to matters relating to her property there. When used of the return of Christ, at the Rapture of the church, it signifies, not merely His momentary coming for His saints, but His presence with them from that moment until His revelation and manifestation to the world. In some passages the word gives prominence to the beginning of that period, the course of the period being implied, 1 Cor 15:23, 1 Thess 4:15, 5:23, 2 Thess 2:1, Jas 5:7, 8, 2 Pet 3:4. In some, the course is prominent, Mt 24:3, 37, 1 Thess 3:13, 1 John 2:28; in others the conclusion of the period, Mt 24:27, 2 Thess 2:8." W. E. Vine, Expository Dictionary of New Testament Words.

I realize that making an argument based on the meaning of Greek words can be fraught with danger, however, there is much more evidence in the Scripture to support this conclusion. First of all, the New Testament writers are very careful to use erchomai when referring to Jesus triumphal entry, whereas they frequently use parousia to refer to the whole period. If the words are interchangeable, why do they not use them as such?

When Jesus left the Temple after declaring to the Jewish leaders, "You shall not see me here again until you learn to cry, 'Blessed is He who comes in the name of the Lord,'" the disciples were not grasping the gravity of His words. They were, instead, preoccupied with the huge stones on the Temple Mount and the magnificence of the whole structure. When Jesus told them that there would not be

---

[43] Vines Expository Dictionary of New Testament Words

one stone left that was not torn down, they were deeply troubled and asked him later, "When will these things be, and what will be the sign of Your coming (parousia) and of the end of the age?"

When we read this, we tend to think that the disciples were asking about a time in the distant future when Jesus would come again. However, this cannot be so. The disciples did not understand that Jesus was going away at this time. They were expecting Him to unveil Himself at any moment in a display of power, bringing judgment on His enemies and ushering in the kingdom age and everlasting righteousness. Even after His resurrection they still were not expecting any "second coming." Therefore, their use of the word "parousia" could not have been in reference to a single event which would take place within a twenty-four hour period thousands of years in the future. They had something else in mind. They were looking for the kingdom, the days of the Son of Man, when Messiah would judge the nations and establish His throne in Israel. They were referring to the Day of the Lord. The fact that the "parousia" is not a single event is evident in the following Scriptures:

"For the coming (parousia) of the Son of Man will be just like the days (plural) of Noah." Mt 24:37

"And He said to the disciples, 'The days shall come when you will long to see one of the days of the Son of Man, and you will not see it.'" Luke 17:22

"And just as it happened in the days of Noah, so it shall be also in the days of the Son of Man...." Luke 17:26

"But woe to those who are with child and to those who nurse babes in those days! But pray that your flight may not be in the winter, or on a Sabbath; for then there will be a great tribulation, such as has not occurred since the beginning of the world until now, nor ever shall. And unless those days had

been cut short, no life would have been saved; but for the sake of the elect those days shall be cut short." Mt 24:19-22

"For we did not follow cleverly devised tales when we made known to you the power and coming (parousia) of our Lord Jesus Christ, but we were eyewitnesses of His majesty. For when He received honor and glory from God the Father, such an utterance as this was made to Him by the Majestic Glory, 'This is My beloved Son with whom I am well-pleased'-- and we ourselves heard this utterance made from heaven when we were with Him on the holy mountain." 2Pet 1:16-18

Peter in his epistle spoke about the parousia with reference to Jesus appearing in glory on the mountain with Moses and Elijah.[44] At that time Jesus was neither coming or going, so why is it called "the parousia?" Another example of the usage of parousia as a time period is found in 2 Thessalonians where Paul refers to the parousia of the Antichrist as being the time of His coming to power and reigning with all kinds of false signs and miracles.[45]

"And then that lawless one will be revealed whom the Lord will slay with the breath of His mouth and bring to an end by the appearance of His coming (parousia); that is, the one whose coming (parousia) is in accord with the activity of Satan, with all power and signs and false wonders..." 2Thess 2:8-9

The time period during which the Antichrist is made known to the world by false signs and wonders is referred to as his "parousia." This fact alone makes the translation of "parousia" as a single event or coming, such as the other Greek word "erchomai" implies, impossible. Also, when we use the English word "coming" with reference to the first coming of Messiah, we acknowledge that we are not speaking about a single event. However, when speaking of the "second coming," how is it we tend to think of a single event?

---

[44] 2Pet 1:16-19
[45] 2Thess 2:9-10

The Scriptures were written by Jews and not Greeks. Most Gentiles think like Greeks, but in order to understand many passages of Scripture, especially prophetic passages, we must think like the ancient Jews did. For Scriptures to skip large quantities of time in one or two verses is not uncommon or unusual. It was, in fact, normal. Remember, the rabbis understood that many passages had more than one meaning or fulfillment, and in some cases several. When Jesus stood up in the synagogue in Nazareth and read Isaiah 61:2, saying that it was fulfilled in their hearing, he left out the rest of the sentence about "the day of vengeance of our God" because it refers to the Day of the Lord at least 2000 years later. The same is true for many New Testament passages and the words of Jesus Himself. Thus many passages that appear to be referring to a single event are often speaking of several. The Olivet Discourse contains examples of this. One is the surrounding of Jerusalem by armies which occurred in 70 AD and will occur again during the Tribulation.

Another example may be the following:

"…and then the sign of the Son of Man will appear in the sky, and then all the tribes of the earth will mourn, and they will see the Son of Man coming on the clouds of the sky with power and great glory." Mt 24:30

Casual reading of this passage leads us to believe that this verse is speaking of one event, but perhaps three events are being referred to which all occur in reasonably close proximity to each other during The Day of the Lord. The Sign of The Son of Man will appear in the Sky. All the tribes of the earth will mourn. They will see the Son of Man coming (erchomai - not parousia) on the clouds of the sky with power and great glory. And Jesus, in Matthew 24, after speaking about His erchomai in the clouds at the end of the Tribulation, goes on to speak about His parousia as being similar to the days (plural) of Noah.[46] He says it will be like that period when everybody will be carrying on as usual, not expecting anything and suddenly it will be upon them. And just as Noah was rescued and the flood washed away the rest, so will it be at the parousia. Suddenly the destruction will come on them, but just as the Lord rescued Noah, one will be taken and one will be left - a clear reference to the Rapture. Please note that the 7th Trumpet of the Book of Revelation does not come in this sudden way - like a thief in the night. On the contrary, the erchomai at the 7th Trumpet of Revelation comes at a time when the earth is reeling to and fro with the judgments being poured out on it and could never be understood to come suddenly. Indeed, it's the parousia, the Day of the Lord and the Rapture that come suddenly (at a time of peace) like a thief.[47]

"For this we say to you by the word of the Lord, that we who are alive, and remain until the coming (parousia) of the Lord, shall not precede those who have fallen asleep. For the Lord Himself will descend from heaven with a shout, with the voice of the archangel, and with the trumpet of God; and the dead in Christ shall rise first. Then we who are alive and remain shall be caught up together with them in the clouds to meet the Lord in the air, and thus we shall always be with the Lord. Now as to the times and the epochs, brethren, you have no need of anything to be written to you. For you yourselves know full well that the day of the Lord will come just like a thief in the night. While they are saying, 'Peace and safety!' then destruction will come upon them suddenly like birth pangs upon a woman with child; and they shall not escape. But you, brethren, are not in darkness, that the day should overtake you like a thief...." 1 Thess 4:15-17, 1 Thess 5:1-4

It is really unbelievable how both Post-Tribbers and Pre-Weekers deny the Rapture clearly spoken of by Jesus in Matthew 24. He says "one will be taken and one will be left." But because the timing is

---

[46] Mt 24:37-41
[47] 1Thess 5:2-4, Mt 24:42-44, 2Pet 3:10, Rev 3:3, 16:15

undeniably identified with the middle of the Last Shemitah Cycle, many are now saying it is a rapture of the wicked. This is a most grievous distortion and alteration of Scripture to support a predetermined position and agenda and there is no support for it anywhere in the Bible. The wicked are not snatched away at any time. They are judged or "gathered up"[48] at the end of the age in the presence of Messiah on Earth and are not suddenly, without warning, snatched away.

Some Post-Tribbers are willing to acknowledge that the coming (erchomai) of Jesus at the end of the Tribulation is a time period of days. Why then can't the parousia be a time period that begins suddenly and lasts for the whole of the Tribulation, since there is more evidence to support that conclusion than there is to suggest it is a single event? Also, when we speak today of Jesus' first coming, we all realize that we are referring to a period of thirty three and a half years. Why then, can't Post-Tribbers accept that His second coming is a time period as well? Indeed, since His first ministry lasted three and a half years, His parousia at the end of the age will last the same amount of time. Thus the redemption and cleansing of the earth will be completed as a seven year period. This was confirmed by Jesus Himself in the synagogue at Nazareth when He read the scroll of Isaiah. He began at Chapter 61 and stopped halfway through the second verse, leaving out the Day of Vengeance of our God. This, of course, is the Day of the Lord and it is also part of Messiah's ministry. It was left out because it was to come at the end of the age, and thus will be fulfilled the verse, *"Behold, I cast out demons and perform cures today and tomorrow, and the third day I reach My goal."*[49]

The Rapture in the New Testament
"For the coming (parousia) of the Son of Man will be just like the days (plural) of Noah. For as in those days which were before the flood they were

---

[48] Mt 13:41-42
[49] Luke 13:32

eating and drinking, they were marrying and giving in marriage, until the day that Noah entered the ark, and they did not understand until the flood came and took them all away; so shall the coming of the Son of Man be. Then there shall be two men in the field; one will be taken, and one will be left. Two women will be grinding at the mill; one will be taken, and one will be left." Mt 24:37-41

Here the coming (parousia) of the Lord is compared to the days of Noah. Just as the people were unprepared and unexpecting of the flood, so the earth will be unprepared and unexpecting of the Day of the Lord. The Day will come suddenly, "as a thief." The clear implication is that just as Noah was prepared and rescued, the righteous will be prepared and rescued. Notice that the Rapture is undeniably linked to the beginning of the Day of the Lord.

Some say that this taking referred to here is a taking away of the wicked. However, because of its connection with the warnings of Jesus to be ready for His "parousia," it is more likely referring to the Rapture of the Bride. Also, there is no way to substantiate a snatching away (implied by the sudden disappearance) of the wicked. If that were the meaning of the passage, then it would mean that the wicked are snatched away just before judgment is poured out on them.

In a discussion about the coming Kingdom (Day of The Lord) in Luke 17, the same statements are repeated with an even clearer link to the middle of the week and the Abom.

"And just as it happened in the days of Noah, so it shall be also in the days of the Son of Man: they were eating, they were drinking, they were marrying, they were being given in marriage, until the day that Noah entered the ark, and the flood came and destroyed them all. It was the same as happened in the days of Lot: they were eating, they were drinking, they were buying, they were selling, they were planting, they were building; but on the day that Lot went out from Sodom it rained fire and brimstone from

heaven and destroyed them all. It will be just the same on the day that the Son of Man is revealed."

Here the text is the same as Mt 24 except that the destruction of Sodom is added as an example of what is coming upon the wicked and the deliverance of Lot as an example of God's deliverance of the righteous before the Great Tribulation. Then in verse 31, the Abom is clearly referenced which is followed immediately by the Rapture.

"On that day, let not the one who is on the housetop and whose goods are in the house go down to take them away; and likewise let not the one who is in the field turn back. Remember Lot's wife. Whoever seeks to keep his life shall lose it, and whoever loses his life shall preserve it. I tell you, on that night there will be two men in one bed; one will be taken, and the other will be left. There will be two women grinding at the same place; one will be taken, and the other will be left. Two men will be in the field; one will be taken and the other will be left." Luke 17:26-36

The statement "on that day" linked with the warning to flee Jerusalem can refer to only one event, the Abom (Abomination of Desolation) which is set up in the middle of the week by the Antichrist (covered in Chapter 5). With this the rest of the Scriptures agree (See Mt 24:15-22, Mark 13:14-20, 1Thes 5:1-3, 2Thes 2:1-4). This is the event which marks the middle of the week, begins the Tribulation, and signals the deliverance of the Bride of Christ in the Rapture. Interestingly enough, many Pre-Weekers stay away from using these verses to refer to the Rapture, and some have tried to change their obvious meaning, because they understand that they place the Rapture in the middle of the Last Shemitah Cycle.

Let us continue now to see the Rapture mentioned in many other places in the New Testament.

Romans

"But because of your stubbornness and unrepentant heart you are storing up wrath for yourself in the day of wrath and revelation of the righteous judgment of God, who will render to every man according to his deeds: to those who by perseverance in doing good seek for glory and honor and immortality, eternal life (Rapture); but to those who are selfishly ambitious and do not obey the truth, but obey unrighteousness, wrath and indignation (Day of the Lord). *Romans 2:5-8*

"Much more then, having now been justified by His blood, we shall be saved (delivered) from the wrath of God through Him." Romans 5:9

1 Corinthians

"For no one can lay any foundation other than the one already laid, which is Jesus Christ. If any man builds on this foundation using gold, silver, costly stones, wood, hay or straw, his work will be shown for what it is, because the day will bring it to light. It will be revealed with fire, and the fire will test the quality of each man's work. If any man's work which he has built upon it remains, he shall receive a reward. If any man's work is burned up, he shall suffer loss; but he himself shall be saved, yet so as through fire (Day of the Lord)." 1 Cor 3:11-15

Paul is here speaking about the foundation of relationship with Jesus that he laid in the believers. He says that those who build upon this foundation must be careful to continue to build with the same material (love for the Bridegroom and not a focus on ministers as is implied by the context) or else their work will be burned up in the Day of the Lord. Yet, he says that they themselves will be saved but they will have to go through the fiery wrath of the Day of the Lord (see 2 Pet 3:10).

"I have decided to deliver such a one to satan for the destruction of his flesh, that his spirit may be saved in the day of the Lord Jesus." 1 Cor 5:5

Paul is saying here that this individual, who claims to be a follower of Messiah but who is living an immoral life, will have to go through the Tribulation. He will have to choose between Christ and his own life. In this way, it is hoped that his spirit will be saved. But he should not be allowed to consider himself a part of the church lest he have false hope of being saved and his influence affect others like leaven.

"Behold, I tell you a mystery; we shall not all sleep, but we shall all be changed, in a moment, in the twinkling of an eye, at the last trumpet; for the trumpet will sound, and the dead will be raised imperishable, and we shall be changed." 1 Cor 15:51-52

This reference to the resurrection and Rapture of the Bride is to take place suddenly at the Last Trump (shophar). Many have confused this Trump with the trumpets in Revelation. However, there is no connection. 1 Corinthians was written many years before the book of Revelation. The trumpets in Revelation were a specific vision given to John concerning the judgments of the Day of the Lord. Paul would have no way of knowing about them. Paul was instead referring to something that his readers would have been familiar with concerning ancient Jewish tradition about the Akeida. The Akeida was a reference to the binding of Isaac. Isaac was a type of Messiah and the ram's horns (shophars) were symbolic of the deliverance of the Jewish people from trouble.

"The Holy One, blessed be He, said to Avraham; 'In a similar manner are your children destined to be caught by iniquities and entangled in troubles, but they will ultimately be redeemed through the horns of the ram' Hence it is written, 'The Lord God will blow the Horn.'" Midrash Rabbah Genesis Vol. 1.56.9, page 498 (Zech 9:14)

The first shophar (ram's horn) was symbolic of the first deliverance from Egypt and it was also symbolic of the covenant at Sinai, which was a marriage covenant between God and the children of Israel.

"Now Mount Sinai was all in smoke because the LORD descended upon it in fire; and its smoke ascended like the smoke of a furnace, and the whole mountain quaked violently. When the sound of the trumpet (shophar) grew louder and louder, Moses spoke and God answered him with thunder." Ex 19:19

Since there are two ram's horns and one has already sounded, there is one left to sound which Paul calls the "Last Trump." This shophar will initiate the Day of the Lord and the wedding of the Messiah Jesus. It will also announce God's second great deliverance of the remnant of Israel which will take place during the Great Tribulation. These two events are indelibly linked in Scripture. Also, in ancient Jewish weddings when the groom came, usually at night, the shophar was blown announcing his arrival. In like manner, when Messiah comes to take His Bride, also at night (see Mt 25:6, Luke 17:34), the Bridal Shophar will be blown to announce the event, and the Bride will be whisked away to the wedding chamber. This Shophar was referred to by Paul as the Last Trump or the Trumpet of God (1Thess 4:16). It is not to be confused with the trumpets in Revelation or the Great Shophar (Shophar Hagadol) that Messiah will blow on Yom Kippur at the end of the Tribulation to call back the remnant of Israel from the all the nations.

Philippians

In Philippians 3, Paul writes one of the most passionate and beautiful portions of Scripture about the hope of the Rapture. Yet, it has been misinterpreted so much over the years that the true meaning has been obscured. The passage begins with Paul expressing his passion to gain Christ. Let's break in at verse 10:

"....that I may know Him, and the power of His resurrection and the fellowship of His sufferings, being conformed to his death, in order that (Lit., if somehow) I may attain to the resurrection from the dead." Phil 3:10-11

Paul's statement here that "if somehow" he might attain to the resurrection or literally "out resurrection from among the dead," has baffled scholars down through the centuries. Why would Paul be so concerned that he be part of the resurrection? Surely, as a believer in Messiah he understood that the resurrection was guaranteed? After all, he was the one who gave us the famous passage in 1 Cor 15 and 1Thess 4:16 about the dead in Christ rising first. But when we see that Paul has the Rapture and resurrection of the Bride in mind what he is saying becomes clear. The resurrection "out from among the dead" takes place first immediately followed by the Rapture of the living. Paul, who was in prison near the end of his ministry, seemed to know that he would likely die before the Rapture. When he spoke of the "out resurrection" he was not referring to the general resurrection of the righteous, as it was known in Hebrew tradition (Dan 12:2, 13), which takes place at the end of the Tribulation. Instead, he was very concerned about being part of the resurrection of the Bride that takes place before the Tribulation and almost simultaneous with the Rapture. This will become clearer in the next few verses.

"Not that I have already obtained it, or have already become perfect, but I press on in order that I may (Lit., if I may even) lay hold of that for which (or, because also) I was laid hold of by Christ Jesus. Brethren, I do not regard myself as having laid hold of it yet; but one thing I do: forgetting what lies behind and reaching forward to what lies ahead, I press on toward the goal for the prize of the upward call (call upward, heavenward - Rapture*) of God in Christ Jesus." Phil 3:12-14*

Paul was acutely aware of his weakness and the grace of God extended to him who was once a persecutor of the church. He speaks about this in the first part of the chapter. This is the context. He says that he has only one goal, to gain Christ and to be clothed in His righteousness. He was not willing to rest on his laurels and trust in his past accomplishments. He was also determined not to allow his failures to drag him down. He was determined to forget the past and keep his eyes on the goal, which he clearly states as the heavenly or upward call. He is not talking here about his ministry, as is commonly taught, but, rather the call to come out to meet the Bridegroom. He is determined to be alert and ready for the Bridal Shophar, whether he is dead or alive at the time. This is his passion, his driving force, to be with Messiah, to be part of that bridal company, to be a wise virgin with his lamp burning bright (Mt 25:1-13, Luke 12:35-36). His whole attitude and focus was for that day. And he now tells his readers that this should also be their attitude.

"Let us therefore, as many as are perfect (mature) have this attitude; and if in anything you have a different attitude, God will reveal that also to you; however, let us keep living by that same standard to which we have attained." Phil 3:15-16

Paul's concern is that he and his readers would be ready for Messiah. He wanted all to be clothed with His righteousness - to be blameless anticipating and living for the Rapture. He said that this was a mature attitude and that if in any way they were not living in accordance with this attitude, God would show them. What he means, I believe, is again emphasized by the admonition to keep "living by that same standard" to which they were already living. This is again repeated in verse 17:

"Brethren, join in following my example, and observe those who walk according to the pattern you have in us." Phil 3:17

Paul is telling his readers that their focus and goal should be preparedness to meet Messiah in the Rapture. If this was their attitude, then they would have to live in a manner that was consistent with this goal. Thus, there is an admonition to imitate his example and let God show them if this attitude was theirs in every aspect of their lives.

Then Paul begins to express his great sorrow over those "Christians" who were not living this way and were following after the desires of the flesh and not taking up the cross.

"For many walk, of whom I often told you, and now tell you even weeping, that they are enemies of the cross of Christ, whose end is destruction, whose god is their appetite (lit., belly), and whose glory is in their shame, who set their minds on earthly things." Phil 3:18-19

These Christians, according to Paul, who do not set their goal to be ready for the bridal call, but rather set their minds on earthly things, will end up facing destruction instead. They will miss the Rapture and have to go through the Day of Wrath and Destruction. This is clearly what he has in mind all along and, I believe, it is proven by the next verse.

"For (because) our citizenship is in heaven, from which also we eagerly wait for a Savior, the Lord Jesus Christ; who will transform the body of our humble state into conformity with the body of His glory, by the exertion of the power that He has even to subject all things to Himself." Phil 3:20-21

Verses 20 and 21 are clearly contrasted with verse 18 and 19. That is the point. Those who are not walking in readiness for the Rapture will miss it, and instead of facing glory, will face shame. Because, he says, we (those who are ready) are waiting eagerly for the Lord Jesus to come from heaven and deliver us and transform our bodies like His own. It does not say that we are waiting for "The Savior," although He is indeed the one, rather "a Savior." This deliverance or saving here is not a saving from sin, but, rather deliverance from the Tribulation.

Colossians

"Set your minds on the things above, not on the things that are on earth. For you have died and your life is hidden with Christ in God. When Christ,

who is our life, is revealed, then you also will be revealed with Him in glory."
Col 3:2-4

This verse again tells us to set our focus on things above. We are to preoccupy ourselves with Christ and the future hope we have in Him. The statement that when He is revealed to mankind we shall be revealed as well in glory, I believe, indicates that we will be with Him prior to that time.

1 Thessalonians

"For the Lord Himself will descend from heaven with a shout, with the voice of the archangel, and with the trumpet of God; and the dead in Christ shall rise first. Then we who are alive and remain shall be caught up together with them in the clouds to meet the Lord in the air, and thus we shall always be with the Lord. Therefore comfort one another with these words." 1 Thess 4:17-18

"But you, brethren, are not in darkness, that the day should overtake you like a thief; for you are all sons of light and sons of day. We are not of night nor of darkness; so then let us not sleep as others do, but let us be alert and sober. For those who sleep do their sleeping at night, and those who get drunk get drunk at night. But since we are of the day, let us be sober, having put on the breastplate of faith and love, and as a helmet, the hope of salvation (deliverance). 1 Thess 5:4-8

In these verses, we have a deliberate contrast to verse 3. While the rest are unaware and caught off guard by the Tribulation, we who belong to Messiah should be awake and alert and ready for the Rapture. We are to have our heads, and by implication, our minds, covered with the helmet of "the hope of deliverance."
"For (Because) God has not destined us for wrath, but for obtaining salvation (deliverance) through our Lord Jesus Christ, who died for us, that whether we are awake or asleep, we may live together with Him. 1 Thes 5:9-10

The word "for" in the beginning of this verse means "because." It is unfortunate that our translators used the word "for" here in its old English usage. We rarely use it that way today and, consequently, we don't realize what is being said when we read this passage.

2 Thessalonians

"And for this reason God will send upon them a deluding influence so that they might believe what is false, in order that they all may be judged who did not believe the truth, but took pleasure in wickedness. But we should always give thanks to God for you, brethren beloved by the Lord, because God has chosen you from the beginning for salvation (deliverance) through sanctification by the Spirit and faith in the truth. And it was for this He called you through our gospel that you may gain the glory of our Lord Jesus Christ. 2 Thess 2:11-14

Again we are told that God has not chosen us for wrath, but for deliverance that we may gain the glory of Messiah. Interestingly enough, some ancient manuscripts say in verse 13 that God has chosen us as "first fruits."

2 Timothy

"….in the future there is laid up for me the crown of righteousness, which the Lord, the righteous Judge, will award to me on that day; and not only to me, but also to all who have loved His appearing." 2 Tim 4:8

Titus

"For the grace of God has appeared bringing salvation to all men, instructing us to deny ungodliness and worldly desires and to live sensibly, righteously and godly in the present age, looking for the blessed hope and the appearing of the glory of our great God and Savior (could also read "the great God and our Savior), Christ Jesus; who gave Himself for us, that he might redeem us from every lawless deed and purify for himself a people for His own possession, zealous for good deeds." Titus 2:11-14

This verse tells us that we are to be looking for the "blessed hope." The NIV translation has removed the "and" from "blessed hope <u>and</u> the appearing of," presumably to suggest that one event is being spoken of. But the "and" is in the Greek and must not be removed. The "and" is telling us that two events are being spoken of. There is a part A and a part B. Part A is the blessed hope, which is our hope of deliverance in the Rapture. Part B is the appearing of the glory of the great God and our deliverer, Jesus. We have already been told that when He appears in glory, we will appear with Him (Col 3:2-4). Therefore, the part A, the Rapture, our "blessed hope" of deliverance must come first.

Hebrews

"...Christ also, having been offered once to bear the sins of many, shall appear a second time for salvation (deliverance) without reference to sin, to those who eagerly await Him." Heb 9:28

When Messiah appears at the end of the Great Tribulation, He comes in wrath and pours out wrath and judgment on His enemies. He also gathers the survivors of the nations together for judgment (Mt 25:31-46). How then can this appearing be "without reference to sin"? This verse is telling us that there is an appearing prior to that, which is only for deliverance and is for some very specific people - "those who eagerly await Him." Again, we see clearly that not all who claim to be Christians will go to meet Him in the Rapture. It is only for those who are waiting for Him with eager anticipation which, of course, implies that they are living a life that is pleasing to Him.

"Let us hold fast the confession of our hope without wavering, for He who promised is faithful; and let us consider how to stimulate one another to love and good deeds, not forsaking our own assembling together, as is the habit of some, but encouraging one another; and all the more, as you see the day drawing near." Heb 10:23-25

Along with the promise of the Rapture, we always have the warning about the judgment of the Day of the Lord.

"For if we go on sinning willfully after receiving the knowledge of the truth, there no longer remains a sacrifice for sins, but a certain terrifying expectation of judgment, and the fury of a fire which will consume the adversaries." Heb 10:26-27

By the way, notice how we can see the Day of the Lord coming which indicates that we can see the signs and understand them.

1 Peter
"Blessed be the God and Father of our Lord Jesus Christ, who according to His great mercy has caused us to be born again to a living hope through the resurrection of Jesus Christ from the dead, to obtain an inheritance which is imperishable and undefiled and will not fade away, reserved in heaven for you, who are protected by the power of God through faith for a salvation (deliverance) ready to be revealed in the last time." 1Pet 1:3-5

We have been born again to a living hope. Notice that this hope is the hope of deliverance. This is not what we call salvation or deliverance from our sins but rather, deliverance from the Day of Wrath and Indignation. Also, notice that Peter talks about receiving an inheritance which is reserved in heaven for us. When Messiah is revealed at the end of the Tribulation, He judges the earth and begins His Millennial reign. If the church is not raptured until that time, then she is just whisked up in the air to come right back down again with Him. How then can she partake of an inheritance that is reserved in heaven? No doubt, Peter has in mind the reward that Jesus spoke about in John 14.

"In My Father's house are many dwelling places; if it were not so, I would have told you; for I go to prepare a place for you. And if I go and prepare a place for you, I will come again, and receive you to Myself; that where I am, there you may be also." John 14:2-3

According to this passage, Jesus promised to take the church to Himself. Also, it seems that Peter fully expected for the church to spend some time in heaven prior to the establishment of the kingdom of God on Earth. If this does not happen prior to the Tribulation, then when does it happen? This is the question that those who believe in a Post-Trib Rapture must answer. The words of the Lord must be fulfilled.

There is a wonderful picture here of the Bridegroom taking His Bride to the wedding Chupah (pronounced "Huppa"). In ancient Jewish weddings, it was customary for the groom to build a tabernacle or Chupah in the house of His father and then, after one or two years, to come and carry His Bride away to this Chupah. This seems to be what Jesus our heavenly Bridegroom had in mind when He spoke these words.

2 Peter

"For if God did not spare angels when they sinned, but cast them into hell and committed them to pits of darkness, reserved for judgment; and did not spare the ancient world, but preserved Noah, a preacher of righteousness, with seven others, when He brought a flood upon the world of the ungodly; and if He condemned the cities of Sodom and Gomorrah to destruction by reducing them to ashes, having made them an example to those who would live ungodly thereafter; and if He rescued righteous Lot, oppressed by the sensual conduct of unprincipled men for by what he saw and heard that righteous man, while living among them, felt his righteous soul tormented day after day with their lawless deeds, then the Lord knows how to rescue the godly from temptation, and to keep the unrighteous under punishment for the day of judgment…" 2Pet 2:4-9

Peter here, having the Day of Judgment in mind, goes to great lengths to illustrate that God will rescue the righteous. This is consistent with Jesus' words on the same subject in the gospels. There He teaches us that the days of the Son of Man will be like the days of Noah and the days of Lot, where there is both deliverance of the righteous and judgment on the wicked.

1 John

"In this way, love is made complete among us so that we will have confidence on the day of judgment, because in this world we are like him. There is no fear in love. But perfect love drives out fear, because fear has to do with punishment. The one who fears is not made perfect in love." 1 John 4:17-18

John tells us that if we walk in the love of God we will have confidence when the Day of the Lord comes and nothing to fear.

Jude

"But you, beloved, building yourselves up on your most holy faith; praying in the Holy Spirit; keep yourselves in the love of God, waiting anxiously for the mercy of our Lord Jesus Christ to eternal life. And have mercy on some, who are doubting; save others, snatching them out of the fire; (likely a reference to the Day of the Lord) and on some have mercy with fear, hating even the garment polluted by the flesh. Jude 1:14-23

Does My Belief in the Rapture Matter?

There is no doubt that theology matters a great deal. But one may ask, "How can my position on the timing of the Rapture make such a difference to my spiritual health and readiness? If I love the Lord and stay focused on Him I will be ok regardless of when it comes." Well that is technically true, but not experientially so. For instance, if the Rapture does not come before the Last Shemitah Cycle, the believers who are thoroughly convinced it will are in danger of not recognizing what is happening around them, or even becoming disillusioned by the fact that they were led astray. However, what about those who believe that the Rapture occurs after the Tribulation? Surely they are better positioned since they are prepared for the Tribulation; and if they are wrong, they will still be raptured. Well, that sounds good, but it is not very comforting.

In reality, there is much more than the timing of the Rapture involved. Our stance toward Christ can be adversely affected by what we perceive His will to be. In addition, our joy in the Holy Spirit can be stolen by fear of what is coming upon the world. When was the last time you heard those who believe in the Post-Tribulation Rapture rejoicing about the Tribulation to come? Indeed, fear is the most common struggle among those who are of this persuasion. However, there is something even more dangerous for Post-Trib Rapture proponents, and that is the idea of preparing for a funeral rather than a wedding. I realize that many are instead preparing for war, however, the preparation for war is quite different still. If they become preoccupied with bringing in the kingdom by force or spiritual striving, they could become absorbed in the work of Christ rather than the person of Christ. There is always the danger of building on the wrong foundation and ending up with wood, hay and stubble.[50] Therefore, no matter how one views the timing of the Rapture or the stance that the church should have, it is clearly foolish to ignore this important subject and act as though it does not matter. Furthermore, it seems that the promise of the Rapture is conditional.

"Now there is in store for me the crown of righteousness, which the Lord, the righteous Judge, will award to me on that day - and not only to me, but also to all who have longed for his appearing. 2 Timothy 4:8 NIV

"...so Christ also, having been offered once to bear the sins of many, will appear a second time for salvation without reference to sin, to those who eagerly await Him." Hebrews 9:28

These verses seem to indicate that Christ is only coming back for those who are longing for Him to come and eagerly awaiting His appearance. Thus those who do not believe in His soon appearing

---

[50] 1Cor 3:11-15 Paul tells us that if a man builds on a foundation other than the person of Christ his work will be burned up and he will have to go through the Tribulation (Day of the Lord).

do not qualify. Right now, that is the majority who seem to think that it does not matter at all. Are they not then by their indifference guaranteeing that they will go through the greatest time of suffering and testing this world has ever known?

Chapter Seven
The Feasts of Israel – Shadows of Things to Come

In ancient Israel the moon was considered a symbol of renewal and resurrection. Having no light of its own, and merely reflecting the sun, the moon goes through a complete cycle each month from darkness to light. The rabbis saw great significance in this. Like the moon, which goes through a complete renewal, we need to constantly be renewed through repentance. As the moon is reborn, so we too must be "born again" through renewal and repentance in Christ. Thus, the moon is referred to as "the faithful witness in the sky."

"Once for all, I have sworn by my holiness-- and I will not lie to David-- that his line will continue forever and his throne endure before me like the sun; it will be established forever like the moon, the faithful witness in the sky." Ps 89:35-37 NIV

This is undoubtedly what Jesus had in mind when He spoke to Nicodemus who came to Him at night. "You must be born again," Jesus said. Perhaps the moon was in view when He said this. In any event, it appears He fully expected Nicodemus to understand what He was referring to.

"Are you the teacher of Israel, and do not understand these things?" John 3:10

The New Moon (Rosh Chodesh), when the disk is dark to the naked eye, was so important to the Jews that they proclaimed a festival at this time every month. The sighting of the New Moon (Rosh Chodesh) was also the event which determined the religious calendar with respect to the Seven Great Feasts of Israel. These feasts were also known as the Appointed Times or Rehearsals (Moedim). All of these festivals were considered "Rehearsals" for the Day of the Lord or the Kingdom of Messiah. Paul alludes to this in the following verse:

Therefore let no one act as your judge in regard to food or drink or in respect to a festival or a new moon or a Sabbath day-- things which are a mere shadow of what is to come; (rehearsals) *but the substance belongs to Christ. Col 2:16-17*

These Appointed Times were known as Passover (Pesach), Unleavened Bread (Hag Hamatzah), First Fruits (Sfirat Haomer), Pentecost (Shavuot), Rosh Hashanah (Yom Teruah), the Day of Atonement (Yom Kippur), and Tabernacles (Sukkot). Each one of these festivals, which the Jews celebrate every year, points to a fulfillment in the Kingdom of Messiah. They are representative of God's perfect plan of salvation in Jesus. The first three appear to have been fulfilled with His first coming. The fourth one, Pentecost, seems to have had a partial fulfillment at that time. But the last three, Rosh Hashanah, Yom Kippur, and Sukkot, all have their future fulfillment in the Day of the Lord at the end of the age.

Pesach (Passover)

"In the first month, on the fourteenth day of the month at twilight is the LORD'S Passover. Then on the fifteenth day of the same month there is the Feast of Unleavened Bread to the LORD; for seven days you shall eat unleavened bread. On the first day you shall have a holy convocation; you shall not do any laborious work. But for seven days you shall present an offering by fire to the LORD. On the seventh day is a holy convocation; you shall not do any laborious work." Lev 23:5-8

Passover was to begin on the 14th of Nissan and Unleavened Bread on the 15th of Nissan (March-April). Because of the proximity of these feasts, the Jews later combined them into one great eight-day festival called Passover or Pesach. On the first day, the Passover

Lamb is eaten in remembrance of the night in Egypt when the death angel passed over the houses of the Israelites because of the blood. Also, at Passover, all the leaven, which is symbolic of sin (1 Cor 5:6-80), is removed from the houses and unleavened bread is eaten. This great feast is a remembrance of the great deliverance from Egypt. Yet, it also pointed to the future when Jesus the Lamb of God was sacrificed on Passover, to take away the sins, not only of the Jews, but of the whole world. He is our Passover Lamb.

Some interesting traditions became part of Passover and have been celebrated for generations. One has to do with the hiding of the matzah during the meal. The matzah, which is striped and pierced, is hidden during the meal and later found by one of the children. This ritual is symbolic of Christ who was striped and pierced and buried in the earth for three days. Though the Jews continue to celebrate this tradition every year, their eyes are still blinded so that they can't see the one who was pierced. Another tradition which was celebrated in New Testament times was the expectation of Elijah at the Pesach meal. During the meal, four cups of wine are drunk. They are the Cup of Sanctification, the Cup of Praise (or the Cup of Plagues), the Cup of Redemption (the New Covenant in Jesus), and the Cup of Elijah. Also, a chair is placed at the table every year for Elijah who is to come and prepare the way for Messiah (Mal 4:5). Jesus Himself confirmed this tradition in a discussion with His disciples.

"And the disciples asked him, saying, 'Why then do the scribes say that Elijah must come first?' And He answered and said, 'Elijah is coming and will restore all things, but I say to you, that Elijah already came, and they did not recognize him, but did to him whatever they wished. So also the Son of Man is going to suffer at their hands.' Then the disciples understood that He had spoken to them about John the Baptist." Mt 17:10-13

Many Christians interpret this passage to mean that John the Baptist was Elijah and the fulfillment of Mal 4:5. The New Spiritualists even use it to authenticate reincarnation. However, Jesus did not mean that John the Baptist was literally Elijah. But, rather, that he was a type of Elijah who was to come and prepare the way for the Lord. The angel told Zacharias that he (John the Baptist) would be a "forerunner" in the "spirit and power of Elijah, to turn the hearts of the fathers back to the children, and the disobedient to the attitude of the righteous; so as to make ready a people prepared for the Lord (Luke 1:17)." John himself was very emphatic that he was not Elijah (John 1:21). Also, by pointing out the role of John the Baptist as a type of Elijah who was to prepare the way before Him in his first advent, Jesus did not negate the fact that Elijah was still coming. In fact, He stated categorically that Elijah is still coming and will "restore all things." This will be fulfilled by the literal coming of Elijah in the Day of the Lord, to turn the hearts of the Jewish people back to "the Fathers" and the hearts of "the Fathers," which he represents, back to their children. He is undoubtedly one of the "Two Witnesses" of Revelation Chapter 11 who comes on Pesach to fulfill the ministry which he did not fulfill while on Earth.

Many teachers, particularly those that downplay the Jewish roots of our faith, interpret these Scriptures as referring to "the church." They do the same with any passage that talks about Zion or the renewed Jerusalem. Though valid applications can be made to the church and the Bride using these Scriptures, it is irresponsible and poor exegesis to deny their plain literal meaning. The Jewish believers of the first century were expecting a literal Elijah to come and not some "Elijah company." When they spoke of "the Jerusalem above" or the "new Jerusalem," they were not undermining the future role of the earthly Jerusalem. On the contrary, they were actually establishing it. It is time for those who teach the Word, especially those of us who are Gentiles, to stop stealing the promises from Israel and remember that the root, which is Jewish, supports us and not the other way around.

The Passover story has an interesting parallel with the Day of the Lord. The plagues which are to take place during this time are very closely paralleled to those that took place in Egypt. Also, there is a contest between Pharaoh, who is a type of Antichrist, and Moses, who is a type of Messiah, and a miraculous deliverance for the Jewish people. It's as though history repeats itself only with different players, and even though it has been fulfilled by Messiah's death, it still points us to the future.

First Fruits – (Sfirat Haomer)

"Then the LORD spoke to Moses, saying, Speak to the sons of Israel, and say to them, 'When you enter the land which I am going to give to you and reap its harvest, then you shall bring in the sheaf of the first fruits of your harvest to the priest. And he shall wave the sheaf before the LORD for you to be accepted; on the day after the Sabbath the priest shall wave it. Now on the day when you wave the sheaf, you shall offer a male lamb one year old without defect for a burnt offering to the LORD. Its grain offering shall then be two-tenths of an ephah of fine flour mixed with oil, an offering by fire to the LORD for a soothing aroma, with its libation, a fourth of a hin of wine. Until this same day, until you have brought in the offering of your God, you shall eat neither bread nor roasted grain nor new growth. It is to be a perpetual statute throughout your generations in all your dwelling places." Lev 23:9-14

This feast, also known as First Fruits, took place on the 16th of Nissan, the "day after the Sabbath" or the first day of the week. It is the early first fruits of the barley harvest and not to be confused with Shavuot which is the first fruits of the wheat harvest. During the ceremony in the Temple, the High Priest would wave the sheaves of the first fruits before the Lord in all directions. The message of this feast was that, since God has been faithful to bless the people with the early harvest, He would also provide for the summer harvest as well.

On First Fruits, Jesus our high Priest was raised from the dead, the first fruits of the resurrection, and ascended to the Father with many of the saints of old as a wave offering (Mt 27:51-53).

"And Jesus answered them, saying, 'The hour has come for the Son of Man to be glorified. Truly, truly, I say to you, unless a grain of wheat falls into the earth and dies, it remains by itself alone; but if it dies, it bears much fruit.'" John 12:23-24

"But now Christ has been raised from the dead, the first fruits of those who are asleep." 1 Cor 15:20

Pentecost (Shavuot)

"You shall also count for yourselves from the day after the Sabbath, from the day when you brought in the sheaf of the wave offering; there shall be seven complete Sabbaths. You shall count fifty days to the day after the seventh Sabbath; then you shall present a new grain offering to the LORD. You shall bring in from your dwelling places two loaves of bread for a wave offering, made of two-tenths of an ephah; they shall be of a fine flour, baked with leaven as first fruits to the LORD. Along with the bread, you shall present seven one year old male lambs without defect, and a bull of the herd, and two rams; they are to be a burnt offering to the LORD, with their grain offering and their libations, an offering by fire of a soothing aroma to the LORD. You shall also offer one male goat for a sin offering and two male lambs one year old for a sacrifice of peace offerings. The priest shall then wave them with the bread of the first fruits for a wave offering with two lambs before the LORD; they are to be holy to the LORD for the priest. On this same day you shall make a proclamation as well; you are to have a holy convocation. You shall do no laborious work. It is to be a perpetual statute in all your dwelling places throughout your generations." Lev 23:15-21

Pentecost is also called the Feast of Weeks and in Hebrew Shavuot. It was one of the three feasts that all male Israelites were required to observe in Jerusalem. When Jerusalem was destroyed in 70AD and the Jews scattered, the feast became more of a celebration of the giving of the Law on Mt. Sinai. The rabbis, having deduced that Moses came down from Sinai on Pentecost, changed the festival somewhat to emphasize this event. However, during New Testament times, this was not the emphasis. It was the feast of the Latter First Fruits of the wheat harvest. And, just like all the other feasts, was rich in symbolism regarding the work of God in redemption and the Day of the Lord. Until the destruction of the Temple, the feast was celebrated according to Lev 23. It was a first fruits celebration similar to that of Sfirat Haomer, except that this time, the first fruits were baked into two loaves which were to be waved before the Lord by the priest. And in an amazing contrast to Unleavened Bread, the loaves were to be leavened. The theme of the Latter First Fruits was similar to Sfirat Haomer. It was a time of thanksgiving for an early harvest and increased hopefulness of an abundant fall harvest.

In the book of Acts, we read the account of the outpouring of the Holy Spirit on the church on Pentecost (Shavuot). Many have referred to this as the birth of the church. But it may be more accurately referred to as the conception of the church or the Bride of Christ. Because of this fulfillment of Pentecost, the feast seems to have a unique connection to the Bride of Messiah. She is a "first fruit company" made up of two loaves, Jew and Gentile that have been made into one. The leaven that is used in the loaves may be symbolic of the inclusion of the Gentiles into this "first fruit company." It may also represent the infilling of the Holy Spirit since, although leaven is usually a reference to sin, Jesus did use it in a positive context in reference to the Kingdom (Mt 13:33).
It seems apparent that the New Testament writers understood the connection of First Fruits with the Bride of Messiah. Consider the following verses:

"And not only this, but also we ourselves, having the first fruits of the Spirit, even we ourselves groan within ourselves, waiting eagerly for our adoption as sons, the redemption of our body." Romans 8:23

"In the exercise of His will He brought us forth by the word of truth, so that we might be, as it were, the first fruits among His creatures." James 1:18

At Pentecost, the first fruits represented by the two loaves, were waved before the Lord with great enthusiasm just as in Sfirat Haomer. We have already discussed the fulfillment of Sfirat Haomer in that Messiah and the saints of old were taken into heaven and waved, so to speak, before the Father. Yet, where was this aspect of Shavuot fulfilled? We know that the outpouring of the Spirit upon Jew and Gentile (a first fruit company from mankind), which may be symbolized by the leavening of the loaves, took place on Pentecost. But since then the process has continued with the Holy Spirit continually poured out on this "first fruit company." Therefore, it would seem, that Pentecost, the middle feast, is only partially fulfilled. Could it be that its final fulfillment will come with the waving of this "first fruit company" before the Throne at the Rapture? Could it be that the Rapture takes place on Pentecost? Considering the fact that every significant event in the ministry of Messiah has taken place on one of the Seven Great Rehearsals, then why would an event as significant as the Rapture be the exception?

As already pointed out, the focus of Shavuot today is more related to the giving of the Law on Sinai. There are two interesting facts about Sinai that correspond to Jesus and His Bridal covenant.

a. The giving of the Law of God to His Bride Israel is repeated in the new bridal covenant between Christ and His Bride that was made on Pentecost. It was then that He gave the Holy Spirit as a pledge or an engagement ring. Consequently we who have received the Spirit are betrothed to Christ.

b. The covenant of Sinai was a marriage covenant. It was the first shophar, and it was a bridal shophar. The second or last shophar is also a bridal shophar announcing the marriage of the Bridegroom Jesus. It is quite probable then that this wedding also takes place on Pentecost.

"This is the covenant that I will make with them. After those days, says the Lord: I will put My laws upon their heart, and upon their mind I will write them...." Heb 10:16

Fall Feasts

The spring feasts of Passover, Unleavened Bread, and First Fruits (Sfirat Haomer) were fulfilled by Messiah's first coming. Pentecost, the early summer feast, was partially fulfilled. And in between is the long hot summer until the fall feasts which will be fulfilled by Jesus at His second appearance in the Day of the Lord. The fall feasts are: Rosh Hashanah (Yom Teruah), Atonement (Yom Kippur), and Tabernacles (Sukkot).

The theme of the fall feasts is repentance and turning to God. Preparation begins in the Summer time in the month of Elul forty days before Yom Kippur on the tenth day of Tishri.

Rosh Hashanah (Yom Teruah)

"Speak to the sons of Israel, saying, 'In the seventh month on the first of the month, you shall have a rest, a reminder by blowing of trumpets, a holy convocation. You shall not do any laborious work, but you shall present an offering by fire to the LORD.'" Lev 23:23-25

Rosh Hashanah (Yom Teruah) is the first day of the seventh month, Tishri (Sept/Oct). It was a day set aside as a Sabbath, a time to blow shophars and be reminded of the fast approaching of the Day of Atonement (Yom Kippur). Since Yom Teruah is also the beginning of the New Year, its name was later changed to Rosh Hashanah which means "head of the year." Rosh Hashanah is the day when the people of Israel take stock of their spiritual condition and make the necessary changes to ensure that the upcoming New Year will be pleasing to God. There is still time. After Atonement (Yom

Kippur) the book is closed. The ten days between Rosh Hashanah and Yom Kippur are called "the Days of Awe." Consequently, Rosh Hashanah is known as "the Day of The Awakening Blast." Four shophars are sounded: Tekia (Blast), Shevarim (Broken notes), Teruah (Alarm), and Tekia Gedolah (The Great Blast). Rosh Hashanah is a wakeup call. It is the sound of an alarm.

Blow a trumpet in Zion, and sound an alarm on My holy mountain! Let all the inhabitants of the land tremble, for the day of the LORD is coming; surely it is near... Joel 2:1

Rosh Hashanah is the official beginning of the Jewish year. It is also the official beginning of the Last Shemitah Cycle and the Day of the Lord Millennium. Besides this, Rosh Hashanah has many other ancient themes. It is the day of concealment, resurrection, and kingly coronation.

Because of the theme of resurrection connected to Rosh Hashanah, many "Pre-Weekers" speculate that the Rapture will take place on Rosh Hashanah at the beginning of the Last Shemitah Cycle. Some "Post-Tribbers" also use this connection to suggest that the Rapture happens on Rosh Hashanah at the end of the Tribulation. However, there is a resurrection on Rosh Hashanah but it is not the resurrection mentioned in 1 Thess 4:17. This is the resurrection of the Bride, those who died in Messiah. The resurrection on Rosh Hashanah, at the end of the Tribulation is what's known to the Jews as the "general resurrection." It is the resurrection of the righteous, the so called "Old Testament Saints" and those believers in Messiah who have been martyred during the Time of Wrath (Dan 12:2, 13, Rev 20:4).

A Unique Day
Rosh Hashanah is unique among all the festivals in that it is the only festival that begins on the New Moon itself.

Blow the trumpet at the new moon, at the full moon, on our feast day. Ps 81:3

This verse is a reference to Rosh Hashanah, the Day of The Awakening Blast. However, the translation of *"kehseh"* into "full moon" which occurs in most of our Bibles is incorrect. There is no feast that occurs on a full moon and a new moon at the same time. The word should have been translated 'set time' or "appointed time." The King James Version has it correctly:

"Blow up the trumpet in the new moon, in the time appointed, on our solemn feast day." Ps 81:3 KJV

The fact that Rosh Hashanah began on the New Moon meant that it was a day that was declared and not merely calculated from the New Moon or beginning of the month. It was known in ancient times as "the day no man knows." Two witnesses were sent out by the Jewish leaders to sight the New Moon. These witnesses were specially chosen and given unique powers. Once they sighted the New Moon they would report back to the Nassi (president of the Sanhedrin) and he would make the determination as to whether or not the sighting was correct. Then he would declare the New Moon and immediately word would go out to all Israel, through a system of fires (like flares) on hilltops that the festival had begun. Thus, the Nassi or leader of the Sanhedrin would be the only one to know of the day or hour. It could not be calculated in advance or determined by any other source. This may very well be what Jesus had in mind when He said that not even He knew the day or the hour but only the Father. Could it be possible that God the Son, the Creator of the universe, did not know when the Millennium was to begin? Would the Father have hidden this thing from His one and only Son? It is possible, but unlikely. Jesus knew everything else, why not this? Could it be that Jesus was merely saying that this was not His call but the Father's, something He had said on other occasions? (Mt

20:23, Acts 1:7) Was He actually referring to the feast? Was he pointing to "the day no man knows?"

Since Rosh Hashanah begins the Last Shemitah Cycle and also the countdown to the visible return of Christ, it may very well be what Jesus meant when he said no one knows. However, concerning the Rapture of the Bride in the middle of the Last Shemitah Cycle it is likely that it has more to do with the Ancient Jewish Wedding and the fact that it is the Father's call when the Bridegroom should go and get His Bride. In either event, the point is not that Jesus did not have the knowledge of the timing but that it was the Father's call. It is an appointed time the Father has fixed by His own authority (Acts 1:7).

"But in those days, after that tribulation, the sun will be darkened, and the moon will not give its light, and the stars will be falling from heaven, and the powers that are in the heavens will be shaken. And then they will see the Son of Man coming in clouds with great power and glory." Mark 13:24-26

This passage is, of course, part of the Olivet Discourse. After explaining the signs leading up to "the end" (the End of The Age or the Day of The Lord) which is initiated by the Abomination of Desolation in verse 14, Jesus now mentions what happens on Rosh Hashanah at the end of the Tribulation. These are the cosmic signs prophesied by the prophets (Joel 2:30-32) as coming before the Millennium - the Day of the Lord proper. This is a parallel passage with Mt 24:29-31.

"But immediately after the tribulation of those days the sun will be darkened, and the moon will not give its light, and the stars will fall from the sky, and the powers of the heavens will be shaken, and then the sign of the Son of Man will appear in the sky, and then all the tribes of the earth will mourn…"

On Rosh Hashanah at the end of the Tribulation, when the New Moon is supposed to take place, a new light appears. It is not the new, renewed light of the moon, neither is it the light of the Sun, but, rather, the "sign of the Son of Man." When this sign appears, there will be great mourning in the earth, particularly in Israel. This mourning is in keeping with Rosh Hashanah, the Day of the Awakening Blast, but this time it is mourning over Him who was pierced. Consider this passage in Zechariah:

"And it will come about in that day that I will set about to destroy all the nations that come against Jerusalem. And I will pour out on the house of David and on the inhabitants of Jerusalem, the Spirit of grace and of supplication, so that they will look on Me whom they have pierced; and they will mourn for Him, as one mourns for an only son, and they will weep bitterly over Him, like the bitter weeping over a first-born. In that day there will be great mourning in Jerusalem, like the mourning of Hadadrimmon in the plain of Megiddo. And the land will mourn, every family by itself; the family of the house of David by itself, and their wives by themselves; the family of the house of Nathan by itself, and their wives by themselves; the family of the house of Levi by itself, and their wives by themselves; the family of the Shimeites by itself, and their wives by themselves; all the families that remain, every family by itself, and their wives by themselves." Zech 12:9-14

Another passage in Zechariah Chapter 14 seems to agree with this and perhaps identifies the feast of Rosh Hashanah.

"Behold, a day is coming for the LORD when the spoil taken from you will be divided among you. For I will gather all the nations against Jerusalem to battle, and the city will be captured, the houses plundered, the women ravished and half of the city exiled, but the rest of the people will not be cut off from the city. Then the LORD will go forth and fight against those nations, as when He fights on a day of battle. In that day His feet will stand on the Mount of Olives, which is in front of Jerusalem on the east; and the Mount of Olives will be split in its middle from east to west by a very large

valley, so that half of the mountain will move toward the north and the other half toward the south. You will flee by the valley of My mountains, for the valley of the mountains will reach to Azel; yes, you will flee just as you fled before the earthquake in the days of Uzziah king of Judah. Then the LORD, my God, will come, and all the holy ones with Him! In that day there will be no light; the luminaries will dwindle. For it will be a unique day which is known to the LORD, neither day nor night, but it will come about that at evening time there will be light. And in that day living waters will flow out of Jerusalem, half of them toward the eastern sea and the other half toward the western sea; it will be in summer as well as in winter." Zech 14:1-8

The prophet indicates that all the nations will be gathered to Jerusalem to battle. And just when they are planning to finish off the remnant of Israel there will be a great earthquake and a valley created through the Mount of Olives on the East through which the remnant will flee. When it says that "His feet will stand on the Mount of Olives," we have tended to think that it is a reference to Jesus Himself. However it may not be Jesus but instead the angel of the Lord since two verses later it says "Then the Lord, my God will come." Also, if the feet are the feet of Jesus the remnant would be seen as fleeing from Him. In any event, we see that the day is a Unique Day and there is not light because the luminaries have dwindled. This is a reference to the cosmic signs spoken about by many of the prophets and the Lord Himself. Then it says that in the midst of the darkness there will be light. Perhaps this light is the sign of the Son of Man that appears throughout the Days of Awe.

The time between Rosh Hashanah and Yom Kippur (Atonement), on the tenth of Tishri, was called "the days of awe." It appears that during these ten days the powers of the heavens will be literally shaken and the sign of the Son of Man will be visible to the earth. Perhaps these cosmic disturbances are caused by the great conflagration known as Armageddon which takes place prior to and during this time. In any event, ten days later on Yom Kippur the

Son of Man is seen coming on the clouds with power and great glory.

"...and they (notice it's not 'you') *will see the Son of Man coming* (erchomai not parousia) *on the clouds of the sky with power and great glory. And then He will send forth the angels, and will gather together His elect from the four winds, from the farthest end of the earth, to the farthest end of heaven." Mk 13:27*

This gathering here which takes place when the Great Shophar is blown on Yom Kippur is not to be confused with the Rapture of the Bride. The term "elect" is a term used of Israel and not of the "church." This is clearly illustrated by Jesus in the same Olivet Discourse when He said that if the Tribulation had not been cut short, no life (Lit. "flesh") would be saved. But for the sake of "the elect" He said, the time was cut short. If all Christians alive during the Tribulation were to be killed this would not be a victory for satan or a defeat for God or the church. Thus cutting the time short would be of no consequence. Jesus is here saying that if the time had not been made short no people would be left. But in order to preserve the remnant of Israel (the natural descendants of Jacob) the time was cut short. If the Jews were to be completely wiped out as a race of people, then God's covenant promises would be made null and void, and satan would have prevented God from fulfilling his promises to the Jewish people. This, of course, cannot happen. A remnant will be delivered and protected.

"Now learn the parable from the fig tree: when its branch has already become tender, and puts forth its leaves, you know that summer is near. Even so, you too, when you see these things happening, recognize that He is near, right at the door. Truly I say to you, this generation will not pass away until all these things take place." Mt 24:32-34

Here Jesus interjects a word of encouragement for His followers. It appears in each of the gospels where the Olivet Discourse is recorded. Its placement toward the end of the discourse may lead some to conclude that the cosmic events at the end of the Tribulation are what Jesus was referring to when He said, "When you see these things take place." However, it seems more likely that He was saying that the generation that sees any of these things take place, will see all of them. This comes out clearly in Luke's account where the phrase "when you see these things begin to take place" is added (Luke 21:28). In this case the reference seems to be the recapture of Jerusalem and the end of the Times of the Gentiles. Another indication that Jesus is referring to the return of Israel to the land and specifically to Jerusalem (Old City), is the reference to the fig tree. Many Bible teachers believe that the fig tree is a type of Israel. Also, for Jesus to say that when you see the cosmic signs and disturbances in the heavens followed by the appearance of the Son of Man in power and great glory, recognize that the end is near, would be completely redundant.

Yom Kippur (The Day of Atonement)

"And the LORD spoke to Moses, saying, 'On exactly the tenth day of this seventh month is the Day of Atonement; it shall be a holy convocation for you, and you shall humble your souls and present an offering by fire to the LORD. Neither shall you do any work on this same day, for it is a day of atonement, to make atonement on your behalf before the LORD your God. If there is any person who will not humble himself on this same day, he shall be cut off from his people. As for any person who does any work on this same day, that person I will destroy from among his people. You shall do no work at all. It is to be a perpetual statute throughout your generations in all your dwelling places. It is to be a Sabbath of complete rest to you, and you shall humble your souls; on the ninth of the month at evening, from evening until evening you shall keep your Sabbath." Lev 23:26-32

Yom Kippur, the Day of Atonement, was and is still considered the holiest day of the year by the Jewish people. It was the day when the High Priest went before God to make atonement, first for himself, and then for the sins of the whole nation. Two goats were chosen. One was sacrificed and the other had the sins of the nation confessed over it and was sent out into the wilderness where it was pushed over a cliff. All this pointed to our atonement in the Messiah who took away our sins and who was the atoning sacrifice. However, besides being the Day of Atonement, Yom Kippur was is also known as the Day of Judgment. Atonement was for those who follow God's way of atonement and repent of their sins. It was not automatically granted to everyone. The rabbis taught that those who were righteous on Yom Kippur were sealed in the book and those who were not would have to wait another year. This tradition continues to this day. Yom Kippur then is the Day of Judgment when Messiah will appear in Jerusalem to bring judgment on the nations, which at that time will be gathered against it, and to bring deliverance to the righteous remnant of the Jews.

At the end of Yom Kippur, when Messiah has appeared and the Great Shophar is sounded, all the exiles of Israel will be gathered back to their land.

"It will come about also in that day that a great trumpet will be blown; and those who were perishing in the land of Assyria and who were scattered in the land of Egypt will come and worship the LORD in the holy mountain at Jerusalem." Isaiah 27:13

We know that this passage points to Yom Kippur because of the phrase "a great trumpet." In Hebrew it is called the Shofar Hagadol. This is different from the Last Shophar or Shophar of God that Paul referred to in 1Cor 15 and 1Thess 4:17 which had a redemption theme. As the gates of the Temple closed at the end of Yom Kippur, a priest blew a long and loud blast signifying the end of the holy convocation and announcing the beginning of Sukkot (Tabernacles) preparations. Jesus made reference to this event on Yom Kippur in the Olivet Discourse.

" ...and they will see the Son of Man coming on the clouds of the sky with power and great glory. And He will send forth His angels with a great trumpet and they will gather together His elect from the four winds, from one end of the sky to the other. Matt 24:30-31

This gathering of the elect (Jewish remnant) from "the four winds of heaven" was prophesied many times by the prophets beginning with Moses.

"'Ho there! Flee from the land of the north,' declares the LORD, 'for I have dispersed you as the four winds of the heavens,' declares the LORD." Zech 2:6

"If your outcasts are at the ends of the earth (Lit. 'sky'), from there the Lord your God will gather you, and from there He will bring (Lit. 'take') you back." Deut 30:4

When Messiah comes in wrath to judge the nations, He will be a man of war. He will execute vengeance on the armies of Antichrist and all the armies of the nations that have gathered against Jerusalem to battle. This time of tribulation will have been so intense that had He not come when He did, there would have been no survivors. He will come in the nick of time to save the Jewish remnant and a remnant from the nations will also be left alive. Considering that the population of the world has now reached seven billion or so, this remnant could be a considerable number. These survivors will be gathered and judged on the basis of how they treated Israel during the Time of Wrath.

"But when the Son of Man comes in His glory, and all the angels with Him, then He will sit on His glorious throne. And all the nations will be gathered before Him; and He will separate them from one another, as the shepherd separates the sheep from the goats; and He will put the sheep on His right, and the goats on the left. Then the King will say to those on His right, 'Come, you who are blessed of My Father, inherit the kingdom prepared for

you from the foundation of the world. For I was hungry, and you gave Me something to eat; I was thirsty, and you gave Me drink; I was a stranger, and you invited Me in; naked, and you clothed Me; I was sick, and you visited Me; I was in prison, and you came to Me.' Then the righteous will answer Him, saying, 'Lord, when did we see You hungry, and feed You, or thirsty, and give You drink? And when did we see You a stranger, and invite You in, or naked, and clothe You? And when did we see You sick, or in prison, and come to You?' And the King will answer and say to them, 'Truly I say to you, to the extent that you did it to one of these brothers of Mine, even the least of them, you did it to Me.' Then He will also say to those on His left, 'Depart from Me, accursed ones, into the eternal fire which has been prepared for the devil and his angels; for I was hungry, and you gave Me nothing to eat; I was thirsty, and you gave Me nothing to drink; was a stranger, and you did not invite Me in; naked, and you did not clothe Me; sick, and in prison, and you did not visit Me.' Then they themselves also will answer, saying, 'Lord, when did we see You hungry, or thirsty, or a stranger, or naked, or sick, or in prison, and did not take care of You?' Then He will answer them, saying, 'Truly I say to you, to the extent that you did not do it to one of the least of these, you did not do it to Me.' And these will go away into eternal punishment, but the righteous into eternal life." Matt 25:31-46

Sukkot (The Feast of Tabernacles)

"Again the LORD spoke to Moses, saying, 'Speak to the sons of Israel, saying, 'On the fifteenth of this seventh month is the Feast of Booths for seven days to the LORD. On the first day is a holy convocation; you shall do no laborious work of any kind. For seven days you shall present an offering by fire to the LORD. On the eighth day you shall have a holy convocation and present an offering by fire to the LORD; it is an assembly. You shall do no laborious work. These are the appointed times of the LORD which you shall proclaim as holy convocations, to present offerings by fire to the LORD - burnt offerings and grain offerings, sacrifices and libations, each day's matter on its own day-- besides those of the Sabbaths of the LORD, and besides your gifts, and besides all your votive and freewill offerings, which you give to the LORD. On exactly the fifteenth day of the

seventh month, when you have gathered in the crops of the land, you shall celebrate the feast of the LORD for seven days, with a rest on the first day and a rest on the eighth day. Now on the first day you shall take for yourselves the foliage of beautiful trees, palm branches and boughs of leafy trees and willows of the brook; and you shall rejoice before the LORD your God for seven days. You shall thus celebrate it as a feast to the LORD for seven days in the year. It shall be a perpetual statute throughout your generations; you shall celebrate it in the seventh month. You shall live in booths for seven days; all the native-born in Israel shall live in booths, so that your generations may know that I had the sons of Israel live in booths when I brought them out from the land of Egypt. I am the LORD your God'"
Lev 23:33-43

The last of the seven great rehearsals is Sukkot, otherwise known as Booths or Tabernacles. It is known as the season of joy. This feast took place five days after Yom Kippur on the fifteenth of Tishri. All of the seven feasts are centered around the theme of harvest, and this one comes at the time of the last great harvest in the fall of the year. It is a time of great rejoicing referred to by the Jews as "the season of our joy." The dwelling in Booths or tents was a reminder of God's presence with and provision for His people in the wilderness when he took them out of Egypt.

The feast is a picture of the Millennial reign of Christ which will be ushered in five days after the Day of Judgment. The Messiah will set up his kingdom, after that last great harvest of the nations has been brought in, and will dwell among His people. It will be a time of great rejoicing and peace for Israel and the whole world. From then on it will be a requirement, not just for the Jews, but for the whole world to go up to Jerusalem and celebrate the feast every year.

"Then it will come about that any who are left of all the nations that went against Jerusalem will go up from year to year to worship the King, the LORD of hosts, and to celebrate the Feast of Booths. And it will be that

whichever of the families of the earth does not go up to Jerusalem to worship the King, the LORD of hosts, there will be no rain on them. This will be the punishment of Egypt, and the punishment of all the nations who do not go up to celebrate the Feast of Booths." Zech 14:16-19

On the last day of Sukkot there was an interesting ritual that took place in Jerusalem. Water was drawn from the pool of Siloam and brought into the Temple area and poured out by the priest in prayer and thanksgiving for the early and latter rains of the coming year. Tishri, of course, is the month when the early rains are expected to begin and without the early and latter rains there would be no crops the next year. Rain, especially in Israel, was and is a very precious commodity indeed. It was a symbol of life and sustenance. The prophets spoke of the outpouring of the Holy Spirit as rain upon dry ground (Joel 2:23, 28-29, Is 44:3, Ezek 34:26). Jesus picks up on this in John's gospel, perhaps as this ritual is underway.

"Now on the last day, the great day of the feast, Jesus stood and cried out, saying, 'If any man is thirsty, let him come to Me and drink, he who believes in Me, as the Scripture said, from his innermost being shall flow rivers of living water.'" John 7:37-39

In the Millennium, all the nations will know that He is the only one who can quench their thirst and satisfy their hunger. Each year they will go up to Jerusalem to celebrate Him and His presence with His people Israel. If they do not go up, they will immediately and swiftly discover their need. In that day, the rain will not fall on the righteous and unrighteous alike but only on the righteous. The Lord alone will be exalted on that day and Israel will be chief among the nations.

~~~~~
**SPRING FEASTS**
1. Passover - 14$^{TH}$ Nisan/Abib — Jesus died
2. Unleavened Bread - 15$^{TH}$ Nisan — Buried in tomb
3. First Fruits - 16$^{TH}$ Nisan — Rose again (with other saints to the Father)
4. Shavuot — Pentecost - 50 days later —Holy Spirit poured out on Jew and Gentile
Two loaves waved — First Fruits - Not about Torah
The Holy Spirit poured out on Jew and Gentile

Long summer _____ 2000years

4. Shavuot fulfilled — Jew and Gentile — Bridal Remnant — Rapture
~~~~~

~~~~~
**Fall Feasts**
5. Rosh Hashanah - (Darkness) Sign of the Son of Man in the sky (Yom Teruah-Awakening Blast) — Days of Awe
6. Yon Kippur (Atonement/ Judgment-10 Days Later) — Jesus appears
7. Sukkot- Tabernacles (5 Days Later) — God with us — Messianic Kingdom
~~~~~

(For an illustration see chart 10 on page 295.)

"Now it will come about that in the last days, the mountain of the house of the LORD will be established as the chief of the mountains, and will be raised above the hills; and all the nations will stream to it. And many peoples will come and say, 'Come, let us go up to the mountain of the LORD, to the house of the God of Jacob; that He may teach us concerning His ways, and that we may walk in His paths.' For the law will go forth from Zion,

and the word of the LORD from Jerusalem. And He will judge between the nations, and will render decisions for many peoples; and they will hammer their swords into plowshares, and their spears into pruning hooks. Nation will not lift up sword against nation, and never again will they learn war.' Isaiah 2:2-4

The seven great rehearsals that God gave to the Jewish people have much to say about the coming kingdom of Christ. Thanks to the Messianic movement, their importance has once again been restored to the church, and Gentiles, as well as Jews, would do well to celebrate them and be reminded of their glorious truths. Each one of them has a literal fulfillment. The first three were literally and sequentially fulfilled by Jesus' death, burial, and resurrection. The middle feast, Shavuot, was literally begun after His ascension and will have its complete literal fulfillment at the Rapture of the first fruit company made up of Jew and Gentile in the middle of the Last Shemitah Cycle. Then on Rosh Hashanah, exactly three and a half years later, He will begin the consummation of the last three on time and in an orderly sequence. Thus all that the prophets have spoken will have come to pass.

The Sixth Door

The sixth door is about the Olivet Discourse. That is the discussion Jesus had with His disciples on the Mount of Olives in Jerusalem. It is found in three of the gospels. Most Christians use it to explain the end of the age but often draw different conclusions. For instance, one will argue that it makes it clear Jesus comes at the end of the Tribulation. Therefore the Rapture occurs then. Another will say it proves the opposite since He comes like a thief in the night and it is like the days of Noah. In Noah's time there was a rescue before the destruction. This implies a rescue (Rapture) before the Tribulation. Jesus actually talks about one being taken and another being left. And in Luke's account He actually says that we can escape the Tribulation period. Thus there is much confusion regarding Jesus words. How can both be right? How can Jesus come at the beginning and also the end? One minute He says His coming is like the days of Noah as a thief in the night. And the next minute He says He comes after the Tribulation when the earth is practically destroyed and the whole world will see Him. Do you see the mystery? Both events are referred to as His coming. How can this be? Again we come to a stone wall with a hidden door. Is there a sixth key that will open it? Amazingly there is!

The Sixth Key

The coming of Christ is a time period called "The Parousia." The Second Coming of Christ is a time period and not a single event. This fact has already been established in Chapter 6. However it is also the sixth key that unlocks the Olivet Discourse. Take it in your hand now and see how Jesus words on that famous afternoon fit perfectly with the End-Time scenario given us throughout Scripture!

Chapter Eight
The Olivet Discourse

When Jesus came out of the Temple for the last time during what we call Passion Week, he was very troubled indeed. He told the Jews that they would not see Him there again until they learned to cry, "Blessed is He who comes in the name of the Lord." However, the disciples were not in tune to Jesus distress and were instead admiring the enormous stones which adorned the Temple complex. It was at that point that Jesus told them that not one stone would be left upon another. They were dismayed by His comments and when they went to the Mount of Olives later, they asked Him about His statement. Then Jesus taught them with regard to the end of the age and the Day of the Lord and His teaching appears in three of the Gospel accounts (Mt 24, Mk 13, Luke 21). This discussion regarding the end of the age which took place on the Mount of Olives is known as the Olivet Discourse.

"As He was sitting on the Mount of Olives, the disciples came to Him privately, saying, 'Tell us, when will these things happen, and what will be the sign of Your coming (parousia), and of the end of the age?'" Mt 24:3

"Tell us, when will these things be, and what will be the sign when all these things are going to be fulfilled?" Mark 13:4

Notice they asked Jesus two questions and not three as is commonly taught:

1. 'When will these things be?' concerning what was to happen to Jerusalem.

2. And what will be the sign of your coming (parousia - presence) and the end of the age - which they understood to be the same event.

Luke's gospel which was written after the others seems to be more concerned with the imminent destruction of Jerusalem and as a result, it focuses on that, while Matthew and Mark focus on the end of the age. This causes some to conclude that the whole discourse is about the first century, but such a conclusion is ludicrous and separates the Olivet Discourse from its own very clear statements about the end of the age (not to mention the whole body of Scripture).

"They questioned Him, saying, "Teacher, when therefore will these things happen? And what will be the sign when these things are about to take place?" Luke 21:7

Luke's gospel answers the question as to what will be the sign of the destruction of Jerusalem.

"But when you see Jerusalem surrounded by armies, then recognize that her desolation is near." Luke 21:20

Of course we know that this event repeats itself at the end of the age when Jerusalem is again surrounded by armies. However, this time it is all the nations against Jerusalem and the result will be very different than the first century. God Himself will fight for them and the Messiah will come (Zech 14). Thus we understand that Luke is clearly speaking about the destruction of Jerusalem in the first century.

"Then those who are in Judea must flee to the mountains, and those who are in the midst of the city must leave, and those who are in the country must not enter the city; because these are days of vengeance, so that all things which are written will be fulfilled. Woe to those who are pregnant

and to those who are nursing babies in those days; for there will be great distress upon the land and wrath to this people; and they will fall by the edge of the sword, and will be led captive into all the nations; and Jerusalem will be trampled underfoot by the Gentiles until the times of the Gentiles are fulfilled." Luke 21:21-24

While Luke focuses on the events of the first century he goes on to talk about the end of the age and the Rapture. However, Matthew and Mark focus exclusively on the sign of the end of the age and say nothing of the destruction of Jerusalem in 70AD.

"Therefore when you see the ABOMINATION OF DESOLATION which was spoken of through Daniel the prophet, standing in the holy place (let the reader understand), then those who are in Judea must flee to the mountains. Whoever is on the housetop must not go down to get the things out that are in his house. Whoever is in the field must not turn back to get his cloak. But woe to those who are pregnant and to those who are nursing babies in those days! But pray that your flight will not be in the winter, or on a Sabbath. For then there will be a great tribulation, such as has not occurred since the beginning of the world until now, nor ever will." Mt 24:15-21

"But when you see the ABOMINATION OF DESOLATION standing where it should not be (let the reader understand), then those who are in Judea must flee to the mountains. The one who is on the housetop must not go down, or go in to get anything out of his house; and the one who is in the field must not turn back to get his coat. But woe to those who are pregnant and to those who are nursing babies in those days! But pray that it may not happen in the winter. For those days will be a time of tribulation such as has not occurred since the beginning of the creation which God created until now, and never will." Mk 13:14-19

It is clear that the disciples were not speaking of Jesus coming to Earth after many years, since at this point they have no idea that He is leaving. To them the "coming" (Greek word *"parousia"* means presence) was His glorification as the Messiah and ruling Monarch in Jerusalem bringing in the end of the age and everlasting righteousness. The idea that the Temple and city would be destroyed was shocking to them and they did not comprehend it until after His resurrection. With that understanding let us look at the Olivet Discourse in all three of the synoptic gospels. I have laid them side by side in chart form to help us see the parallels.

Mt 24	Mark 13	Luke 21
"And Jesus answered and said to them,	*"And Jesus began to say to them,*	*"And He said,*
Words of Warning and Encouragement for the First Century Church		
"See to it that no one misleads you. For many will come in My name, saying, 'I am the Christ,' and will mislead many. You will be hearing of wars and rumors of wars. See that you are not frightened, for those things must take place, but that is not yet the end." **(DOTL Tribulation is not yet)**	*'See to it that no one misleads you. Many will come in My name, saying, "I am He!" and will mislead many. When you hear of wars and rumors of wars, do not be frightened; those things must take place; but that is not yet the end."* **(DOTL Tribulation is not yet)**	*'See to it that you are not misled; for many will come in My name, saying, "I am He," and, "The time is near." Do not go after them. "When you hear of wars and disturbances, do not be terrified; for these things must take place first, but the end does not follow immediately."* **(DOTL Tribulation is not yet)**

Jesus begins all three accounts with a warning about deception and false Messiahs that will be coming, such as; Bar Kochba (135AD). He makes it clear to them that much has to happen before the end of the age comes. Luke's account seems to add clarity when he says, "the end does not follow immediately." He also warns them about wars and rumors of wars that will be swirling. Undoubtedly He is preparing them for the War of the Jews which lasted from 66AD to 72AD when Jerusalem was destroyed and the people scattered to the nations. Then Jesus jumps to the end of the age when He describes the cosmic signs that will accompany it. Again Luke's account makes this clear since he adds "terrors and great signs from heaven." Famines and earthquakes alone would not suggest the end of the age but the terrors and great signs from heaven do. Thus these are not ordinary earthquakes, if you would, but the increase of shaking at the end of the age which will culminate in the great cosmic signs.

Signs Which Will Accelerate at the End/DOTL

Mt 24	Mark 13	Luke 21
For nation will rise against nation, and kingdom against kingdom, and in various places there will be famines and earthquakes. But all these things are merely the beginning of birth pangs.	*For nation will rise up against nation, and kingdom against kingdom; there will be earthquakes in various places; there will also be famines. These things are merely the beginning of birth pangs.*	*"Then He continued by saying to them, 'Nation will rise against nation and kingdom against kingdom, and there will be great earthquakes, and in various places plagues and famines; and there will be terrors and great signs from heaven.'"* **Cosmic Signs in the DOTL**

After outlining the earmarks of the end of the age Jesus now returns to what awaits His first century hearers. He warns them of what they will suffer as they bring forth testimony and how they will hated by all for the sake of the gospel. He then comforts them with words of His eternal protection and reward.

Mt 24

"Then they will deliver you (early church) to tribulation, and will kill you, and you will be hated by all nations because of My name. At that time many will fall away and will betray one another and hate one another. Many false prophets will arise and will mislead many. Because lawlessness is increased, most people's love will grow cold. But the one who endures to the end, he will be saved."

All This Happened to Them in the First Century

Mk 13

"But be on your guard; for they will deliver you to the courts, and you will be flogged in the synagogues, and you will stand before governors and kings for My sake, as a testimony to them."

Luke 21

"But before all these things, they will lay their hands on you and will persecute you, delivering you to the synagogues and prisons, bringing you before kings and governors for My name's sake. It will lead to an opportunity for your testimony. So make up your minds not to prepare beforehand to defend yourselves; for I will give you utterance and wisdom which none of your opponents will be able to resist or refute. But you will be betrayed even by parents and brothers and relatives and friends, and they will put some of you to death, and you will be hated by all because of My name. Yet not a hair of your head will perish. By your endurance you will gain your lives."

After warning His disciples what they will suffer for the witness of the gospel in their generation, Jesus states categorically that the message would be preached in the entire world, and then the end of the age would come. Both Matthew and Mark record this.

Mt 24	Mark 13	Luke 21
"This gospel of the kingdom shall be preached in the whole world as a testimony to all the nations, and then the end will come."	"The gospel must first be preached to all the nations	**The Destruction of Jerusalem in 70 AD**

Luke 21 — The Destruction of Jerusalem in 70 AD

"But when you see Jerusalem surrounded by armies, then recognize that her desolation is near. Then those who are in Judea must flee to the mountains, and those who are in the midst of the city must leave, and those who are in the country must not enter the city; because these are days of vengeance, so that all things which are written will be fulfilled. Woe to those who are pregnant and to those who are nursing babies in those days; for there will be great distress upon the land and wrath to this people; and they will fall by the edge of the sword, and will be led captive into all the nations; and Jerusalem will be trampled underfoot by the Gentiles until the times of the Gentiles are fulfilled.
Fulfilled in 1967

For two thousand years the gospel has been preached to every nation and tongue as a witness. Please note that Jesus did not say the world would believe and be saved but only that the gospel would be preached as a witness. By this statement He also made it clear that this did not need to be done over and over again. A witness was to be preached to the nations, period. Some would argue that, since there are a few small tribes in remote places that do not yet have a Bible in their own language, the commission is unfulfilled. However, even if that were so, the experts tell us with modern technology it will be accomplished in a few years. Thus there is no "Post-Christian" era - the end of the age is upon us now!

Luke's account does not speak about the gospel going forth here, but instead the answer to the first question regarding the sign of the destruction of Jerusalem in the first century.

Notice that Jerusalem is surrounded in the Day of the Lord as well as 70AD. This one however, is clearly first century since it refers to the destruction of Jerusalem and the scattering of the Jewish people.

Since Jesus has declared what will happen to that generation and that the gospel must be preached in all the nations before the end can come, He now answers the question regarding the sign of the period known as the end. Both Matthew and Mark record this answer as the Abom (Abomination of Desolation. Luke, since he is focused on the events of the first century, records Jesus' words about the destruction of Jerusalem here.

The End Comes – The DOTL Tribulation – The ABOM – Warning for All to Flee Judea

Mt 24

"*"Therefore when you see the ABOMINATION OF DESOLATION which was spoken of through Daniel the prophet, standing in the holy place (let the reader understand), then those who are in Judea must flee to the mountains. Whoever is on the housetop must not go down to get the things out that are in his house. Whoever is in the field must not turn back to get his cloak. But woe to those who are pregnant and to those who are nursing babies in those days! But pray that your flight will not be in the winter, or on a Sabbath. For then there will be a great tribulation, such as has not occurred since the beginning of the world until now, nor ever will. (the Day of the Lord Tribulation) Unless those days had been cut short, no life would have been saved; but for the sake of the elect (Jews) those days will be cut short."*

Mark 13

"*But when you see the ABOMINATION OF DESOLATION standing where it should not be (let the reader understand), then those who are in Judea must flee to the mountains. The one who is on the housetop must not go down, or go in to get anything out of his house; and the one who is in the field must not turn back to get his coat. But woe to those who are pregnant and to those who are nursing babies in those days! But pray that it may not happen in the winter. For those days will be a time of tribulation such as has not occurred since the beginning of the creation which God created until now, and never will. Unless the Lord had shortened those days, no life would have been saved; but for the sake of the elect, whom He chose, He shortened the days."*

The term "elect" or "chosen" used here refers to the believing Jews. No one on the Mount of Olives would have known otherwise since there were no Gentiles among them and they had no knowledge at this time that Gentiles were going to become Christians.

Great Deception in the Day of the Lord

Mt 24	*Mark 13*
"Then if anyone says to you, 'Behold, here is the Christ,' or "There He is,' do not believe him. For false Christs and false prophets will arise and will show great signs and wonders, so as to mislead, if possible, even the elect. Behold, I have told you in advance. So if they say to you, 'Behold, He is in the wilderness,' do not go out, or, 'Behold, He is in the inner rooms,' do not believe them. For just as the lightning comes from the east and flashes even to the west, so will the coming of the Son of Man be.'"	*"And then if anyone says to you, 'Behold, here is the Christ'; or, 'Behold, He is there'; do not believe him; for false Christs and false prophets will arise, and will show signs and wonders, in order to lead astray, if possible, the elect (JEWS). But take heed; behold, I have told you everything in advance.*

← Here Jesus uses *"parousia"* to refer to the end of the period.

Not the days of Noah
Not as a thief

Jesus used the word parousia to refer to the whole of the Tribulation period. Here He uses it to refer to the end of the period when He comes through the clouds. Later on He will refer to the beginning of the period (days of Noah) and also call it the parousia.

Since Jesus warned His followers not to be deceived in the Tribulation period or the Day of the Lord. Does this suggest that all believers will go through the Tribulation? Not at all! Jesus is aware that there will be believers during the Tribulation. Besides, he may have been speaking to the remnant of Israel that will be coming to Him during this time. The term "elect" used here refers to Jews just as in the previous passage.

Please note that in the last two pages Luke's gospel was silent. Now we will continue to lay all three side by side!

Mt 24	Mark 13	Luke 21
"Wherever the corpse is, there the vultures will ← gather."	Here Mathew adds a phrase that can only refer to the armies gathering against Jerusalem. It also appears in Luke 17:37 where it has the same context and meaning.	

Cosmic Signs at the End of DOTL Tribulation

"'But immediately after the tribulation of those THE SUN WILL BE DARKENED, AND THE MOON WILL NOT GIVE ITS LIGHT, AND THE STARS WILL FALL from the sky, and the powers of the heavens will be shaken."	"But in those days, after that tribulation, THE SUN WILL BE DARKENED AND THE MOON WILL NOT GIVE ITS LIGHT, AND THE STARS WILL BE FALLING from heaven, and the powers that are in the heavens will be shaken."	"There will be signs in sun and moon and stars, and on the earth dismay among nations, in perplexity at the roaring of the sea and the waves, men fainting from fear and the expectation of the things which are coming upon the world; for the powers of the heavens will be shaken."

The Son of Man to be Revealed to the World in Power and Glory

"And then the sign of the Son of Man will appear in the sky, and then all the tribes of the earth will mourn, and they will see the SON OF MAN COMING ON THE CLOUDS OF THE SKY with power and great glory.	"Then they will see THE SON OF MAN with great power and glory."	"Then they will see THE SON OF MAN COMING IN A CLOUD with power and great glory."

Many have confused this trumpet blowing and regathering of Jews with the Rapture of believers. However, this is the same event as Moses spoke of in Deuteronomy 30 verse 4.

"If your outcasts are at the ends of the earth (lit. sky), from there the LORD your God will gather you, and from there He will bring you back." Deut 30:4

It is also spoken of in Isaiah 27:13 as the great trumpet that brings back the exiles.

"And it will come about in that day, that the LORD will start His threshing from the flowing stream of the Euphrates to the brook of Egypt; and you will be gathered up one by one, O sons of Israel. It will come about also in that day that a great trumpet will be blown; and those who were perishing in the land of Assyria and who were scattered in the land of Egypt will come and worship the LORD in the holy mountain at Jerusalem." Is 27:12-13

This Great Trumpet is the Shophar HaGadol that is blown on Yom Kippur. Yom Kippur is the Day of Judgment when Jesus will come to judge all the earth.

Mt 24	Mark 13	Luke 21
And He will send forth His angels with A GREAT TRUMPET and THEY WILL GATHER TOGETHER His elect from the four winds, from one end of the sky to the other.'"	*"And then He will send forth the angels, and will gather together His elect from the four winds, from the farthest end of the earth to the farthest end of heaven."*	

Please note Luke's account does not contain this verse.

Then Jesus told them a parable about the fig tree. When the fig tree blossoms summer is near and when you see these things happening His coming is near. It is possible that Jesus is merely using a fig tree as an example. However, many believe the fig tree is a reference to the restoration of Israel (Jer 24). In any event, the point remains the same. Luke adds "when you see these things begin to take place." This of course leads us to the beginning of these events which is previously mentioned as Jerusalem no longer trodden down by Gentile rulers. Thus "these things" began in 1967.

Last Generation - That Sees the Fig Tree Blossom
Israel Restored to Her Land 1948/1967

Mt 24

"'Now learn the parable from the fig tree: when its branch has already become tender and puts forth its leaves, you know that summer is near; So, you too, when you see all these things, recognize that He is near, right at the door. Truly I say to you, this generation will not pass away until all these things take place. Heaven and earth will pass away, but My words will not pass away."

Mark 13

"Now learn the parable from the fig tree: when its branch has already become tender and puts forth its leaves, you know that summer is near. Even so, you too, when you see these things happening, recognize that He is near, right at the door. Truly I say to you, this generation will not pass away until all these things take place. Heaven and earth will pass away, but My words will not pass away."

Luke 21

"'But when these things **begin** to take place, straighten up and lift up your heads, because your redemption is drawing near.' Then He told them a parable: 'Behold the fig tree and all the trees; as soon as they put forth leaves, you see it and know for yourselves that summer is now near. So you also, when you **see** these things happening, recognize that the kingdom of God is near. Truly I say to you, this generation will not pass away until all things take place. Heaven and earth will pass away, but My words will not pass away.'"

Mt 24	Mark 13	Luke 21
"But of that day and hour no one knows, not even the angels of heaven, nor the Son, but the Father alone."	*"But of that day or hour no one knows, not even the angels in heaven, nor the Son, but the Father alone."*	

The English word "but" does not really make clear what Jesus means here. The Greek is "*peri de*" and it is a digression - literally "now concerning." Jesus is digressing to talk about the timing. It would be better rendered, "Now concerning the day or the hour...."

Also, please notice that this verse is a lead into the next passage which talks about the beginning of the Tribulation and the Rapture which is the Father's call!

Here Jesus used parousia to refer to the beginning of the Tribulation which is like the days of Noah.

Mt 24	Mark 13	Luke 21
"'For the coming (parousia) of the Son of Man will be just like the days of Noah. For as in those days before the flood they were eating and drinking, marrying and giving in marriage, until the day that Noah entered the ark, and they did not understand until the flood came and took them all away; (destruction) *so will the coming of the Son of Man be. Then there will be two men in the field; one will be taken and one will be left. Two women will be grinding at the mill; one will be taken and one will be left."* (Rapture)	*"Take heed, keep on the alert; for you do not know when the appointed time will come. It is like a man away on a journey, who upon leaving his house and putting his slaves in charge, assigning to each one his task, also commanded the doorkeeper to stay on the alert. Therefore, be on the alert - - for you do not know when the master of the house is coming, whether in the evening, at midnight, or when the rooster crows, or in the morning -- in case he should come suddenly and find you asleep. What I say to you I say to all, be on the alert!"*	*"Be on guard, so that your hearts will not be weighted down with dissipation and drunkenness and the worries of life, and that day will not come on you suddenly like a trap; for it will come upon all those who dwell on the face of all the earth. But keep on the alert at all times, praying that you may have strength to escape all these things that are about to take place, and to stand before the Son of Man."* (Rapture)

When Jesus said that His coming or parousia would be like the days of Noah, there is no doubt He was talking about the beginning of the Tribulation or the Day of the Lord. Both the Day of the Lord and the Rapture come like a thief. There is no way that the end of the Tribulation can be referred to as the "days of Noah." The whole point of this terminology is that all will be going on as usual and then sudden destruction will come like a thief. Then there will be a rescue (rapture) and a judgment! The period at the end of the Tribulation, when the earth is practically destroyed, cannot fit this scenario.

In the above passages, please notice that Luke also mentions the Rapture. In his account, Jesus spoke about "the Day" or the Tribulation coming like a trap which would mean that those who were unprepared were caught in it. Then He said that we could have the strength to escape all these things (the Day of the Lord Tribulation) and stand before the Son of Man who will not be on Earth during this time.

Matthew's gospel continues on this theme while the others end.

Mt 24

"Therefore be on the alert, for you do not know which day your Lord is coming. But be sure of this, that if the head of the house had known at what time of the night the thief was coming, he would have been on the alert and would not have allowed his house to be broken into. For this reason you also must be ready; for the Son of Man is coming at an hour when you do not think He will. Who then is the faithful and sensible slave whom his master put in charge of his household to give them their food at the proper time? Blessed is that slave whom his master finds so doing when he comes. Truly I say to you that he will put him in charge of all his possessions. But if that evil slave says in his heart, 'My master is not coming for a long time,' and begins to beat his fellow slaves and eat and drink with drunkards; the master of that slave will come on a day when he does not expect him and at an hour which he does not know, (Clearly implying that those who are on the alert will know) *and will cut him in pieces and assign him a place with the hypocrites; in that place there will be weeping and gnashing of teeth.*

This parable tells us clearly that those who are awake and alert and walking with Christ will know when He is coming and will not be taken off guard. However, the Christian who is not on the alert will not know or be prepared for the coming of Christ!

Matthew 25 is a continuation of the Olivet Discourse and therefore is referring to the time of the parousia or the Day of the Lord just like Matthew 24. Notice it begins by saying "Then" or "At that time."

Two stories are given to illustrate the need for diligent preparedness and obedience in order to be prepared for His return.

Mt 25

"Then (at that time) the kingdom of heaven will be comparable to ten virgins, who took their lamps and went out to meet the bridegroom. Five of them were foolish, and five were prudent. For when the foolish took their lamps, they took no oil with them, but the prudent took oil in flasks along with their lamps. Now while the bridegroom was delaying, they all got drowsy and began to sleep. But at midnight there was a shout, 'Behold, the bridegroom! Come out to meet him.' Then all those virgins rose and trimmed their lamps. The foolish said to the prudent, 'Give us some of your oil, for our lamps are going out.' But the prudent answered, 'No, there will not be enough for us and you too; go instead to the dealers and buy some for yourselves.' And while they were going away to make the purchase, the bridegroom came, and those who were ready went in with him to the wedding feast; and the door was shut. Later the other virgins also came, saying, 'Lord, lord, open up for us.' But he answered, 'Truly I say to you, I do not know you.' Be on the alert then, for you do not know the day nor the hour."

This parable has to do with being ready for the Rapture - the return of the Bridegroom to whisk His Bride away. It is a beautiful picture of being filled with the Spirit (represented by the oil) and staying awake or alert. Though the virgins in the story are attendants of the bride and not the bride herself, they represent Christians. Since Christ is referring to two groups of Christians it was necessary to use the virgin attendants rather than the actual bride in the wedding parable. After all, like any parable the details are not to be taken literally. The parable is about going to the wedding versus missing out. One group of Christians is taken to be with the Bridegroom, whereas; the others are left behind. Notice it says "At that time (the Day of the Lord) the kingdom will be <u>like</u> ten virgins who went out to meet the Bridegroom." The ten virgins represent the believers in Christ who were all waiting for the Bridegroom to come yet the foolish ones were not prepared. Their attitude was that they had enough already. The wise virgins could not get enough oil and made sure that they would not run out. They represent the Bride of Christ that has made herself ready and is raptured by the Bridegroom. Thus the Rapture is clearly taught in the Olivet Discourse (in Mt 24 & 25) and is connected with the Abomination of Desolation which occurs in the middle of the Last Shemitah Cycle and begins the Tribulation period.

The second parable in Matthew 25 concerns rewards and judgments that accompany the return of Christ. It is similar to the parable of the virgins in that there are some that are rewarded and enter into the joy of the Master and one who is cast out because he produced no fruit. This parable, although it has the same theme seems to be more about the way we live for Christ in anticipation of His coming. The one servant does not see His Master correctly and does not know His heart and is afraid of His coming.

The Sheep and Goats

This last section is identified with the erchomai of Christ when He appears in glory at the end of the Tribulation and sets up His throne. Then it says he will gather the nations before Him. This is the surviving remnant from all the nations after the Tribulation. Remember if it were not cut short to three and a half years no life would be saved. However, it was and there are survivors. Then Jesus tells us clearly that these survivors will be gathered into two groups (sheep and goats) and judged based on how they treated the Jews (brothers of Jesus) during the Tribulation. Did they help them or were they oblivious to their suffering? Both groups are astonished since they have no idea that the Jews are suffering because of who they are, and that God is watching the way they treat them. Though the brothers of Jesus are clearly Jews in this passage, it can also apply to the treatment of Christians since we are Christ's spiritual brothers.

Because of Replacement Theology the church has so twisted the meaning of this passage. It is usually explained in an almost secular humanist way - that the poor of the world are the brothers of Christ that have to be cared for because we "see Jesus in them." While it is absolutely right that we must care for the poor, this passage is about caring for Israel. As we can see clearly today, those who mistreat Israel are the goats and those who help them are the sheep.

The Seventh Door

The Seventh door is about the last book of the Bible called "The Revelation." I'm sure you must have heard someone incorrectly call it "Revelations." Over the centuries it has been neglected and completely misunderstood. Yet it is the only book in the Bible that is written exclusively about the end of the age. It gives us the whole scenario. Yet it is considered by many to be the most confusing book in the Bible. There must literally be hundreds of interpretations. What is the primary reason for all this confusion? How can there be so many versions of the trumpets and the bowls? Why is this little book that we are blessed to read so mysterious? Why have so many great preachers and spiritual minds been unable to make it clear? There must be a lost key. Actually there is! But why has it not been discovered you may ask? The reason is actually simple. Unless one comes through the six doors the seventh key cannot be found. That's right! It is the other keys that expose it and make it visible! Now that we have come this far we can see it clearly!

 ## The Seventh Key

The Book of Revelation is not chronological. It is a series of visions that are all about the period of time known as the Day of the Lord or the Tribulation. There it is! The missing key lost for so many centuries. Can it really be that simple? Why don't you take it in your hand and find out? Let's see if we can comprehend the visions and symbols. You will definitely want to spend some time here!

Chapter Nine
The Revelation

The book of Revelation was written to encourage the church in the midst of trial. Yet, most Christians today are afraid to even read the book or try to comprehend its mysteries. There are several reasons for this. Besides the fact that many are afraid to think about the coming of the Lord, centuries of faulty interpretation have fostered the idea that its message is incomprehensible. But how can this be? Why would God write an incomprehensible book to Christians to help them endure trial? That simply makes no sense. How could veiled passages and illustrations about doom and destruction, that so frighten Christians today, be an encouragement to the church at the latter part of the first century? The answer appears obvious. It could not have been veiled to them the way it has been to subsequent generations. They must have understood its message and symbolic language enough to be greatly encouraged. If this is so, and I believe it is, then we need to discover what knowledge these early Christians had that has been lost to the modern church.

What is it About?

I think the greatest mistake that Gentile scholars have made in attempting to unlock the Revelation given to John, is that they have failed to see its Jewishness and have interpreted it with a Gentile mindset and understanding. But it is a Jewish book with a message and content that is very typical of the Hebrew prophets. After all, it was penned by a Jewish apostle and student of the Jewish prophets. It covers the period known as the Day of the Lord which was the predominant theme of the prophets. This is clearly stated by John in Chapter 1 verse 10.

"I was in the Spirit on the Lord's Day, and I heard behind me a loud voice like the sound of a trumpet, saying, "Write in a book what you see....."" Rev 1:10

The "Lord's Day" here is clearly the Day of the Lord. There is no other way to understand this verse except that John is describing how he was caught up in the Spirit into the Day of the Lord and told to write down what he saw. The notion that John was referring to the Sabbath, or Sunday, is not acceptable. If he were referring to the Sabbath, namely, the last day of the week, he would have likely said, "One Shabbat I was caught up in the Spirit." But he didn't say Sabbath, which certainly wouldn't have been Sunday, but, rather on "the Lord's Day." The use of the article here signifies that it was a specific time period known as "the Day of The Lord."

Much of the symbolism in the book of Revelation is not new. It is, for the most part, repetitive of the revelations given to Isaiah, Joel, Zechariah, Ezekiel, Micah, and the other prophets. What is new is merely detail on the same events which they depicted. In order to unlock the book of Revelation, one cannot start with the Revelation itself, but with a thorough understanding of the theme of the Day of the Lord as prophesied by the prophets.

The Revelation is Not a Chronological Book

Perhaps the second greatest mistake made by Bible students and scholars, is to approach the book of Revelation as a chronological book. It simply cannot be understood this way. This approach causes one to invent all sorts of theories and hypotheses which are at odds with other portions of Scripture and lead to much confusion. This reasoning is usually taken from verses which say things like, "After these things I looked" and "After this I saw." But these statements usually mean that after seeing one vision John saw another vision which unveiled more detail on the same events. There are many proofs throughout the book that this is the way it is to be understood. For example, in Chapter 6 there is a description of the opening of the sixth seal which unleashes the great destruction at the end of the Great Tribulation. This is clear by the description of events such as the great earthquake, the sun turning black, the moon to blood, and the stars falling from the sky. These are the cosmic signs which were prophesied by the prophets and covered throughout this book. Then we are told that the sky is split apart like a scroll and that every mountain and island are moved out of their places and men are hiding in caves and rocks to get away from the wrath of the Lamb (Is 2:9-11). Then in Chapter 7, John says that "after this" he saw four angels standing at the four corners of the earth, holding back the four winds of the earth, and another angel told these angels not to harm the earth or the sea or the trees until the remnant of Israel is sealed. It seems hard to imagine how Chapter 7 can be in chronological order with Chapter 6. To interpret it this way, as the Pre-Weekers do, means that the command not to harm the earth, sea, or trees comes after a time of the greatest destruction the earth has ever known. Also, how can the events of the sixth seal take place at the beginning of the Last Shemitah Cycle during a time of "peace" as the Pre-Weekers also teach? This, therefore, is very clear proof that the words "after this" do not necessarily refer to a particular sequence of events but simply mean that after one vision had ended another appeared.

Seven Churches (Chapters 2 & 3)

The first part of the Revelation to John, after he is caught up in the Spirit into the Day of the Lord, is a message to "the seven churches." Though these churches existed at the time and the message was for them, they are representative of the whole church. This pattern of seven as the number of completeness is well established in the Hebrew Scriptures and is used in the same passage of Revelation to refer to the Holy Spirit ("the Seven Spirits" Rev 1:4). Some Bible teachers, recognizing that "the seven churches" represent the whole church, came up with the idea that each one identifies a period in church history down through the centuries. As fascinating as this theory is, and despite the remarkable parallels that exist between these churches and various segments of church history, the theory breaks down in many places, particularly with the church in Laodicea. This church is thought to be symbolic of the last days church which is portrayed as lukewarm and backslidden. Yet, the church today worldwide is much more committed to Christ than the church which existed in the dark ages. Besides, it is the last days church that Messiah is coming back for. How then can she be represented by the church at Laodicea?

A much more reasonable interpretation of the identity of "the seven churches" is that they are symbolic of the church that is in existence prior to the Day of the Lord. This interpretation is very natural and does not require the force fitting of passages to accommodate the facts of church history. Also, since John began the Revelation stating that he had been taken in the Spirit into the Day of the Lord, and this is the theme of the rest of the book, this view is most likely. How else can we understand the promise to the church in Philadelphia to "keep them from the hour of trial which is about to come upon the whole inhabited earth." This is clearly a reference to the Tribulation. Also, the continual warnings to "wake up" and the promises to those who "overcome" and who "keep My deeds until the end," seem to clearly refer to the church at the end of the age.

The use of numeric symbolism throughout the Book of Revelation is profound and pervasive and is used to underscore the divine origin and completeness of the Day of the Lord. This does not mean that the events are not literal, but that numbers are used in a biblical prophetic sense to illustrate God's hand in the orchestration of events. Thus they are not all to be taken literally.

The Sevens of Revelation

Seven Churches
Seven Seals 5:6
Seven Trumpets
Seven Bowls
Seven Lampstands
Seven Spirits
Seven Stars
Seven Lamps 4:5
Seven Promises to Overcomers 2 & 3
Seven Horns 5:6
Seven Eyes 5:6
Seven Angels 8:2, 6, 15:1, 6, 7, 8
Seven Thunders 10:3, 4
Seven Thousand 11:13
Seven Heads 12:3
Seven Crowns 12:3
Seven Plagues 15:1
Seven Mountains 17:9
Seven Kings 17:10, 11
Seven Features of Christ
Seven Personages 12 & 13 (Woman, Man-Child, Red Dragon, Beast, False Prophet, Michael, the Lamb)

Scene in Heaven (Chapters 4&5)

In the beginning of Chapter 4, John is taken in the Spirit to heaven where he sees another vision. He then goes on to describe the things he saw in heaven. The throne of God is mentioned and twenty-four thrones with twenty-four elders upon them. There has been much speculation as to the identity of the twenty-four elders. Most Pre-Weekers believe that they are representative of the church, and that their presence in heaven proves that the church is raptured prior to the Last Shemitah Cycle. However, I do not believe it is necessary to conclude that the twenty-four elders are representative of the church. This number may have more to do with the heavenly sanctuary and the priesthood than the church (see 1Chron 24, 25, Rev 5:8, 15:5, Heb 9:23-25). Also, if the twenty-four elders are representative of the church, why do they sing, "Thou hast made them to be a kingdom and priests to our God; and they will reign upon the earth" (5:10) rather than, "thou hast made us to be a kingdom and priests to our God and we will reign upon the earth?" I realize that the KJV translates it this way but it is all alone and not a single interlinear concurs. Furthermore, if these elders represent the church, how could John the Beloved Apostle be left out?

In Chapter 5, God is seen upon His throne with a scroll sealed with seven seals. The Messiah, the Lion of the tribe of Judah, the Lamb that was slain, is the only one worthy to take the scroll and open its seals. This scroll is the scroll of dominion over the earth. It is the title deed to the kingdoms of the earth and its opening ushers in the Day of the Lord and the Millennial Reign. This is why all of heaven rejoices and ascribes glory and dominion to Him who sits upon the throne and to the Lamb and they sing about those whom Messiah has purchased from every tongue and people and nation to reign with Him. This vision is the same as that given to Daniel in Dan 7:9-14.

The Seven Seals (Chapters 6-8)

When Messiah breaks the first seal, the reign of Antichrist begins. He is pictured on a white horse impersonating Messiah with a bow in his hand. Also, a crown (kingdom) has been given to him, and he goes out conquering and to conquer. Interestingly enough, Antichrist is said to have a bow but there is no mention of arrows. Perhaps this is assumed, but this language could also suggest that he conquers without warfare. This first horse represents the first part of the Last Shemitah Cycle when Antichrist signs a covenant of "peace" with Israel, and through skill and diplomacy, solidifies the other nations behind him. (See chart 11 on page 296)

Diplomacy is regarded as a primary means of settling territorial disputes today. Though wars have increased, nations now view diplomacy, dialogue, trade agreements, etc., as being equally or even more effective in settling disputes. The nation of Israel is obsessed with the need for "peace and security" and the whole world seems to be committed to the "peace process." The one who succeeds in bringing this peace will likely be the rider of the white horse in the first seal. Peace will come for a while and then it will suddenly be broken and all out destruction will begin. The events which follow - wars, famines, plagues, earthquakes, darkness, etc. - are all common themes of the Day of the Lord. While they are saying "peace and security" then suddenly destruction will come upon them like birth pangs upon a woman with child, and they will not escape. This is the time of Jacob's Distress, but the Lord will deliver a remnant from it.

When Jesus breaks the second seal, Antichrist rides out on a red horse. This red horse is symbolic of war. A great sword is given to him, and he takes peace from the earth. In the middle of the week, Antichrist breaks his covenant with Israel, sets up the Abomination of Desolation, and the time of "peace" comes to an end (1 Thess 5:3). Notice that in order for him to take "peace" from the earth, the earth must have been experiencing a time of peace. This can hardly be said at the moment, but it is the main preoccupation of the nations today, especially in the Middle East.

When the third seal is broken, a black horse is released and its rider has a pair of scales in his hand. Then a voice cries out saying, "A quart of wheat for a denarius...." This is a picture of great famine brought on by the destruction of war and possibly by the persecution of the Antichrist who forbids buying and selling except by the mark of the Beast (Rev 13:17).

When Messiah breaks the fourth seal, an ashen horse is released. He who sat on it had the name Death, and Hades was following with him. A fourth of the earth is slaughtered by a combination of war, famine, pestilence, and wild beasts. This is undoubtedly a result of the beginning of the Armageddon campaign. At present, a fourth of the earth would equal at least one and a half billion people. For this to happen before the Tribulation is unimaginable.

When the fifth seal is broken, a vision appears of the martyred saints underneath the altar. The altar is the place of justice, and the blood of the martyrs is seen here as crying out for justice to be done. They are told to be patient a little longer until the rest of their martyred brethren join them. This illustrates the great multitude that will not bow down to the devil taking the mark of the Beast and are martyred as a result.

The Sixth Seal compares directly to Isaiah 2

"I looked when He broke the sixth seal, and there was a great earthquake; and the sun became black as sackcloth made of hair, and the whole moon became like blood; and the stars of the sky fell to the earth, as a fig tree casts its unripe figs when shaken by a great wind. The sky was split apart like a scroll when it is rolled up, and every mountain and island were moved out of their places. Then the kings of the earth and the great men and the commanders and the rich and the strong and every slave and free man hid themselves in the caves and among the rocks of the mountains; and they said to the mountains and to the rocks, "Fall on us and hide us from the presence of Him who sits on the throne, and from the wrath of the Lamb; for the great day of their wrath has come, and who is able to stand?" Rev 6:12-17

The pride of man will be humbled and the loftiness of men will be abased; and the LORD alone will be exalted in that day, but the idols will completely vanish. Men will go into caves of the rocks and into holes of the ground before the terror of the LORD and the splendor of His majesty, when He arises to make the earth tremble. In that day men will cast away to the moles and the bats their idols of silver and their idols of gold, which they made for themselves to worship, in order to go into the caverns of the rocks and the clefts of the cliffs before the terror of the LORD and the splendor of His majesty, when He arises to make the earth tremble. Isaiah 2:17-21

At the opening of the sixth seal, the wrath of Messiah is poured out. This happens toward the end of the Tribulation.

The events of the Sixth Seal are conclusive and only happen once. They are clearly identified by many verses of Scripture as marking the end of the Tribulation or the Day of the Lord.

➢ Sun like sackcloth
➢ Moon like blood
➢ Stars fall from the sky
➢ Every mountain and island moved out of their places
➢ Sky split apart like a scroll

Below is a sampling of verses on the cosmic signs at the end of the Tribulation.

"But immediately after the tribulation of those days THE SUN WILL BE DARKENED, AND THE MOON WILL NOT GIVE ITS LIGHT, AND THE STARS WILL FALL from the sky, and the powers of the heavens will be shaken. And then the sign of the Son of Man will appear in the sky, and then all the tribes of the earth will mourn, and they will see the SON OF MAN COMING ON THE CLOUDS OF THE SKY with power and great glory." Mt 24:29-30

"In that day there will be no light; the luminaries will dwindle. For it will be a unique day which is known to the LORD, neither day nor night, but it will come about that at evening time there will be light." Zech 14:6-7

"I will display wonders in the sky and on the earth, blood, fire and columns of smoke. The sun will be turned into darkness and the moon into blood before the great and awesome day of the LORD comes. And it will come about that whoever calls on the name of the LORD will be delivered; for on Mount Zion and in Jerusalem there will be those who escape, as the LORD has said, even among the survivors whom the LORD calls." Joel 2:30-32

"Behold the day of the LORD is coming, cruel, with fury and burning anger, to make the land a desolation; and He will exterminate its sinners from it. For the stars of heaven and their constellations will not flash forth their light; the sun will be dark when it rises and the moon will not shed its light. Thus I will punish the world for its evil and the wicked for their iniquity; I will also put an end to the arrogance of the proud and abase the haughtiness of the ruthless. I will make mortal man scarcer than pure gold and mankind than the gold of Ophir. Therefore I will make the heavens tremble, and the earth will be shaken from its place at the fury of the LORD of hosts in the day of His burning anger." Is 13:9-13

Peace & Security

"For you yourselves know full well that the day of the Lord will come just like a thief in the night. While they are saying, 'Peace and safety!' then destruction will come upon them suddenly like birth pangs upon a woman with child; and they shall not escape." 1 Thess 5:2-3

Daniel's Seventieth Week or Last Shemitah Cycle is divided into two halves of three and a half years each. The first part is a time of "Peace and Security" which is abruptly broken by "sudden destruction." This destruction is a common theme of Scripture. It refers to the Tribulation which begins with the revealing of the "Man of Lawlessness" in the Temple, and ends with the Armageddon campaign and the revealing of the Messiah. This time of "destruction" is also known as the "Day of Wrath" or the "Day of The Lord." Proponents of the Pre-Shemitah Cycle Rapture (Pre-Week) refer to all seven years of this period as "the Tribulation." However, this cannot be correct. "The Tribulation" is the last part of the Shemitah Cycle which is marked by the breaking of the covenant with the Jews and the setting up of the Abomination of Desolation. With this all of the Scriptures agree.

Sudden Destruction

Since the Day of the Lord begins in the middle of the Shemitah Cycle, and this is known as "The Time of Destruction" which comes suddenly upon those living in "Peace and Security," how can the beginning of the Shemitah Cycle also be a time of destruction? This is the primary problem with the Pre-Week or Pre-Shemitah Cycle view. It is impossible for a time of "Peace and Security" to be also a time of gloom, doom, darkness, distress, desolation, and destruction. The Day of the Lord does not initially bring peace, but war and judgment upon the wicked. I have yet to hear someone from a Pre-Week or Pre-Shemitah Cycle point of view explain this. Almost all of them believe that the events of the first six seals of Revelation Chapter 6 take place before the middle of the Shemitah Cycle. This is a complete impossibility.

Two Remnants (Chapter Seven)

As has already been stated, the events of Chapter 7 are not sequential to Chapter 6. John sees another vision of four angels who are being told to hold back harm from the earth until the remnant of Israel is sealed on their foreheads. Apparently this remnant that goes through the Tribulation is shielded and protected by God from harm. John hears the number of the remnant. The number of Jews sealed is 144,000; 12,000 from every tribe of Israel. Though the prophets prophesied that only a remnant of Jews would return to God at the end of the age, it seems very difficult to accept that this number is to be taken literally. It is my belief that it is a representative number symbolizing the remnant of Israel. Twelve is a representative number in Israel. Israel had twelve patriarchs and twelve tribes. Twelve men were sent out by Moses to spy out the land of Canaan. Solomon had twelve princes. Messiah chose twelve apostles. The number twelve means "government" and "thousand" means "maturity" or "fullness." The fact that numerical symbolism is rampant in Revelation adds weight to this conclusion.

The Revelation 7 Church

In the second part of the chapter, John looks again and sees another remnant. However, no number is given since the multitude is said to be more than anyone can count. They are those from every nation, tribe, and tongue that have come "out of" the Great Tribulation. It is said that they have washed their robes in the blood of the Lamb. I believe this statement implies their need to be washed in the blood and get right with God prior to the Tribulation; otherwise they would have been raptured. When the Bride is mentioned later in Chapter 19, attention is drawn to her righteousness and not her need to be cleansed from sin. This information identifies them as the Lukewarn Church and not militant apostolic intercessors. They washed their robes, presumably because they were dirty. They were not walking in righteousness but needed to repent and get right with God. Secondly, it is clear they were not protected from the judgments in some city of refuge, since they are comforted from the effects of the various plagues, namely hunger, thirst, intense heat, and many tears.[51]

The fact that this great multitude goes through the Tribulation, and that many of them are martyred, is borne out by verse 16 which implies that they have gone through the famine, pestilence, and intense heat associated with the Great Tribulation.

"They shall hunger no more, neither thirst anymore; neither shall the sun beat down on them, nor any heat; for the Lamb in the center of the throne shall be their shepherd, and shall guide them to springs of the water of life; and God shall wipe every tear from their eyes." Rev 7:16-17

The church in Revelation 7 is presented as a great multitude from every tribe and tongue. They are presented alongside the remnant of Israel which is sealed. They are a believing remnant of the nations that come through the Tribulation and have been saved by the Blood of the Lamb. In fact, we are clearly told that they have washed their robes and made them white in the Blood.

---

[51] Rev 7:16-17

Jewish Evangelists?

Many Pre-Shemitah Cycle Rapture proponents say that the 144,000 Jews mentioned in Revelation 7 are Jewish evangelists. Though they are undoubtedly evangelistic, it is clear from the context that they are the remnant of Israel sealed from harm during the Tribulation. Consider the following verses on the promised remnant:

"For I do not want you, brethren, to be uninformed of this mystery, lest you be wise in your own estimation, that a partial hardening has happened to Israel until the fullness (or full number) of the Gentiles has come in; and thus all Israel will be saved; just as it is written, 'The Deliverer will come from Zion, He will remove ungodliness from Jacob.'" Rom 11:25-26

"Now it will come about in that day (the Day of the Lord) that the remnant of Israel, and those of the house of Jacob who have escaped, will never again rely on the one who struck them, but will truly rely on the LORD, the Holy One of Israel. A remnant will return, the remnant of Jacob, to the mighty God. For though your people, O Israel, may be like the sand of the sea, only a remnant within them will return; a destruction is determined, overflowing with righteousness. For a complete destruction, one that is decreed, the Lord GOD of hosts will execute in the midst of the whole land." Is 10:20-23

"The sun will be turned into darkness, and the moon into blood, before the great and awesome day of the LORD comes. And it will come about that whoever calls on the name of the LORD will be delivered; for on Mount Zion and in Jerusalem there will be those who escape, as the LORD has said, even among the survivors whom the LORD calls." Joel 2:31-32

"And Isaiah cries out concerning Israel, 'Though the number of the sons of Israel be as the sand of the sea, it is the remnant that will be saved; for the Lord will execute His word upon the earth, thoroughly and quickly.' And just as Isaiah foretold, 'Except the Lord of Sabaoth had left to us a posterity, we would have become as Sodom, and would have resembled Gomorrah.'" Romans 9:27-29

Ask now, and see, if a male can give birth. Why do I see every man with his hands on his loins, as a woman in childbirth? And why have all faces turned pale? Alas! for that day is great, there is none like it; and it is the time of Jacob's distress, but he will be saved from it. Jer 30:6-7

The Saved Remnant Born

"Before she travailed, she brought forth; before her pain came, she gave birth to a boy. Who has heard such a thing? Who has seen such things? Can a land be born in one day? Can a nation be brought forth all at once? As soon as Zion travailed, she also brought forth her sons. 'Shall I bring to the point of birth, and not give delivery?' says the LORD. 'Or shall I who gives delivery shut the womb?' says your God." Is 66:7-9

This time of "birth pains" for Israel is not in vain. Israel does give birth. Zion does bring forth sons and the result is life from the dead (Rom 11:15). The sons are a reference to the remnant delivered in the Time of Wrath. "Can a nation be born in a day?" Some have interpreted this word to be a reference to the rebirth of the State of Israel in 1948. Though that was absolutely miraculous, and certainly would be another fulfillment of the prophecy, it doesn't seem to be what the prophet is directly referring to. Israel was declared a State in one day but it is stretching it a bit to say that the State was born in a day. It seems more likely, given the context of Jacob's Distress, that this is a reference to the spiritual rebirth of a remnant that comes to Messiah shortly after the time of travail begins.

"As soon as Zion travailed, she also brought forth her sons."

This is borne out by the fact that God pours out a Spirit of grace and supplication at this time.

"And it will come about in that day that I will set about to destroy all the nations that come against Jerusalem. And I will pour out on the house of

David and on the inhabitants of Jerusalem, the Spirit of grace and of supplication, so that they will look on Me whom they have pierced; and they will mourn for Him, as one mourns for an only son, and they will weep bitterly over Him, like the bitter weeping over a first-born." Zech 12:9-10

There are several factors that impact Israel at this time, leading to repentance and a turning to Messiah. They are as follows:

A. The Abomination of Desolation (They realize Antichrist is the false Messiah when the Holy Place is desecrated)
B. The Rapture of the Bride will have a devastating affect worldwide
C. The ministry of the Two Witnesses which begins in the middle of the week (likely at Passover - Rev 11:3-12).

The sons that Israel brings forth in a day, a renewed, born-again remnant of the nation, are spoken of many places in Scripture as being sealed or protected during this time. While the earth is being devastated and there is all-out war on the Jews, the Lord delivers a remnant, concealing them from the wrath.

"Alas! for that day is great, there is none like it; and it is the time of Jacob's distress, but he will be saved from it." Jer 30:7

"...for on Mount Zion and in Jerusalem there will be those who escape, as the LORD has said, even among the survivors whom the LORD calls." Joel 2:32

"Come, my people, enter into your rooms, and close your doors behind you; hide for a little while, until indignation runs its course." Is 26:20

When the Abomination of Desolation is set up, Jesus warned that every Jew (those in Judea) should flee to the mountains. It would appear that there is a remnant that heed His words and flee. Many have speculated that they will go to Petra in Jordan, since Jesus said to flee Judea and Messiah is expected from the east (Is 63:1-7).

Now please note the following about the flight of the remnant:

A. With regard to the warning of Jesus to flee Jerusalem found in the gospels, consider the following:

The warning to leave immediately without turning back is intended to convey the urgency of the need to flee, and does not mean that all will flee at the same time or on the same day. Jesus told them to pray that their flight would not be in winter or on a Sabbath. There is no doubt that had He been referring to the actual day that the Abomination of Desolation is set up (if indeed it's a 24-hour period); He would have known whether it was in winter or on a Sabbath.

B. The remnant will begin to flee at this time but will continue to flee from Antichrist and the Gentile armies right up to the end (Zech 14:5 "You will flee by the valley of My mountains").

C. This remnant is not only a remnant of the Jewish nation as a whole; it is also a remnant of the nation existing at that time. A great number of the apostasizing Jews will be slaughtered by Antichrist. This is why it says that "brother will betray brother to death." This is also true of Christians living at this time.

D. Though the conflict is centered in Jerusalem (it is Jacob's Distress), it will affect the whole world and thus the Jews brought back from the nations by Messiah when He comes (Mt 24:31, Is 27:13), will also be part of the remnant that escapes, provided of course they have become believers.

E. When it says in Romans 11:26 that "all Israel will be saved (delivered)," it is not referring to every Jew but the remnant that survives as a representative body. This will truly be all Israel and it will be all of Israel that is left.

F. It is for the sake of the remnant of the Jews that the Tribulation has been cut short. They are "the elect" referred to by Jesus in Matthew 24 and elsewhere. The devil's intent is to wipe out the natural seed of Jacob and thus nullify God's promises. The Christians cannot be wiped out by death.

When we get to Chapter 12 we will see that there is another remnant to whom Israel gives birth!

Remnants Are Nothing New

God has always had His righteous remnants, and He continues to have them today. When Elijah was having a pity party thinking that he was the only righteous person left in Israel, God rebuked him with the news that there were seven thousand others who had not bowed the knee to Baal. Paul picks up on this in Romans 11:1-10. He points out that even though Israel's leaders, and thus the nation, had rejected Messiah; there was a significant remnant of Jewish believers alive at that time, just as there also is today. This remnant, together with a remnant from the Gentile nations, has been made into "one new man" in Christ. This is something that the church, because of centuries of bad theology, fails to understand or stubbornly resists. That is, that God has remnants among Jews and Gentiles. In the Day of the Lord there will be remnants sealed, concealed, and delivered, and there will be remnants that come through the fire. So far we have seen that there is a Jewish remnant protected in the Day of Wrath. There is also a Jewish remnant which is part of the Bride of Christ that is raptured out. There is a Gentile remnant that is raptured out in the Bride of Christ and apparently a very large one that comes out of the Tribulation knowing Messiah (Rev 7). Then there are survivors of the Tribulation from all the nations that are judged by Jesus (Mt 25) based on how they treated the Jews (and Christians) during that time. These will likely be the ones to populate the renewed earth during the Millennial reign. Does this trouble you? Why should it? What good is a kingdom, if there is no one to govern? How can Israel be head of the nations (Is 2) if there are no nations to be head of? The church is not going to reign over itself, is it? Why is this so difficult for Bible teachers to accept? I believe it's because there is still resistance among Gentile believers, and even some Jewish believers, to the fact that the root of the tree is Jewish (Rom 11:17-24). Also, years of Amillennialism and Augustinian theology have created a bias in the way Bible schools and denominational leaders interpret Scripture. The reality that heaven is coming to Earth is still hard to grasp.

The Seventh Seal (Chapter Eight)

The first six seals that Messiah broke contained an overview of events during the Day of the Lord or the Tribulation. The seventh seal is then opened and within it are a series of visions relating to the time of wrath and judgment that is poured out on the earth. These various judgments are pictured as seven angels with seven trumpets. Again the number seven is used symbolically to show the fullness of the judgment and wrath. However, before the judgment is released we are told that there is silence in heaven for half an hour. This verse is telling us how serious this judgment of mankind is and how it pains God to pour it out. All of heaven, which is usually triumphant in song, observes, as it were, a half hour of complete silence because of the magnitude of suffering that is about to be experienced on Earth. Then verses 3-5 reveal the role of God's people as priests and how the unleashing of this judgment is in direct response to their worship (represented by the incense) and intercession. Then the seven angels sound their trumpets, and seven great judgments are released upon Earth. They are as follows:

1. **Destruction on the earth** - Hail and fire mixed with blood. A third of the earth, a third of the trees, and all the green grass was burned up.

2. **Destruction on the sea** - Something like a great mountain burning with fire was thrown into the sea. A third of the sea became blood, a third of the creatures in the sea died, and a third of the ships were destroyed.

3. **Destruction on the rivers and springs** - A great star fell from heaven, burning like a torch, and it fell on a third of the rivers and springs of water and they became bitter and many men died.

4. **Darkness** - A third of the sun and a third of the moon and a third of the stars were smitten - darkness for a third of the day and night.

5. **Locusts releasing torment** - torment men for five months. They are not allowed to kill and they are not allowed to harm the servants of God. Their king is the destroyer himself, Antichrist. (The description of these locusts given in Chapter 9 implies that they are not insects at all but likely some sort of man-made weapons. Perhaps they are helicopters or drones that release chemical weapons. Though they are man-made, they are inspired by satan himself (the star that <u>had</u> fallen) who unleashes a horde of demons to round them up. This is the typical picture that exists throughout the book of Revelation of supernatural and natural forces working together in unison.)

6. **Armageddon** - Four angels that are bound at the Euphrates are released. These are satanic forces, principalities of war, which prepare the way for the 200 million army to come from the east. A third of mankind is killed by this action. John, not knowing what he was looking at, called the weapons he saw horses, but the descriptions he gave could only be matched by modern armament - weapons of mass destruction.

7. Seventh Trumpet - Christ Reigns

"And the nations were enraged, and Your wrath came, and the time came for the dead to be judged, and the time to reward Your bond-servants the prophets and the saints and those who fear Your name, the small and the great, and <u>to</u> destroy those who destroy the earth. And the temple of God which is in heaven was opened; and the ark of His covenant appeared in His temple, and there were flashes of lightning and sounds and peals of thunder and an earthquake and a great hailstorm." Rev 11:18-19

When the seventh angel sounds, the Messiah appears and pours out wrath on the nations gathered against Jerusalem. The general resurrection takes place when the prophets and saints of old are raised together with those believers that were martyred during the Tribulation. Also mentioned is the great earthquake and hailstorm which climax the Tribulation. Though Messiah's appearing is not actually mentioned until Chapter 14, it is implied by these events. This is another reason why the book of Revelation cannot be chronological since the events of the Sixth Seal, the Seventh Trumpet, and the Seventh Bowl are the same and each ends with the return of Messiah to judge.

There is a fascinating similarity between the trumpet plagues and the bowl judgments! That is why I am inclined to believe they are the same. They each appear to end with the return of Christ. What is the significance of the "one-third?" Could it be that it is also symbolic since many of the numbers are?

Plagues
1. Fire on the Earth
2. Water to Blood
3. Waters Made Bitter
4. Darkness
5. Locusts – Chemical Warfare
6. Armageddon
7. Thy Wrath

~~~~~

Chapter 9 – Parallel to Joel Chapter 2

Rev 9:7-11	Joel 2:1-10
"The appearance of the locusts was like horses prepared for battle; and on their heads appeared to be crowns like gold, and their faces were like the faces of men. They had hair like the hair of women, and their teeth were like the teeth of lions. They had breastplates like breastplates of iron; and the sound of their wings was like the sound of chariots, of many horses rushing to battle. They have tails like scorpions, and stings; and in their tails is their power to hurt men for five months. They have as king over them, the angel of the abyss; his name in Hebrew is Abaddon, and in the Greek he has the name Apollyon."	For the day of the LORD is coming; surely it is near, a day of darkness and gloom, a day of clouds and thick darkness......A fire consumes before them and behind them a flame burns. The land is like the garden of Eden before them but a desolate wilderness behind them, and nothing at all escapes them. Their appearance is like the appearance of horses; and like war horses, so they run. With a noise as of chariots they leap on the tops of the mountains, like the crackling of a flame of fire consuming the stubble, like a mighty people arranged for battle. Before them the people are in anguish; all faces turn pale. They run like mighty men, they climb the wall like soldiers; and they each march in line, nor do they deviate from their paths....They rush on the city, they run on the wall; they climb into the houses, they enter through the windows like a thief. Before them the earth quakes, the heavens tremble, the sun and the moon grow dark and the stars lose their brightness."

Whatever these creatures are in Chapter 9, they are definitely not real locusts. Joel saw a swarm of locusts devouring the land. It was a vision of the Day of the Lord. John saw the same thing but gave us much more detail. These are undoubtedly weapons systems of some kind. They could be helicopters or missiles or perhaps new bug-like drones. It would appear that they attack with chemical weapons because of the sores and burns and they move with great precision. They do not deviate from their paths. They hurt men for five months and their king is said to be the angel that is released from the abyss. This is a fallen angel that has been chained in the abyss (Jude 1:6), as opposed to satan who is not yet there.

Chapter 10 – Similar to Ezekiel 3 & Zechariah 14
Sandwiched between the sixth trumpet of Chapter 9 and the seventh trumpet of Chapter 11 verse 15, is a little bit of digression that sounds like it is taken right out of the prophet Zechariah. John sees a very powerful angel coming down out of heaven and putting his right foot on the sea and his left on the land. The possibility that this angel is the seventh angel who sounds the seventh trumpet, seems clear from verse 7 of Chapter 10 and verse 15 of Chapter 11. Also, judging from the striking similarity of Chapter 10 and 11 to the book of Zechariah, it seems likely that it is the same angel who places his feet on the Mount of Olives causing the great earthquake (Zech 14:4) and who is immediately followed by the Messiah appearing in glory.

"I saw another strong angel coming down out of heaven, clothed with a cloud; and the rainbow was upon his head, and his face was like the sun, and his feet like pillars of fire; and he had in his hand a little book which was open He placed his right foot on the sea and his left on the land; and he cried out with a loud voice, as when a lion roars; and when he had cried out, the seven peals of thunder uttered their voices. When the seven peals of thunder had spoken, I was about to write; and I heard a voice from heaven saying, 'Seal up the things which the seven peals of thunder have spoken and do not write them.' Then the angel whom I saw standing on the sea and

on the land lifted up his right hand to heaven, and swore by Him who lives forever and ever, WHO CREATED HEAVEN AND THE THINGS IN IT, AND THE EARTH AND THE THINGS IN IT, AND THE SEA AND THE THINGS IN IT, that there will be delay no longer, but in the days of the voice of the seventh angel, when he is about to sound, then the mystery of God is finished, as He preached to His servants the prophets." Rev 10:1-7

"In that day His feet will stand on the Mount of Olives (Angel of the Lord), which is in front of Jerusalem on the east; and the Mount of Olives will be split in its middle from east to west by a very large valley, so that half of the mountain will move toward the north and the other half toward the south. You will flee by the valley of My mountains, for the valley of the mountains will reach to Azel; yes, you will flee just as you fled before the earthquake in the days of Uzziah king of Judah Then the LORD, my God, will come (Jesus), and all the holy ones with Him!" Zech 14:4-5

John is told to take the little book out of the angel's hand and eat it. Then he is told that he must prophesy again concerning many peoples, nations, tongues, and kings. The scroll is sweet because it is the word of God. It makes his stomach bitter because it is the judgment of God. Notice the similarity to Ezek 3:1-4.

"Then the voice which I heard from heaven, I heard again speaking with me, and saying, 'Go, take the book which is open in the hand of the angel who stands on the sea and on the land.' So I went to the angel, telling him to give me the little book. And he said to me, 'Take it and eat it; it will make your stomach bitter, but in your mouth it will be sweet as honey.' I took the little book out of the angel's hand and ate it, and in my mouth it was sweet as honey; and when I had eaten it, my stomach was made bitter. And they said to me, 'You must prophesy again concerning many peoples and nations and tongues and kings.'" Rev 10:8-11

When this prophesying takes place is not apparent and this has caused some to speculate that John is one of The Two Witnesses mentioned in Chapter 11. Though this is possible, it is highly unlikely. Perhaps the fulfillment is merely the rest of the judgments of the Day of the Lord that follow in the Revelation.

CHAPTER 11 – Detail on the Holy Place
Then John is told to measure the Temple, the altar, and the worshipers.

"Then there was given me a measuring rod like a staff; and someone said, "Get up and measure the temple of God and the altar, and those who worship in it. Leave out the court which is outside the temple and do not measure it, for it has been given to the nations; and they will tread underfoot the holy city for forty-two months. And I will grant authority to my two witnesses, and they will prophesy for twelve hundred and sixty days, clothed in sackcloth. These are the two olive trees and the two lampstands that stand before the Lord of the earth. And if anyone wants to harm them, fire flows out of their mouth and devours their enemies; so if anyone wants to harm them, he must be killed in this way. These have the power to shut up the sky, so that rain will not fall during the days of their prophesying; and they have power over the waters to turn them into blood, and to strike the earth with every plague, as often as they desire."Rev 11:1-6

The word translated "temple" here is the word "*naos*," a word that refers to the Holy of Holies specifically. Interestingly enough, John is told only to measure the Holy of Holies and the Altar and to leave out everything else since it has been "given to the nations." This implies that the entire structure which encompassed the first and second temples will not be in Jewish hands during the first three and a half years of the Last Shemitah Cycle but only an area covering the Holy of Holies and an altar. Also, Jerusalem (the Old City) will become an international city for at least forty two months or three and a half years – the first three and a half years of the Shemitah Cycle. Then in a way that seems connected to the Holy Place, the Two Witnesses and their three and a half year ministry are mentioned. This of course, occurs during the second half of the Last Shemitah Cycle - the Tribulation period. The identity of these witnesses is likely Moses, and almost certainly, Elijah. When Jesus revealed His glory to His disciples on the Holy Mountain, Moses and Elijah appeared with Him. They were discussing what He was about to accomplish at Jerusalem. This indicates that Moses and Elijah play a pivotal role in the Day of the Lord and the dawning of the Millennial Kingdom. Jesus acknowledged that Elijah himself was coming and would restore all things (Mt 17:11). This is the restoration of the Jewish people back to God - turning the hearts of the children back to the fathers. Jesus also said that John the Baptist was a fulfillment of this prophecy although he was not actually Elijah - he came in the Spirit and power of Elijah (Luke 1:17). John himself also said that he was not Elijah. However, he was the messenger (Mt 11:10) the voice of one crying in the wilderness (Mt 3:3). John came before Jesus' first coming to prepare the Jews, and Elijah himself will come before His second coming to prepare the Jews. There is a strong tradition at the Passover Seder where a chair and a cup are prepared for Elijah. They truly expect him to come again!

Another point that must be made from this passage and the Two Witnesses is that they seem to be the same ones referenced by Zechariah. Note the similarity between these two passages.

"Then I said to him, 'What are these two olive trees on the right of the lampstand and on its left?' And I answered the second time and said to him, 'What are the two olive branches which are beside the two golden pipes, which empty the golden oil from themselves?' So he answered me, saying, 'Do you not know what these are?' And I said, 'No, my lord.' Then he said, 'These are the two anointed ones who are standing by the Lord of the whole earth.'" Zech 4:11-14

And I will grant authority to my two witnesses, and they will prophesy for twelve hundred and sixty days, clothed in sackcloth. These are the two olive trees and the two lampstands that stand before the Lord of the earth. Rev 11:3-4

Moses and Elijah together represent the Law and the Prophets which all pointed to the ministry of Messiah. Also, the miracles that the Two Witnesses perform, shutting up the sky, calling down fire, turning the waters into blood, smiting the earth with every plague, are trademarks of the ministry of Moses and Elijah and also correspond with the plagues poured out by God during the Great Tribulation. Likely this means that these plagues are a direct result of a showdown between the Jewish people led by Moses and Elijah and the Gentile nations led by Antichrist. (See chart 15 on page 298)

The Passover Replay

There is a great similarity between the plagues of Egypt and the plagues of the Tribulation. There is also an uncanny resemblance in the cast of characters. Jesus clearly fulfilled Passover in His first advent by being crucified as the Passover Lamb that takes away the sins of the world. However, He also hinted at a possible future fulfillment.

"And He said to them, "I have earnestly desired to eat this Passover with you before I suffer; for I say to you, I shall never again eat it until it is fulfilled in the kingdom of God." Luke 22:16

Take a look at the following charts:

~~~~~
Pharaoh - Antichrist
Moses & Aaron - Moses & Elijah
Jannes & Jombres - Antichrist & False Prophet
Armies of Pharaoh buried in Red Sea
Armies of Antichrist swallowed by the earth (Rev 12:16)
~~~~~

Plagues of Egypt	Plagues of Revelation
1. Water to blood	1. Fire (1/3 Earth burned up)
2. Frogs	2. Waters (rivers and springs & sea) to blood
3. Gnats or lice	3. Waters made bitter
4. Flies	4. Locusts (chemical weapons?)
5. Disease on livestock	5. Loathsome sores
6. Boils	6. Intense heat
7. Hail	7. Frogs (demons performing signs to gather armies)
8. Locusts	8. Hail
9. Darkness	9. Darkness
10. Death of first born	10. Death (1/3 of mankind)

Chapter 12 –Detail on the Remnant of Israel and the Remnant Bride

"A great sign appeared in heaven: a woman clothed with the sun, and the moon under her feet, and on her head a crown of twelve stars; and she was with child; and she cried out, being in labor and in pain to give birth. Then another sign appeared in heaven: and behold, a great red dragon having seven heads and ten horns, and on his heads were seven diadems. And his tail swept away a third of the stars of heaven and threw them to the earth. And the dragon stood before the woman who was about to give birth, so that when she gave birth he might devour her child." Rev 12:1-4

The great sign that John saw was the woman Israel about to give birth. We know that the woman is symbolic of Israel because the symbolism is old (see Gen 11:9-10). The woman is in pain and about to give birth. In other words, John sees a vision of Israel entering into the time of the Tribulation about to give birth. The context of the prophecy is the Day of the Lord, the Tribulation, or the time of Birth Pains. All of these names refer to the same time period. The prophecy, in a typical Jewish way, depicts the event as happening in heaven while in fact it is happening on the earth. This is clearly illustrated in the second part of the vision, which we will deal with next. The events that happen in heaven directly affect the events on the earth and the events that transpire on Earth directly affect events in heaven. To a first century Jew, there were two levels of reality, the spiritual and the natural, and they were both closely connected (1 Cor 15:40-50).

What is in Heaven Represents What is on Earth!

Now notice the position of the dragon. He is directly before the woman (Israel) which of course is where satan positions himself in the beginning of the Tribulation with the Abomination of Desolation. Also, notice that he is called "the dragon," "the serpent of old" which indicates that he is no longer masked in any way. That's because he has just been cast out of the heavenlies by Michael and his angels and knows that his time is short. When the "man of lawlessness" is revealed, there are no more disguises. Notice that the dragon has seven heads and ten horns. The dragon, who is working through and empowering Antichrist, represents the ten kingdoms of the Revived Roman Empire, and the Seven Heads which represent the city of Rome and the seven great empires that persecuted Israel (see Chapter 3). Then the woman (Israel) gives birth to a son, "a male child who is to rule the nations with a rod of iron." Then she fled into the wilderness where she had a place prepared by God where she would be nourished for three and a half years.

"And she gave birth to a son, a male child, who is to rule all the nations with a rod of iron; and her child was caught up to God and to His throne. Then the woman fled into the wilderness where she had a place prepared by God, so that there she would be nourished for one thousand two hundred and sixty days." Rev 12:5-6

The Child is Not Jesus

Most Bible teachers and scholars consider the "male child" to be Jesus, and the above verse a reference to His birth and ascension into heaven. However, this position is untenable for the following reasons.

➢ The Bride of Christ or the "overcomers" were also given the promise of ruling the nations with a rod of iron (Rev 2:26-27, 3:21).

➢ The son is immediately snatched to heaven. The Greek word that is translated "caught up" is "harpazo" which means "to snatch away." It's the same word used in 1 Thess 4:17 from which we get the word "Rapture." It is a violent and sudden snatching away. Jesus was not, in any way, snatched into heaven. He left intentionally, and His disciples saw Him depart. The word used in Acts 1:9 is not "*harpazo*" but "*epairo*" which means to raise up. It was neither violent nor sudden. He was not snatched away from the clutches of satan as the male child is in this passage.

➢ After Messiah ascended to heaven, there was no subsequent fleeing of Israel to the desert to a place prepared by God. In fact, Israel received no such help at all after Jesus' ascension, but forty years later the Jews were massacred and the rest scattered to the nations. Those who claim that all these events are past have a serious problem with history and missing data. There is no record in the first century of Israel being protected in the wilderness for three and a half years. On the other hand, those who claim that the first part of the prophecy is past and the rest future, have a serious contextual problem. If they believe that the rest of the chapter is future, then how can they separate this one event, the birth of the male child, from its clearly defined context which can only take place at the end of the age? For example, in verse 5 the woman is said to give birth and her child raptured. But in verse 4 the devil is cast out of the heavens and is poised to devour the child before he is born. The second part of the vision is merely a repeat of the first part (it is all one vision) with more detail. Thus satan would have to have been cast out of the heavens around 32AD and the Abomination of Desolation set up, followed by Armageddon and the Millennium. Preterists, of course, believe this.

➢ If we accept that the vision applies to the future Day of the Lord, then I believe the simplest interpretation is that the male child is the Bride of Christ who is destined to sit next to her Bridegroom and rule all the nations.

The Bride of Christ is the overcoming church that is to sit down with Jesus on His throne according to the following verses.

"He who overcomes, and he who keeps My deeds until the end, TO HIM I WILL GIVE AUTHORITY OVER THE NATIONS; AND HE SHALL RULE THEM WITH A ROD OF IRON, AS THE VESSELS OF THE POTTER ARE BROKEN TO PIECES, as I also have received authority from My Father; and I will give him the morning star." Rev 2:26-28

"He who overcomes, I will grant to him to sit down with Me on My throne, as I also overcame and sat down with My Father on His throne." Rev 3:21

Now let's look at the rest of the vision.

"And there was war in heaven, Michael and his angels waging war with the dragon. And the dragon and his angels waged war, and they were not strong enough, and there was no longer a place found for them in heaven. And the great dragon was thrown down, the serpent of old who is called the devil and satan, who deceives the whole world; he was thrown down to the earth, and his angels were thrown down with him." Rev 12:7-9

At the midpoint of the Last Shemitah Cycle, the devil is cast out of the heavenly realm. His being thrown to Earth is the factor that begins the labor pains of Israel. It is the event which transforms the Antichrist and causes him to break the covenant with the Jews and set out to destroy them. Notice that he will first set his attention on the Bride of Christ, but she will be snatched away just in the nick of time.

"And I heard a loud voice in heaven, saying, 'Now the salvation, and the power, and the kingdom of our God and the authority of His Christ have come, for the accuser of our brethren has been thrown down, who accuses them before our God day and night. And they overcame him because of the blood of the Lamb and because of the word of their testimony, and they did not love their life even to death. For this reason, rejoice, O heavens and you who dwell in them. Woe to the earth and the sea, because the devil has come down to you, having great wrath, knowing that he has only a short time.'" Rev 12:10-12

The casting out of satan from the heavenlies is a great victory for the saints of God and causes great rejoicing in heaven. This is undoubtedly the event that Jesus foresaw in Luke 10:18-21 that caused Him to rejoice greatly. It also underscores the role that the Bride plays in his downfall. When it says "they overcame him," it is a reference to the godly living of the Bride and her spiritual warfare which have contributed greatly to satan's demise. These overcomers are representative of all their brethren who have gone before them who willingly laid down their lives for Christ (Rev 6:9-11). Also, when it says they "did not love their life even to death" it does not mean they were martyred. If that were the case then they would not be snatched away from the clutches of satan. What it means is that they were totally given to Christ and were not afraid to die for Him if need be.

After satan is cast out, the long-awaited salvation (deliverance) of the church comes, and with it the Kingdom of God or the Day of the Lord when Messiah cleanses the earth of His enemies and begins His reign. Despite the great rejoicing in heaven, there is a sad note. Michael the archangel, who has restrained satan's attempts to destroy Israel for centuries, steps aside and hurls the devil and his cohorts to the earth, where he vents all of his fury on a rebellious planet, and begins his last attempt to annihilate the Jews.

"And when the dragon saw that he was thrown down to the earth, he persecuted the woman who gave birth to the male child. And the two wings of the great eagle were given to the woman, in order that she might fly into the wilderness to her place, where she was nourished for a time and times and half a time, from the presence of the serpent. And the serpent poured water like a river out of his mouth after the woman, so that he might cause her to be swept away with the flood. And the earth helped the woman, and the earth opened its mouth and drank up the river which the dragon poured out of his mouth." Rev 12:13-16

When the devil loses his footing in the heavens, he realizes that his time is up. The reality finally gets to him. He has only one card left to play and that is the destruction of the Jewish people. In this way he hopes to thwart the purpose of God and keep Him from fulfilling His promises. But as always, he miscalculates. God has a special deliverance in store for this remnant who turn to him for help and flee the wrath of the serpent. There is a place prepared for them in the desert, probably east of the Dead Sea in Jordan. The Antichrist pours water out of his mouth like a flood after them. This is figurative language referring to armies (Dan 9:26, Nah 1:8). When the armies come, there is a great earthquake and the ground literally swallows them (see Zech 14:4).

"And the dragon was enraged with the woman, and went off to make war with the rest of her offspring, who keep the commandments of God and hold to the testimony of Jesus." Rev 12:7-17

Failing in his attempts to destroy the Jewish remnant that are sealed and protected by God, the devil sets his attention on the rest of the Jews and all the Christians who are left. By this time I believe that there will be multitudes turning to Messiah from among the Jews and Gentiles. As dark a day as the Tribulation is, it has a glorious end. Yet, they will suffer greatly. Notice that the male child (Bride) that is caught up to God is spoken of as overcoming the Antichrist. On the other hand, those who remain, though they will rise again and reign with Messiah will be overcome and killed (Rev 13:7).

The Remnant Bride in the Prophets?

We examined Isaiah 66 with regard to the Jewish remnant in Chapter 7. Now let us go back to the same passage where we see another remnant that is birthed from Israel (Zion).

"Before she travailed, she brought forth; before her pain came, she gave birth to a boy." Is 66:7

We have discussed already the sons of Zion that are mentioned in verse 8 as having been born "as soon as Zion goes into labor" (the Tribulation). Then who is this "boy" or son that is born before Zion goes into labor? The fact that he is born before the labor causes the prophet to ask: "Who has heard such a thing?" It has been taught widely that this boy is Jesus Himself, who was born before the labor pains of the Day of the Lord - almost 2000 years to date. Yet, though Messiah is the Son born to the virgin, could the time gap be telling us that the prophet had someone else in mind? We have many examples in Scripture of prophecies that have more than one meaning or type. What about this one? The context seems to suggest that there is a birth immediately after the birth pains and immediately before them. Wouldn't it make more sense if the prophet were referring to the Bride of Christ, raptured just before the birth pains begin in earnest? This would certainly make the word "before" more meaningful. The Bride of Christ certainly qualifies. We are the offspring of Israel, birthed by the Jewish Messiah Himself on Pentecost in the city of Jerusalem. However, the Bride is yet in the birth canal, so to speak, since we have not yet received our full number and come to maturity. This interpretation is certainly plausible. But wait; there is more on this "boy" in the Hebrew Scriptures.

"Writhe and labor to give birth, daughter of Zion, like a woman in childbirth, for now you will go out of the city, dwell in the field, and go to Babylon. There you will be rescued; there the LORD will redeem you from the hand of your enemies. And now many nations have been assembled against you who say, `Let her be polluted, and let our eyes gloat over Zion.' But they do not know the thoughts of the LORD, and they do not understand His purpose; for He has gathered them like sheaves to the threshing floor. Arise and thresh, daughter of Zion, for your horn I will make iron and your hoofs I will make bronze, that you may pulverize many peoples, that you may devote to the LORD their unjust gain and their wealth to the Lord of all the earth. Now muster yourselves in troops, daughter of troops; they have laid siege against us; with a rod they will smite the judge of Israel on the cheek. But as for you, Bethlehem Ephrathah, too little to be among the clans of Judah, from you One will go forth for me to be ruler in Israel. His goings forth are from long ago, from the days of eternity. Therefore, He will give them up until the time when she who is in labor has borne a child. Then the remainder of His brethren will return to the sons of Israel. And He will arise and shepherd His flock in the strength of the LORD, in the majesty of the name of the LORD His God. And they will remain, because at that time He will be great to the ends of the earth." Mic 4:10-5:4

This passage is clearly talking about the end of the age (Micah 4:1), the battle of Armageddon (4:13-5:1), and the time of Jacob's Distress (4:10). Then there is a digression to the rejection of Messiah (which is typical of the Hebrew prophets) and the statement that "he will give them up until the time when she who is in labor has borne a child." Just as in Isaiah 66, this passage has also been interpreted to be referring to Mary, the mother of Jesus, giving birth to Messiah. But this simply does not fit for several reasons:

➢ The Messiah is being spoken of as the one who is being rejected by Israel in 5:1, born in Bethlehem, going forth to be ruler in Israel in 5:2, and the one who does the giving up (of Israel) in

5:3. Therefore, since He is the one who gives her up "until the time when she who is in labor gives birth," how can He be the one born?

➤ It says that He (the Messiah) gives them up "until she who is in labor has borne a child." The word "until" means that after the child is born He will no longer give them up, but will instead begin to shepherd His flock and usher in His Millennial reign (5:4). If Jesus is the One spoken of as being the child that is born, then why did He not establish His rule and why did He give them up at that time?

➤ In verse 4 we are told that, after the time that the child is born, Israel lives securely and enters into a time of great peace and prosperity. If Mary was the one spoken of in the prophecy and Jesus the child born, then where did the peace go and why were the Jews scattered to all the nations?

I believe that the prophecy is telling us the following:

➤ Messiah gave up the nation of Israel after His rejection. This is consistent with the rest of Scripture (Mt 23:36-39, Mt 21:43, Rom 11:25). He did not reject Israel, but He allowed the prophesied judgment to come on them, and He turned His focus on the Gentiles. Jerusalem, and sadly, the Jewish people, were trodden underfoot by the Gentiles.

➤ The "time when she who is in labor" refers to the Day of Jacob's Distress. This is the context of the passage (4:10). The child born to Israel at this time is the Messianic community, the Bride of Christ made up of Jew and Gentile.

➤ "Then the remainder of His brethren will return to the sons of Israel" (5:3). This is a reference to the remnant being brought back by Jesus from the ends of the earth to join their brothers in Israel. Thus, He will arise and shepherd His flock (5:4).

➤ The one born of Israel at this time cannot be the remnant that is sealed because it is said that He gives up the sons of Israel until after this one is born. This giving up is not complete rejection. Neither does it imply that God is not working on behalf of Israel. He continues to watch over Israel. However, He is not fellowshipping with them as a nation, until that time when the veil is removed and there is healing in their relationship. It is interesting to note the key role the Rapture of the Bride plays in the repentance of Israel and the removing of the hardness that is still over their hearts.

~~~~~

The False Church (Harlot) rides the Beast and sits on seven mountains, whereas the Bride is attacked by the Beast and is identified with Israel her mother and Mount Zion in Jerusalem!

~~~~~

The Overcoming Church

I believe wholeheartedly in an overcoming church that moves in the power of the Spirit and does great exploits in the Name and authority of Jesus. Such a church is certainly presented in the book of Revelation. "They overcame him by the blood of the Lamb and the word of their testimony," and that they were willing to suffer even death for His sake.[52] However, this overcoming church is found in the context of Revelation 12 where they triumph over satan and that triumph results in his expulsion from the heavenlies. That is very clear if we keep the verse in its context. Satan is cast out and they are victorious. Of course, Post-Tribbers, although they agree that this chapter is all about the Day of the Lord and Israel being persecuted for three and a half years, always insist that

---

[52] Rev 12:11

verse 5 is about Jesus and was fulfilled in the first century. They will appeal to the historical church to substantiate this claim - the same church that came to this conclusion based on Replacement Theology and Amillennialism. However, the son that is raptured (harpazo) is not Jesus but the overcoming Bride. Jesus was not snatched away from the clutches of satan as this child is.[53] Neither was Israel taken into the desert for three and a half years after Christ's ascension. When satan is cast down he tries to devour the overcoming Bride, who was instrumental in his ousting, but the overcomers are snatched away to meet the Bridegroom, who has moved into the heavens which have been cleansed. This is at the beginning of the Day of the Lord and Christ has now begun to exercise His authority as King with His raptured Bride by His side. Then satan is said to persecute the woman Israel and make war with the rest of her offspring, which are indentified as the remaining believers in Christ on Earth. I realize that this interpretation will be a shock to some who have never studied this chapter in its contextual order. I also realize that satan has been busy obscuring verse 5 and blinding the church to its obvious meaning.

The only other place that the overcoming church is shown in Revelation is in Chapter 14 where they are with Christ in the heavenly Zion. Of course, Post-Tribbers argue that there is an overcoming church throughout the book and cite several passages, including Rev 12:17. However, in this verse we see the saints essentially on the run from the devil. When it says, "woe to the earth and the sea," it is understood that the people on the earth are not excluded, and that includes Jews and Christians who are at the top of the devil's hit list. What we see with regard to Israel is that God protects and seals a believing remnant of the nation that repents and turns to their true Messiah. This is the whole point of the Tribulation – that the remnant of Israel will return to the mighty God and never again rely on the one who struck them.[54] But

---

[53] See Rev 12:4
[54] Rom 11:26, Is 10:20, 59:20

what is not understood by most Christians is that the protection given to Israel is very specific and very different from that offered to the church. And there is good reason for this distinction. The church enters the Millennium as a spiritual people; whereas the remnant of Israel must enter it in the natural. This was Jesus' clear meaning when He said that for the sake of the Elect the days would be cut short.[55] When Christians are martyred it is a gain for them and only a temporary victory for the devil. However, if the enemy were able to wipe out the seed of Jacob, it would be a permanent victory for him, since it would annul God's plan and promises. Surely the deceiver has known this throughout history since he has tried over and over again to eliminate the whole race of Jews. The Tribulation will be his final attempt – his final solution. Gentile believers in Christ on the other hand, although God will certainly give them grace and comfort, do not have the same need to be physically preserved. Thus there will be wholesale slaughter of believers during this time.

Revelation Chapter 13

This chapter deals with the rise of the Beast (Antichrist), his ten nation confederacy, and the false prophet. It discusses the Abomination of Desolation and the mark of the Beast which is forced upon mankind and is the seal of his ownership placed upon their forehead or right hand. There has been much speculation as to what the mark of the Beast is and most of it is entirely meaningless. It is likely some kind of computer chip since it is needed for buying and selling. In any event, it will become clear at the time what it is and that taking it will mean selling your soul to Antichrist.

The Revelation 13 Church

Replacement Theology causes the church to view the word "saints" or "holy ones," occuring in both the Hebrew and Greek Scriptures, as referring to "Christians." This view is so pervasive that most Bible

---

[55] Mt 24:22

teachers never even consider the possibility that it might be referring to Jews. But prior to the New Testament it was always used of the Jewish people, and afterwards, especially when it comes to prophecy, it is occasionally used that way.[56] This may very well be the case in Chapter 13 where the Antichrist is said to "make war on the saints and overcome them,"[57] and authority over every tribe and nation was given to him.[58] Then it says all who dwell on the earth will worship him; all whose names are not written in the Book of Life. The next verse says if anyone is destined for captivity, to captivity he goes and whoever is destined for the sword, with the sword he must be killed. And then it says, "Here is the perseverance and the faith of the saints."[59] Now if we accept that this passage refers to Jews or Christians or both, it is hardly a picture of a powerful opposition. Certainly, their perseverance and faith is noteworthy, but they are fleeing for their lives here.

Revelation Chapter 14

The first part of this chapter is given in deliberate contrast to Chapter 13. Here the Bride of Christ is pictured in heaven with the mark of the true Messiah on their foreheads.

"And I looked, and behold, the Lamb was standing on Mount Zion, and with Him one hundred and forty-four thousand, having His name and the name of His Father written on their foreheads. And I heard a voice from heaven, like the sound of many waters and like the sound of loud thunder, and the voice which I heard was like the sound of harpists playing on their harps. And they sang a new song before the throne and before the four living creatures and the elders; and no one could learn the song except the one hundred and forty-four thousand who had been purchased from the earth. These are the ones who have not been defiled with women, for they have kept themselves chaste. These are the ones who follow the Lamb wherever He goes.

---

[56] Mt 24: 22, 31, 27:52
[57] See Dan7:21
[58]Rev 13:7
[59] Rev 13:10

These have been purchased from among men as first fruits to God and to the Lamb. And no lie was found in their mouth; they are blameless." Rev 14: 1-5

We have already looked at the 144,000 in Chapter 7 that were the sealed remnant of Israel. Most Pre-Shemitah Cycle Rapture proponents believe that this 144,000 mentioned in Chapter 14 is the same group. However, this cannot be true. The 144,000 mentioned here are very different from those mentioned in Chapter 7 for the following reasons:

➢ The 144,000 mentioned in Chapter 7 are clearly stated to have been sealed from the 12 tribes of Israel. They are Jews, plain and simple. The 144,000 spoken of here in Chapter 14 are taken from among men, both Jew and Gentile. They are the "One New Man," (the Bride).

➢ The 144,000 Jews in Chapter 7 are clearly stated to be on earth. That is why the angel says not to harm the earth or the sea or the trees until they are sealed. This, of course, is a direct reference to the judgment and destruction to follow. The 144,000 mentioned here, on the other hand, are not on earth but in heaven. They are in the heavenly Mount Zion and not the earthly, since it is given over to the Antichrist during this time (Rev 11:2). They are singing a new song before the throne in heaven.

This 144,000 in Chapter 14 are spoken of in bridal language. They are "chaste virgins." They "have not been defiled with women." This is poetic language. It is the language of love. It is not to be taken literal. They are taken from among mankind, purchased by the Lamb. They love Him and follow Him wherever He goes. They are in love with Jesus, singing Him love songs. The song they sing is the song of the Bride. It is a love song. Not being "defiled with women" cannot mean that they are celibate men. To interpret it this way is to say that men who have been married are "defiled." This would mean that marriage is sinful. On the contrary, marriage is sacred and a precious type of the relationship of Christ with His church. The reference to virginity and not being sexually defiled has to do with purity and devotion to Messiah. This is the language of the prophets concerning Israel. It is also the language of Jesus and the apostles (Mt 25:1-13, 2Cor 11:2). This same language is used elsewhere in the book of Revelation with reference to the false church or "harlot" (Rev 17). This group has stayed pure. They are holy and blameless. They have not committed spiritual adultery and have kept themselves unstained by the world. They are a "first fruit" company conceived on Pentecost. They are the overcomers having the name of the Groom and the name of the Father on their foreheads.

"He who overcomes, I will make him a pillar in the temple of My God, and he will not go out from it anymore; and I will write upon him the name of My God, and the name of the city of My God, the new Jerusalem, which comes down out of heaven from My God, and My new name." Rev 3:12

"And he who overcomes, and he who keeps My deeds until the end, to him I will give authority over the nations; and he shall rule them with a rod of iron, as the vessels of the potter are broken to pieces, as I also have received authority from My Father; and I will give him the morning star." Rev 2:26-28

Why 144,000?

There is much debate over whether 144,000 is a literal number. However, there is no reason to assume this. It is a figurative number representing, in Chapter 7 the remnant of Israel, and here the Bride of Christ. Numbers and word pictures are used throughout the book of Revelation in a symbolic way. This does not mean that every verse or reference is symbolic, as some suggest, but, rather, those references which are symbolic and which are literal have to be determined from the context and an understanding of the rest of the Scriptures. Here are some examples of this use of symbolism in numbers and descriptions:

➢ There are Seven Spirits of God mentioned in Rev 1:4, yet there is only one Spirit
➢ The Seven Churches are representative of the whole church
➢ There are twenty-four elders in heaven.
➢ There are Seven Seals, Seven Trumpets, Seven Bowls
➢ Messiah is a Lamb
➢ The Devil is a Dragon
➢ The Antichrist is a Beast
➢ The Harlot sits on many waters
➢ Messiah rides on a white horse
➢ The number of the Beast is 666
➢ The Bride is a city

The number twelve in the Bible is a representative number. There are twelve tribes of Israel, twelve spies were sent out to spy the land, and there are twelve apostles of the Lamb. One hundred and forty four thousand is divisible by twelve. Whatever this signifies, I believe that we have little basis on which to claim that it is a literal number. The context here is completely symbolic. There is no hint anywhere in Scripture that the Bride of Christ or the remnant of Israel is limited to a specific number even though it is a remnant. Chapter 14 closes with a description of Jesus coming in glory and trampling the armies gathered against Jerusalem in the wine press of God's wrath, the final battle of Armageddon.

Another Sign - Detail on the Last of the Plagues (Chapter 15 & 16)

In Chapter 15 and 16, we are given more detail on the wrath of God poured out on the kingdom of Antichrist. Two visions appear. First, we are given a picture of seven angels holding seven bowls of God's wrath ready to pour them out. This is a similar picture to what transpires in Chapter 8 of Revelation where the pouring out of judgment seems to be a direct response to the prayer and worship of the saints. Now, before the seven bowls are poured out, we are given a picture of all those saints who have gone through the Tribulation and been martyred by Antichrist, both Jews and Gentiles, rejoicing in heaven. Then the seven angels pour out their bowls. They are as follows:

1. **Loathsome and malignant sores** upon those who worship the beast.
2. **Sea becomes blood.** All marine life dies.
3. **Rivers and springs become blood.** "Thou hast given them blood to drink."
4. **Fierce heat.** The sun becomes much hotter scorching men with intense heat.
5. **Darkness.** Gnawed their tongues because of pain.
6. **Euphrates dried up** for the armies of the east. This sixth bowl corresponds to the sixth trumpet in Chapter 9 and the gathering of the 200 million man army from the east.
7. **The final battle of Armageddon**, the great earthquake and the great hailstorm take place. Jerusalem is split into three parts and the cities of the nations fall. Every island "fled away" and the mountains were not found. This corresponds to the events of the sixth seal of Chapter 6.

Then we are told that Babylon the great was remembered before God and a specific judgment was poured out upon her. Chapters 17 and 18 are then devoted to Babylon and the judgment that is poured out (See Chapter 3).

The Similarity of the Trumpets and Bowls

There is a striking similarity between the seven trumpet judgments and the seven bowl judgments. It is possible that they are both describing the same events but from a different angle. This seems inescapable when we see how they both end. For instance, the 6th Trumpet and the 6th Bowl produce the exact same result. Both concern the Euphrates being prepared for the armies from the East. Then both the 7th Trumpet and 7th Bowl deal with the great earthquake and the hail and the return of Messiah. In Chapter 15 we are told that the bowls are "the last" because in them the wrath of God is finished or complete. Could this be the whole point? It is the full or complete wrath of God that is being emphasized. The number seven is about completeness and oftentimes to underscore His seriousness God says things twice. Two is the number of decision and judgment. The Ten Commandments were given twice! The promises of God were spoken twice to Abraham and many others. Pharaoh had two dreams and Gideon had two fleeces. It's the same as when Jesus says, "Verily, verily" meaning this is really important. Could it be that we have two accounts of the judgment for emphasis but they are in fact one and the same? This seems very likely. In any event, they each end with the return of Christ. (See charts 13 & 14 on page 297)

The Revelation 15 Church

This group is pictured in heaven and standing on a sea of glass mixed with fire. They are singing the song of Moses and of the Lamb and it is said that they are the ones who have "come off victorious from the beast and from his image and from the number of His name." These are obviously martyred believers in Christ, both Jew and Gentile, who have not taken the mark of the beast. That is clearly what is meant by his image and his name. All who will not take the mark will be killed. These believers refused to compromise and instead were murdered. Though we rejoice in their perseverance and victory over death, one can hardly view them as this end-time "apostolic greater works church," that has released powerful judgments on the Antichrist (as many Post-Tribbers claim). Indeed, they are blessed to have not surrendered to the mark and stayed true to their faith.

Revelation Chapters 17 & 18 - Destruction of Babylon

Chapter 17 and 18 are about the specific judgment of Babylon, the great city. This is covered in Chapter 3.

Revelation Chapter 19: Two Great Suppers

Chapter 19 begins with great rejoicing over the destruction of Babylon and the ushering in of the Messianic kingdom. Then two great suppers are depicted, "the marriage supper of the Lamb," and the "great supper of God" where all the birds of the air are called upon to eat the flesh of the enemies of Messiah destroyed in the last great battle of the Armageddon campaign. This contrast of the two suppers is deliberate and typical for the book of Revelation. It is the contrast of the fate of the righteous and the fate of the wicked. Another such contrast is the religious system or Harlot, pictured in Chapter 17, who is identified with the city of Rome and the Bride of Messiah who is identified with a revived Jerusalem.

The marriage supper of the Lamb is the long anticipated celebration that takes place in Jerusalem at the start of the Messianic Kingdom. The fact that it begins with a great feast is a well-established Jewish expectation which Jesus Himself confirmed.

"I say to you that many will come from east and west, and recline at the table with Abraham, Isaac and Jacob in the kingdom of heaven; but the sons of the kingdom will be cast out into the outer darkness; in that place there will be weeping and gnashing of teeth." Matt 8:11-12

"The LORD of hosts will prepare a lavish banquet for all peoples on this mountain; a banquet of aged wine, choice pieces with marrow, and refined, aged wine. And on this mountain He will swallow up the covering which is over all peoples, even the veil which is stretched over all nations. He will swallow up death for all time, and the Lord GOD will wipe tears away from all faces, and He will remove the reproach of His people from all the earth; for the LORD has spoken." Isa 25:6-8

The Greek word "*gamos*" can be translated "wedding" or "wedding feast." In this case, because of the context, it is translated "wedding feast." This raises the question as to whether the wedding takes place at the Rapture and is followed afterwards by the wedding feast, as I am inclined to believe, or whether both take place at the commencement of the Messiah's earthly rule. In either case, it's not an event to be missed, although, sadly, many will miss it.

One interesting aspect of the wedding feast is the statement in verse 9, "Blessed are those who are invited to the marriage supper of the Lamb." This confirms again what I have established over and over in this book, that is, the separation of a bridal company prior to the beginning of the Day of the Lord proper. The Bride, after all, is not invited to her own wedding. Those righteous who come through the Tribulation will be invited to this great global celebration.

The Great Supper of God

"And I saw heaven opened, and behold, a white horse, and He who sat on it is called Faithful and True, and in righteousness He judges and wages war. His eyes are a flame of fire, and on His head are many diadems; and He has a name written on Him which no one knows except Himself. He is clothed with a robe dipped in blood, and His name is called The Word of God. And the armies which are in heaven, clothed in fine linen, white and clean, were following Him on white horses. From His mouth comes a sharp sword, so that with it He may strike down the nations, and He will rule them with a rod of iron; and He treads the wine press of the fierce wrath of God, the Almighty. And on His robe and on His thigh He has a name written, 'KING OF KINGS, AND LORD OF LORDS.' Then I saw an angel standing in the sun, and he cried out with a loud voice, saying to all the birds which fly in midheaven, 'Come, assemble for the great supper of God, so that you may eat the flesh of kings and the flesh of commanders and the flesh of mighty men and the flesh of horses and of those who sit on them and the flesh of all men, both free men and slaves, and small and great.' And I saw the Beast and the kings of the earth and their armies assembled to make war against Him who sat on the horse and against His army." Rev 19:11-19

The "great supper of God" that is mentioned in the second part of Chapter 19 corresponds to Ezekiel Chapters 38 and 39. It is the destruction of Gog and Magog and all the nations that gather with them against Jerusalem.

"As for you, son of man, thus says the Lord GOD, speak to every kind of bird and to every beast of the field, 'Assemble and come, gather from every side to My sacrifice which I am going to sacrifice for you, as a great sacrifice on the mountains of Israel, that you may eat flesh and drink blood. You will eat the flesh of mighty men and drink the blood of the princes of the earth, as though they were rams, lambs, goats and bulls, all of them fatlings of Bashan. So you will eat fat until you are glutted, and drink blood until you are drunk, from My sacrifice which I have sacrificed for you. You will be glutted at My table with horses and charioteers, with mighty men and all the men of war,' declares the Lord GOD. And I will set My glory among the nations; and all the nations will see My judgment which I have executed and My hand which I have laid on them. And the house of Israel will know that I am the LORD their God from that day onward. The nations will know that the house of Israel went into exile for their iniquity because they acted treacherously against Me, and I hid My face from them; so I gave them into the hand of their adversaries, and all of them fell by the sword." Ezek 39:17-23

Some have speculated that this battle with Gog and Magog takes place prior to the Day of the Lord. However, from the description of the battle in Ezekiel Chapters 38 and 39, it seems apparent that this cannot be so. The following are some examples of this:

➢ Many nations with you (Ezek 38:15)
➢ After this battle God will no longer allow His name to be profaned (inconceivable to have the Great Apostasy and the rise of Antichrist after this)
➢ Nations will know God's blessing on Israel (Ezek 39: 23-29)
➢ People of Israel living securely ("Peace and Security" Ezek 38:14, 1 Thess 5:3)

- ➢ Great earthquake in the land of Israel (everything shakes in God's presence - mountains thrown down)
- ➢ Pestilence and blood - "I shall rain on him, a torrential rain, with hailstones, fire, and brimstone"
- ➢ Making firewood out of weapons (Ezek 39:10)
- ➢ Every man's sword will be against his brother (Ezek 38:21, Hag 2:21-22, Zech 14:13)

This great cleansing of the earth and judgment upon the nations gathered against Jerusalem takes place when the Messiah appears in glory. The Antichrist and his False Prophet will be seized and thrown into the lake of fire. Then the kingdom of Messiah, Jesus our Savior will finally come.

Revelation Chapter 20 – The Millennium

Chapter 20 begins with the binding of satan and his 1000 year prison sentence in the abyss. What a celebration that will be for the planet when the prince of darkness is removed and the will of God is finally done on Earth as it is in heaven. Who can comprehend the glory and the joy that will be realized when Messiah Himself governs the affairs of men from a restored and rebuilt Jerusalem? We can only imagine how wonderful it will be when God's will is accomplished and the whole earth follows Jesus. Yet, it would appear that there is still resistance in the human race despite one thousand years of His benevolent reign and the absence of the devil. It's as though mankind is being tested one more time and satan is loosed to finish the purging. Then he is banished forever to the lake of fire.

"And I saw thrones and they sat upon them..." Rev 20:4

The "they" here is likely a reference to the Bride mentioned at the end of Chapter 19. Then John mentions another group that rises up at the end of the Tribulation and also reigns with Christ. These are the believers who have been martyred during the Tribulation because they would not bow to Antichrist. This, we are told, is the first resurrection and the rest of the dead are not raised until after the Millennial Reign of Christ.

The First Resurrection

The resurrection mentioned here that is called the "first resurrection" does not imply a numerical first, but is the general resurrection at the end of the age or the Last Day resurrection which was well understood by the Jewish people in the first century (John 11:24, Dan 12:13). The numerical first resurrection was Messiah Himself the "first fruits" (1 Cor 15:23) followed by the second "first fruits" resurrection of the Bride at the Rapture prior to the Tribulation. Then comes the general resurrection which is not the "first fruits" but a great harvest of righteous souls.

The mention of a specific group as being resurrected at the first general resurrection does not necessarily imply that they are the only ones resurrected at this time. The promise of resurrection at the end of the age was given to the Old Testament saints as well. Some would say that the Old Testament saints were raised up with Jesus at His resurrection. However, though some evidently were raised (Mt 27:51-53), it was likely a small number. It would appear that Daniel was not among those raised because the promise to him was that he would rise "at the end of the age" (Dan 12:13), unless, of course, we believe that the end of the age took place in the first century.

At the end of Chapter 20, we are told of the second great resurrection and judgment. John remarks in the vision that heaven and earth "fled away" from the presence of God's throne and that "no place was found for them." This seems to suggest that the earth just disappears. However, if that is the case, then what happens to those on the earth? Do they disappear as well? Also, if the earth simply disappears in verse 11, why does he speak in verse 13 of the sea giving up the dead that are in it? Then we are told in Chapter 21 that John saw a new heaven and a new earth, and that the first heaven and the first earth have "passed away." The Greek word "*kainos*" that is translated "new" means qualitatively new and not merely a replacement. Thus, it is likely that God reshapes the planet and the heavens in such a fashion that it is qualitatively new, and all traces of corruption and decay are forever erased.

Revelation Chapters 21 & 22 – The New Jerusalem

Chapters 21 and 22 of the book of Revelation are a wonderful ending to a wonderful book. The revelation contained in these chapters is so glorious and so captivating that it seems almost too good to be true. But it is. The heavenly city, the New Jerusalem coming to rest on a totally new planet Earth filled with the glory and presence of God. For centuries the church, inspired by Augustinian theology, has pictured it more as a state of eternal bliss than a literal place. And those who espouse Replacement Theology continue to interpret it in this non-literal, figurative sense. According to them, it is "the church" the Bride of Christ and not a city. When they speak of the future reign of Messiah, they will usually skip right over the Millennial Reign in a literal Jerusalem the capital of a restored Israel, likely because it's too Jewish. They prefer to emphasize the role of the church, which is today largely Gentile in its make up, and "spiritualize" all the promises made to the literal descendants of Jacob. To them, the fact that the eternal city is called "Jerusalem" and not "Rome" or "New York" is of no consequence. They capitalize on the mention of the Bride the wife of the Lamb, which to them proves that it is not a place, and interpret all of the subsequent measurements and descriptions of a city, including the twelve gates which have written on them the names of the twelve tribes of Israel, as figurative, allegorical references to the church. This position, however, is inconsistent with all of Scripture, especially the prophets and the book of Revelation itself. Despite the symbols and figurative language of the book, the judgments are poured out on a literal Earth. The plagues are real plagues which do real damage and kill real people. The Antichrist is a real person and, thankfully, so is the Messiah who is coming to reign over a real people, in a real city, Jerusalem. The city of Rome is a real city (Rev 17:18) even though it is referred to as a "woman" and "Babylon the Great, the Mother of Harlots." In the same way, the New Jerusalem is a real city that comes down out of heaven even though it is referred to as the "Wife of the Lamb." It is the Bridal city, forever identified with the Lamb and His Bride. It is the eternal fulfillment of the city that Abraham longed for, David reigned from, and Messiah wept over. It has no temple because it is the temple, the sanctuary of God. It is the heavenly temple of which the tabernacle in the wilderness and the temple in Jerusalem were miniature replicas.

Many evangelicals struggle with the reality of heaven coming to Earth. This is particularly so with the Millennial Kingdom of Messiah reigning from a literal Jerusalem. The root of this difficulty lies, not only in Replacement Theology, but also in an inability to accept that spiritual and physical realities exist together on the same plane. It is easier to believe in one or the other but not in the two existing together in total harmony. However, this is exactly what is in store for us. The kingdom of heaven is coming to Earth and the will of God will be done on Earth as it is in heaven. The tabernacle of God will be among men and God Himself will be among them. Amen. Come Lord Jesus.

Chapter Ten
The Day and the Hour – What Can We Know?

"But of that day and hour no one knows, not even the angels of heaven, nor the Son, but the Father alone." Mt 24:36

It is true that there have been many false dates predicted for the return of Christ. It is also true that many continue to use this as an excuse to say that the Day is unknowable and we should not be concerned with it. Recently a friend, who is in Christian ministry declared, "No one knows when Jesus is coming back and honestly I don't care anymore." This sounds really mature and accepting and all that, but it is in fact an attitude that is contrary to Scripture and the Bridal love which should consume believers. Indeed, instead of the five foolish virgins who were not ready for the Bridegroom's return, this is the attitude of the five "turned off virgins" that have gone home and stopped waiting. However, the admonition of Jesus to be alert because no one knows the Day or the Hour, is not intended to motivate us to complacency. On the contrary, it is intended to cause us to be watching and waiting. And how can we be watching if we are not aware of the hour we live in and the signs that Scripture says will accompany the time of His return. Furthermore, the attitude of the early church was that they expected the Lord to come in their lifetime. This is clearly the desire of Christ for them when He concealed from that generation the dates which the Father had fixed. He said that it was not for them to know (Acts 1:7). This does not mean that it would be concealed from every generation and especially from the generation during whose lifetime it would come to pass. But it makes it very clear that the expectancy of the Apostles and the early church was God given and God ordained. He wanted them to be on the edge of their seat and He told them so. Thus all believers in every generation were expected to live with a sense of anticipation that Christ was coming soon, and any other belief would be regarded as out of step with the faith of the Apostles and fathers of the church. This in itself is enough reason for every believer to be alert and watching for His soon return. How much more then, should we be on the alert and filled with expectancy since all of the prophecies in Scripture indicate that we are living in the last generation?

Apparent Contradiction

"But you, brethren, are not in darkness, that the day would overtake you like a thief; for you are all sons of light and sons of day. We are not of night nor of darkness; so then let us not sleep as others do, but let us be alert and sober." 1 Thess 5:4-6

If Jesus said that no one knows the Day or the Hour, then why did Paul say that we are not of the darkness that the Day should overtake us? Is there a contradiction here? Apparently Paul did not interpret Jesus' words like many Christians do today. He said very clearly that those who were walking in the light, as believers ought to be, would not be overtaken by the Day of the Lord. In other words, we would be aware of the signs and know when it was happening. It would not come on us in surprise even though it comes like a thief in the night. Indeed, the whole point of Bible prophecy is to alert us to what is coming and when it is coming. And Jesus, together with all of the prophets gave us many signs to watch for so that we would know when He was coming. Could it be possible then that we have misunderstood Jesus words regarding the Day and the Hour?

No One Knows?

When Jesus said that no one knows except the Father, I do not believe that it was factual information that was being withheld from Him. Such a detail would hardly have been concealed to the Son of God especially since He Himself is also the Creator. Instead I believe He was saying that it was the Father's call and not His. In the ancient

Jewish wedding ritual the bridegroom could not choose the day to go and take his bride. Rather, that time was decreed by the father. Thus Jesus does not know the day or the hour because it is chosen or declared by the Father.

"But of that day and hour no one knows, not even the angels of heaven, nor the Son, but the Father alone. For the coming of the Son of Man will be just like the days of Noah. For as in those days before the flood they were eating and drinking, marrying and giving in marriage, until the day that Noah entered the ark, and they did not understand until the flood came and took them all away; so will the coming of the Son of Man be. Then there will be two men in the field; one will be taken and one will be left. Two women will be grinding at the mill; one will be taken and one will be left. Therefore be on the alert, for you do not know which day your Lord is coming." Mt 24:36-42

Here Jesus says that His coming (parousia) is like the days (plural) of Noah when people were unsuspecting and the flood came and took them all away. Noah and his family however, were rescued. In the same way He will come suddenly and rescue His Bride while the world will experience the Day of the Lord (the Tribulation). Then He makes a clear reference to the Rapture when He says that one will be taken and one will be left.

At the end of this passage in Matthew 24, Jesus seems to clearly answer the question as to who will know and who will not. He says that the master of the wicked lazy slave will come on a day and hour that he does not expect. The clear implication is that the believer who is walking in the will of the Lord will not be taken off guard but will know when He is coming. In Luke 12 there is a parallel passage which indicates that it was an answer to this question asked by Peter.

"Blessed are those slaves whom the master will find on the alert when he comes; truly I say to you, that he will gird himself to serve, and have them

recline at the table, and will come up and wait on them. Whether he comes in the second watch, or even in the third, and finds them so, blessed are those slaves. But be sure of this, that if the head of the house had known at what hour the thief was coming, he would not have allowed his house to be broken into. You too, be ready; for the Son of Man is coming at an hour that you do not expect. Peter said, "Lord, are You addressing this parable to us, or to everyone else as well?" Luke 12:37-41

Above is Peter's question and below is Jesus' answer!

"And the Lord said, "Who then is the faithful and sensible steward, whom his master will put in charge of his servants, to give them their rations at the proper time? Blessed is that slave whom his master finds so doing when he comes. Truly I say to you that he will put him in charge of all his possessions. But if that slave says in his heart, "My master will be a long time in coming,' and begins to beat the slaves, both men and women, and to eat and drink and get drunk; the master of that slave will come on a day when he does not expect him and at an hour he does not know, and will cut him in pieces, and assign him a place with the unbelievers. And that slave who knew his master's will and did not get ready or act in accord with his will, will receive many lashes, but the one who did not know it, and committed deeds worthy of a flogging, will receive but few. From everyone who has been given much, much will be required; and to whom they entrusted much, of him they will ask all the more." Luke 12:42-48

The Abom & the Rapture

We have seen already that the sign of Christ's parousia is the Abomination of Desolation (Abom - Mt 24:15). And we have also concluded that the Day of the Lord begins at this time and that the Rapture and the Day of the Lord are simultaneous. Another passage that confirms this (as though we needed more) is Luke 17:26-37. We know this because of the admonition to get out of Judea and not go down to get anything out of the house. This can only be referring to the time of the unveiling of the Abomination of Desolation which begins the Tribulation as is clearly taught in Matthew 24 and Mark

13. However, this passage goes even further and seems to pinpoint the night of the event. Can you see it below?

"And just as it happened in the days of Noah, so it will be also in the days of the Son of Man: they were eating, they were drinking, they were marrying, they were being given in marriage, until the day that Noah entered the ark, and the flood came and destroyed them all. It was the same as happened in the days of Lot: they were eating, they were drinking, they were buying, they were selling, they were planting, they were building; but on the day that Lot went out from Sodom it rained fire and brimstone from heaven and destroyed them all. It will be just the same on the day that the Son of Man is revealed. On that day, the one who is on the housetop and whose goods are in the house must not go down to take them out; and likewise the one who is in the field must not turn back. Remember Lot's wife. Whoever seeks to keep his life will lose it, and whoever loses his life will preserve it. I tell you, on that night there will be two in one bed; one will be taken and the other will be left. There will be two women grinding at the same place; one will be taken and the other will be left. Two men will be in the field; one will be taken and the other will be left." Luke 17:26-36

Is it a Sin to Speculate?

There is no lack of strange predictions and teachings regarding Jesus' coming. Much of it, of course, is from cults and strange characters in the deeper recesses of the internet. Many were surprised when Harold Camping's book came out with 1994 as the chosen year. Then he did it again with his May 21, 2011 date. But there have been many others. A whole movement was founded upon William Miller's predictions of the end in 1844 but it never happened. As a result, many were disillusioned. The same scenario has repeated itself many times over, down through the centuries, reaching fever pitch at the end of the 20th Century. In most cases, people were doing foolish things, like selling their homes, quitting their jobs and heading for the hills to escape Antichrist and wait for Jesus. Consequently, the church has gone dumb on the subject.

Speculation of any kind is considered harmful and those who set any kind of time frame are branded as heretics.

Recently, a well-known and well-respected evangelical was asked on national TV, "Are we in the End-Times?" His response was, "Only God knows." Are we to believe this well-known author has no clue if we are in the End-Times? Is there no way to know? I suspect his answer is a result of fear and denial. The fear that any kind of speculation would be sin, therefore it is safe to say, "No one really knows." But is this the way Jesus wants us to be about His coming? Is it wrong to speculate at all, even if we see the signs Jesus warned us about? What does the Scripture say we should do? Did the early church have this attitude? Is speculation a sin?

To answer this question we must turn to Scripture itself. If we can find speculation prohibited there, that would be sufficient to outlaw the practice. On the other hand, if it is not prohibited there, then who has the right to do so today? We have already discovered that Jesus, in His Olivet Discourse, expected us to be watching and waiting for that day. If He considered speculation as to the end-time events and the time of their fulfillment to be dangerous, then He would have warned us to avoid it. Perhaps you are one of those who believe He did warn us, and you don't accept my conclusions drawn here. Fine! But unless the rest of Scripture can support that position, it is not a correct understanding of Jesus' words. However, let's now consider Paul. If he addressed the subject of end-time speculation, wouldn't you accept his conclusions? Let's consider what he had to say to the Thessalonians.

"Now we request you, brethren, with regard to the coming of our Lord Jesus Christ and our gathering together to Him, that you not be quickly shaken from your composure or be disturbed either by a spirit or a message or a letter as if from us, to the effect that the day of the Lord has come. Let no one in any way deceive you, for it will not come unless the apostasy comes first, and the man of lawlessness is revealed, the son of destruction, who opposes

and exalts himself above every so-called god or object of worship, so that he takes his seat in the temple of God, displaying himself as being God. Do you not remember that while I was still with you, I was telling you these things? And you know what restrains him now, so that in his time he will be revealed. For the mystery of lawlessness is already at work; only he who now restrains will do so until he is taken out of the way. Then that lawless one will be revealed whom the Lord will slay with the breath of His mouth and bring to an end by the appearance of His coming; that is, the one whose coming is in accord with the activity of Satan, with all power and signs and false wonders, and with all the deception of wickedness for those who perish, because they did not receive the love of the truth so as to be saved. For this reason God will send upon them a deluding influence so that they will believe what is false, in order that they all may be judged who did not believe the truth, but took pleasure in wickedness. But we should always give thanks to God for you, brethren beloved by the Lord, because God has chosen you from the beginning for salvation through sanctification by the Spirit and faith in the truth. 2 Thess 2:1-13

First of all, I want to point out that Paul had been teaching the believers at Thessalonica about End-Times, even though they were new converts and he had just been there a few weeks. Why was he not afraid to teach this subject to young immature believers? Imagine teaching brand new believers the eschatology of the book of Daniel! Pastors today are afraid to teach it at all, let alone to new believers. However, it is obvious that Paul considered an understanding of End-Times as foundational material. Furthermore, he was not afraid that teaching such material concerning the Antichrist and the Abomination of Desolation would lead to instability or crazy predictions. If he felt that speculation with regard to the time of the end was wrong and dangerous, then he had the perfect opportunity to say so in his second letter. He has already written them one letter in which he addresses their discouragement over End-Times and their fear that their dead loved ones had missed it. Now word has reached him, apparently through Timothy, that the Thessalonians had received some kind of letter about the Day of the Lord. The letter, which they believed came from Paul, suggested that the end of the age or the Day of the Lord had already come. As a result, they were discouraged and thought they had missed it. Also, it appears many were not working and were behaving like busybodies; presumably because of the false report they had received.

This scenario sounds very much like what we have been discussing, where people predict dates and times and believers are discouraged because they have not come to pass. What a perfect opportunity for Paul to address the subject of speculation. If it is wrong to consider times and dates, why not tell them so? But Paul does not admonish them for their interest in End-Times. He does absolutely nothing to restrain their speculation or excitement regarding the Day of the Lord. On the contrary, he takes them back to the book of Daniel and reminds them of the teaching. He tells them that unless they see Antichrist taking his seat in the Temple, the time of the end has not come. In any event, Paul merely exhorts the Thessalonians to get it right and not to stop looking. If they are rebuked at all, it is not for speculating or wanting to know. It is for getting it wrong and not watching for the biblical signs. "Don't you remember?" he said, "What I was telling you when I was there?" Furthermore, he does not concern himself with condemning the individual who wrote the letter, other than to say it is clearly wrong and why.

When we carefully analyze Paul's letters to the Thessalonians, a church that seems to have been preoccupied with End-Times, we do not see the apostle admonishing them for their preoccupation. In fact, we can only conclude that they got this emphasis from him. He himself was the one who told them to watch and wait and observe the signs. They were eagerly anticipating the return of Jesus and appear to have been expecting Him to deliver them from the time of wrath. Consider these verses from his first Epistle:

"For they themselves report about us what kind of a reception we had with you, and how you turned to God from idols to serve a living and true God, and to wait for His Son from heaven, whom He raised from the dead, that is Jesus, who rescues us from the wrath to come." 1 Thess 1:9-10

Fear of Getting it Wrong

It is important to understand that there is a difference between a false prophet and one who brings a false prophecy. Is there a difference between a false teacher and one who brings a teaching that is false? Before you say no, consider that you may be judging yourself. Have you ever brought a teaching you later rejected? Indeed, who but the Master Himself has not had that experience? I am not talking of course about the essentials of the faith, but rather about the fact that our understanding grows – particularly in the area of Eschatology.

Paul, speaking of prophecy in the church, said that we prophesy in part. He exhorted the leaders to judge prophecy and to hold on to that which is good. If everyone were expected to get it absolutely right all the time, there would be no need for his exhortations. I have heard a lot of prophets and prophecy over the years. For the most part, none have been right one hundred per cent of the time. Is this an excuse for missing the target in prophecy? No! But neither is it reason to assume that everyone who misses it occasionally is a false prophet or false teacher. Why then is there a different standard applied to those who seek to understand and teach the church with regard to the End-Times? Why are they labeled as "false prophets" if something they say turns out to be wrong? Indeed, if we judge this way, then all of our heroes in the faith would be false prophets or teachers or both. The early apostles expected the Messiah to come in their generation. This fact is undeniable! Does that make them false prophets? Many of the reformers taught things that were untrue and which we now reject, does that make them false teachers? Martin Luther and many of his contemporaries believed the Pope was the Antichrist, and that the Jews should be rejected and mistreated. Therefore, was the reformation a false movement? Luther also set a date that proved false and so did John Wycliffe, Jonathon Edwards and even John Wesley. Were these men of God or not? We can't have it both ways. Obviously, these men did not believe it was a sin to speculate or try to understand the signs of the times. They were simply wrong in their predictions. They were not false prophets and teachers. False teachers and false prophets lead people away from Christ. Not only is their teaching wrong but their character as well.

It is time to reject this kind of thinking. What's wrong with looking and waiting? What's wrong with examining the signs? If we are teaching believers to walk with Jesus and grounding them in the truth, they will not be foolish or reckless. Surely, mature Christians should be able to examine these things without becoming irresponsible, quitting their jobs and heading for the hills. Perhaps that's the real issue. We need to educate people and teach them to live as examples of Christ without being clueless about eschatology. To be sure, many who predicted the end of the world in their lifetime were wrong. Likewise, those who say that Jesus' coming is a long way off are equally wrong. Which is better, to expect Jesus soon or not to expect Him soon? If he doesn't come in your lifetime, then you were wrong, but at least you lived expecting. But what if you don't expect the end in your lifetime and it comes on you unexpectedly. Is that better? Wouldn't it be more sensible to keep watch even if you made a mistake and got the timing wrong?

Following Signs

"The Pharisees and Sadducees came up, and testing Jesus, they asked Him to show them a sign from heaven. But He replied to them, 'When it is evening, you say, "It will be fair weather, for the sky is red." 'And in the morning, "There will be a storm today, for the sky is red and threatening." Do you know how to discern the appearance of the sky, but cannot discern the signs of the times? An evil and adulterous generation seeks after a sign;

and a sign will not be given it, except the sign of Jonah.'" And He left them and went away. Matt 16:1-4

In the above passage, Jesus is scolding the Pharisees for not recognizing the signs of the times. Yet, we are also told they were asking Him for a sign from heaven to show that He was the Messiah. It almost seems contradictory. However, what Matthew is saying is that the Pharisees were asking for proof, for some greater evidence that He was the Messiah and the Messianic Age had come. They did not believe in Him and their question was insincere, since they had already made up their minds. Jesus rebukes them for not seeing the signs already there and for the hardness of their hearts. He declares that they will only see the sign of Jonah, which refers to His death, burial and resurrection. Because of their hardness and unbelief, these religious leaders remained blind and failed to recognize their visitation.

There is a similar atmosphere among believers today, at the end of the age, as there was in the first century. These religious Jews studied Torah. They knew their Bibles. They knew about the Messianic Age and prophesy. They knew where the Messiah was to come from and what He was to do. They truly wanted Him to come. But Jesus did not meet their criteria and their understanding of prophecy; therefore, no matter how many signs they saw, they would not believe. Yet the signs were everywhere. It is estimated that Jesus fulfilled over three hundred specific prophesies from Scripture. What was the problem? Why did they miss it?

There was, of course, a remnant of people who were alert and watching. They saw the signs. Angels appeared to shepherds. Anna and Simeon were watching and praying and recognized the Son of God. Nicodemus was a righteous Pharisee (imagine that) who pondered it all and put the signs together. There were many others. But the religious leaders looked on them with disdain. They viewed them as foolish, uneducated speculators. "If He is the Messiah, then

He will establish the Kingdom and liberate us from Rome," they said. That was all that mattered to them. They didn't want to look foolish in the eyes of the world or be persecuted. They wanted political proof. They adopted a "wait and see" and "I'll believe it when I see it" attitude. But they missed the clear signs of God's word. If it happened then, could it not happen again? Is this not the primary warning of Scripture and history? Is this not what Jesus was concerned about at the end of the age? Was it not that His disciples would be asleep and not watching and miss the signs of His return?

Some will argue that we should not look for signs at all since the enemy will show signs also. After all, Jesus warned that there would be false signs and wonders attempting to deceive God's people. But since when do we abandon the real item simply because there is a counterfeit? Do we reject the gospel because there are people preaching a false gospel? Do we reject signs, wonders and miracles because the enemy can produce counterfeit ones? I think not! Because there will be counterfeit signs does not give us license to be complacent and ignore the real ones. In fact, is it not all the more reason we should be alert and watching, discerning the signs of the times? We are not those who are in darkness that the day should overtake us, are we? Heaven forbid! Yet, the Scripture is clear. The last generation of believers will be no different than the first century generation. Some will be waiting and watching and ready for His return. The rest will be caught up in the things that matter to them and making excuses for their complacency.

Four Sources Agree on the Date of 7th Day
Now that I have gotten that off my chest I would like you to consider with me some possibilities of a timeframe for what the Lord is about to do. We know that we are waiting for the Last Shemitah Cycle when the Peace Treaty is signed, beginning the countdown to the Rapture and the Day of the Lord. We know what that will look like and what it will entail. We also see the signs it is imminent. Therefore, is there any indication in prophecy or history as to when

those events will take place? I would like to suggest that we have some clear indications from biblical prophecy, and biblical history, as to when this will all go down. There are at least four sources that correlate on this time frame. It is certainly not conclusive, although I am reasonably convinced. However I want to make it clear that it is speculative and should not be taken as an absolute fact. We will begin with the modern Jewish calendar.

The Modern Jewish Calendar

The modern Jewish calendar year is based on the Seder Olam Rabbah which was composed by a Jewish rabbi in the second century AD. It is based on the Bible chronology. However, after the destruction of Jerusalem and the advent of the Persian Empire its calculations are inaccurate. It appears the rabbi followed the seventy Shemitah cycle prophecy of Daniel 9, and tried to avoid the conclusion of Jesus as the Messiah. As a result, the years of the Persian and Greek rule are shortened. Thus the current Jewish calendar is approximately 200 years short. Jewish sources openly concur with this fact.

Taking this into consideration, and assuming that the date for the destruction of the Temple from the Seder Olam (3340) is correct, and adding 70 years until the Temple was rebuilt (3410), we will now correlate the Jewish calendar to the secular one. We will begin with the date of 3410/516BC, which we trust.

Secular Calendar from 516BC

From 516 BC to 1967.8 when the Holy Place came back under Jewish control is 2483.8 of our calendar years. Please keep in mind that our calendar years of 365.25 days have to be converted to Jewish biblical years of 360 days.

$$\sim\sim\sim\sim\sim$$
$$-516BC +1967.8 =2483.8 *365.25 /360 = 2520$$
$$3410 + 2520 = 5930$$

Thus the year 1967 was **5930** on the Jewish calendar.

$$5930+49=5979 = 2015/2016$$
$$\sim\sim\sim\sim\sim$$

The current Jewish year is **5979** (2015) from the date of creation and not 5776. This would leave 21 years to the 6000th year or the 7th Day (the Millennium) which would begin in **2036/2037**. Thus this is the first source - the corrected Jewish calendar.

The Last Generation from 1967

As we have already seen in the beginning of the book (Pg. 21-22), a biblical generation is considered to be seventy years. In the Jubilee year of 1967 the prophecy of Jesus was fulfilled as Israeli soldiers took possession of the Old City of Jerusalem and the Temple Mount. Exactly seventy years earlier the World Zionist Congress began the effort to establish a Jewish State and in one generation it was complete. Jesus told us in Luke Chapter 21 that those who saw this happen would see all that the prophets of Israel had spoken come to pass. Thus the generation born in 1967 is the last generation.

If it took one generation to restore Israel to the Land, completing phase one of their return, then why would it not take seventy more years to complete phase two (their spiritual return)? When we add seventy years to 1967 we get 2037. Thus we have two more amazing confirmations of the year 2037 for the beginning of the Millennium. That is, Ezekiel 36:24-28 (Phase One and Two) and Luke 21 (Jesus' prophecy about Jerusalem and the last generation).

~~~~~

1. Ezekiel 36:24-28 - 1897 +70 = 1967 (Phase 1), 1967+70 (Phase 2) = **2037**
2. Corrected Jewish Calendar – 5979 (2015/2016) + 21 = **6000**
3. Last Generation - 1967 + 70 = **2037**

~~~~~

Prophecy of Hosea Chapter 6

Another source that confirms this date of 2037 as the Millennium is the prophecy of Hosea Chapter 6.

"Come, let us return to the LORD. For He has torn us, but He will heal us; He has wounded us, but He will bandage us. He will revive us after two days; He will raise us up on the third day, that we may live before Him". Hosea 6:1-2

The early rabbis understood this passage to refer to the Messianic era. The Jewish people would be wounded for two days, but on the third day they would be healed. For two thousand years they would suffer, and in the third millennium the Kingdom would come. Thus on the third day or third millennium they would be healed.

For centuries the church viewed this prophecy as proof that the year 2000AD was the Third Day. However, they assumed that the first day began with the birth of Jesus or with His death. Once again because of Replacement Theology their understanding was darkened. The prophecy does not speak about the Messiah but the wounding of the Jewish people. This is clear from the context in Hosea Chapter 5 and 6.

In 66 AD the wounding and scattering of Israel began in what came to be known as the War of the Jews. Israel was rejected by God, but only for a season. She would be wounded for two millennia and healed on the third. Then she would be completely accepted again. Since we know the date the first millennium began, 66 AD, we can determine when the third millennium will begin. This time we have to convert the biblical prophetic years into our calendar years. To do that we must multiply by 360 and divide by 365.25.

~~~~~

2000 years of 360 days (biblical years) x 360 = 720000 days
720000 days/365.25 (days in our years) = **1971** our years
66 AD + 1971 = **2037**

~~~~~

Amazingly once again, the year of the Millennium happens to be 2037 - the year that begins with the end of the calendar Shemitah! Can all four of these sources be wrong? Surely one of them would be significant? Nevertheless they are all pointing to the same year for the beginning of the reign of Christ! Now if we accept this, all we have to do is subtract seven years and we know the beginning of the Last Shemitah Cycle (Daniel's Seventieth Week). This would be Rosh Hashanah 2029. Then three and a half years later, or half way through the fourth year, the Abomination will be set up and the Rapture will take place.

Ezekiel 36:24-28:1897+70 (1967) +70 = **2037**
Corrected Jewish calendar: 5979 + 21 = **6000**
Last generation (Luke 21): 1967 + 70 = **2037**
Hosea Chapter 6: 66AD + 1971= **2037**

~~~~~

I realize that many of you are now upset with me and are going back to the mantra that nobody knows the day or the hour. It just troubles you to think that we could actually have a clue as to when Jesus would return. You seem to be convinced that Jesus wants us in the dark about this. Yet you have seen throughout this book that the opposite is true. Those who are eagerly awaiting Him, and doing His will, are able to see the signs and know the day. It will not come on them suddenly like a thief and overtake them.

However, if you are still troubled, you can comfort yourself with the fact that I only gave a possible year and not a twenty-four hour period.

2015-2016
The year beginning in September 2014 to September 2015 was a Shemitah year. But it was not only a Shemitah year it was the seventh Shemitah. Therefore, the year beginning in September 2015 and ending in September 2016 is a Jubilee year. This is very significant indeed.

Besides the Jubilee there were other significant signs during this Shemitah year. Blood Moons or lunar eclipses have taken place on Passover and Sukkot on both 2014 and 2015. The last time that happened was 1967-1968. And the time before that was during the War of Independence in 1949. Also, during this Shemitah there was a solar eclipse on the Jewish Religious New Year and there was another one on Rosh Hashanah.

The Jubilee is the time when everyone in Israel returned to his family inheritance and all debts were cancelled. The last Jubilee was 1967 when Israel recovered its ancient capital Jerusalem. There is a very good possibility that in this coming year Israel will consecrate the Holy Place and begin to rebuild the Temple. We shall see what happens. However, if not that, we expect something that will significantly advance the prophetic timetable.

The Shemitah Cycle & the Millennium
Daniel's Seventieth Week is the last of the Seventy Shemitah periods decreed for the Jewish people. We know it begins when a treaty is made with an EU leader. This treaty allows for Jewish worship in the Holy Place, and also admits Israel to the European body. In this chapter, we have observed how four sources of biblical prophecy all converge around the year 2037. However there is another intriguing convergence taking place. This last prophetic

Shemitah appears to also coincide with the last calendar Shemitah. The year from Rosh Hashanah 2028, to Rosh Hashanah 2029, is a Shemitah period. Thus Rosh Hashanah 2029 begins a new Shemitah cycle, which appears to be the last. This would seem to suggest that the "peace treaty" will be signed on this date.

~~~~~

Rosh Hashanah 2029 to Rosh Hashanah 2036 is the Last Shemitah Cycle

Rosh Hashanah 2029 (5993) + 7 = Rosh Hashanah 2036 (6000)

Rosh Hashanah 2036 to Rosh Hashanah 2037 is the year 6000

~~~~~

The Jewish year begins on Rosh Hashanah, which means that the year 2029 is the year 5993 (from our corrected calendar). Thus seven years later would be Rosh Hashanah 6000, beginning a new year. Some would argue that Rosh Hashanah 6001 is the beginning of the Millennium but it is actually Rosh Hashanah 6000. In other words, Rosh Hashanah 6000 to Rosh Hashanah 6001 is the first year of the Millennium. Therefore, Rosh Hashanah 2029 is the beginning of the calendar Shemitah Cycle and also the prophetic Shemitah Cycle. And Rosh Hashanah 2036 is the end of the Last Shemitah and the beginning of the reign of Christ. Thus the year 2037 is the year that Israel is healed and all that the prophets have spoken is accomplished. Whether this is right or not, one thing is clear, those who are eagerly awaiting Him will not miss the obvious signs!

Chapter Eleven
Great Sifting & Apostasy

"See to it that you do not refuse Him who is speaking for if those did not escape when they refused him who warned them on earth, much less will we escape who turn away from Him who warns from heaven. And His voice shook the earth then, but now He has promised, saying, 'YET ONCE MORE I WILL SHAKE NOT ONLY THE EARTH, BUT ALSO THE HEAVEN.' This expression, 'Yet once more,' denotes the removing of those things which can be shaken, as of created things, so that those things which cannot be shaken may remain. Therefore, since we receive a kingdom which cannot be shaken, let us show gratitude, by which we may offer to God an acceptable service with reverence and awe; for our God is a consuming fire." Heb 12:25-29

The above verses speak of the shaking of the Day of the Lord. However, that shaking has already begun. God is sifting and shaking all mankind in a sieve. The wheat is ripening and so are the tares. He is getting ready to harvest the earth. He will bring in the First Fruits, then the Harvest, and then the Gleanings. The wheat will be gathered into His barn and the tares will be burned up with fire. Everything that can be shaken will be and the time is now. All who can be deceived will be deceived. Only the true kingdom of Christ will remain. In this chapter we will look at the continued parallel restoration of Israel and the church and examine how the church, Israel, and the nations are currently being sifted by God.

The Last Great Sifting of Israel

"For behold, I am commanding, and I will shake the house of Israel among all nations as grain is shaken in a sieve, but not a kernel will fall to the ground." Amos 9:9

As we saw in Chapter 2, there is a continued restoration of Israel taking place. Since 1967 we have been in the second phase of that restoration which is spiritual - bringing the nation back to God. In 1993 there was the signing of a seven year agreement called the Oslo Accords. This was a precursor to the seven year treaty that begins the Last Shemitah Cycle. It was a complete failure and the situation is much worse now than it was then. Storm clouds are brewing throughout the world as a Middle-East war is well underway. The pressure on Israel has been unbearable. The nations expect them to divide the land and Jerusalem. Israel is more and more isolated by the nations and this situation will continue until the false peace of the Last Shemitah Cycle. Already the nations have sent armies to the Middle-East and it is unlikely that they will ever return home. However, what many do not see is that this conflict is not just about land. It's about Israel itself. The land is covenanted to her forever. But this crucible is intended to turn her heart back to God. The pressure will continue to increase and there will be nowhere to turn except to the Father. Perhaps we see the beginnings of that turning in the nation right now as more and more people are becoming religious - especially the youth. A recent study shows that by 2030 the majority of Jews will be religious Jews. Also, another recent poll indicated, that for the first time, 64% of Israelis were in favor of rebuilding the Temple. All this, of course, is in keeping with the End-Time prophetic Scriptures! The great stumbling block of Israel has been the cross of Christ. The rejection of the Messiah has brought them millennia of pain. But the Scripture says that they will be reconciled very soon. They will look upon Him whom they have pierced and mourn for Him like an only Son. This is the future of the remnant of Israel.

The Great Apostasy

As previously discussed, Paul was very clear that the Day of the Lord and the Rapture could not come until the Apostasy came first. This Apostasy occurs when the leaders of Israel are duped into signing a covenant of "peace" with the person who is later revealed as the Antichrist. This is their covenant with Sheol that abruptly ends three and a half years later ushering in the Tribulation period of Jacob's Distress. This period is also known as the Day of the Lord which is why it can't come until the Apostasy comes first. Hopefully by now I have made this clear to you and you know that the Day of the Lord and the Rapture are simultaneous events, both appearing suddenly like a thief. Nevertheless, besides the Apostasy of Israel mentioned by Paul that must come first, we are also taught that there will be a great apostasy among Christians prior to Jesus' return.[60] Not only is there parallel restoration, there is also parallel apostasy. The apostasy in the church has already begun and is going to increase to where the Harlot is clearly separated from the remnant Bride. Israel on the other hand must fight another war and somehow get the courage and conviction to rebuild the Temple. The scenario to bring that to pass seems to already be underway. However, Israel will become religious before they return with their heart to God Himself. This leader of the EU will be very shrewd and will use this to broker a deal that is accommodating to religious concerns as well as guaranteeing political and financial security. Israel's leaders will fall into this trap and place their trust in this personage as the Messiah. Then the Day of the Lord judgment will come and a remnant nation will turn to the true Messiah and be delivered.

---

[60] 1Tim 4:1-3, 2Tim 3:1-5, 2Pet 3:3-4, Jude 17-18

Sifting of the Nations

"His breath is like an overflowing torrent, which reaches to the neck, to shake the nations back and forth in a sieve, and to put in the jaws of the peoples the bridle which leads to ruin." Isaiah 30:28

In the first century, the nation of Israel stumbled over the stumbling stone of Jesus and the cross, and their stumbling brought life to the Gentiles (Rom 11:20). However, they were not alone in their stumbling. The Gentiles have also stumbled very badly, but over a different stone. This is the story yet to be told. And just as the Jewish people have paid a high price for their error, the nations of the earth will be punished most severely for their Anti-Semitism and jealousy of Israel. From the very beginning of the nation, they have despised Jacob and tried to wipe him out. Because of the envy in their own hearts they have repeatedly succumbed to a demonic plot to kill the Jews and take their land. And when God Himself chose to chasten His people for their sin and idolatry, the nations of the earth took advantage of the opportunity. The prophets had much to say about this. Consider these words from the prophet Zechariah:

"So the angel who was speaking with me said to me, 'Proclaim, saying, "Thus says the LORD of hosts, I am exceedingly jealous for Jerusalem and Zion. But I am very angry with the nations who are at ease; for while I was only a little angry, they furthered the disaster."'" Zech 1:14-15

The fact that God used the Gentile nations to chasten Israel does not mean He condoned their actions. On the contrary, He was very angry with them and brought their evil on their own heads. Yet, throughout the centuries they have gloated and rejoiced in Israel's suffering, doing everything they possibly could to make it harder. Kings, tyrants, sultans, and even US presidents claiming to be Christians, have butchered them and stolen their God-given land. But the Lord continues to be exceedingly jealous for Jerusalem and Zion. The story is far from over. Those who suppose that God is no longer angry over Jerusalem and Anti-Semitism need to get reacquainted with these verses:

"If I forget you, O Jerusalem, may my right hand forget her skill. May my tongue cling to the roof of my mouth if I do not remember you, if I do not exalt Jerusalem above my chief joy." Ps 137:5-6

"Behold, I am going to make Jerusalem a cup that causes reeling to all the peoples around; and when the siege is against Jerusalem, it will also be against Judah. It will come about in that day that I will make Jerusalem a heavy stone for all the peoples; all who lift it will be severely injured. And all the nations of the earth will be gathered against it. 'In that day,' declares the LORD, 'I will strike every horse with bewilderment and his rider with madness. But I will watch over the house of Judah, while I strike every horse of the peoples with blindness.'" Zech 12:2-4

This is not referring to the events that happened in 586BC or 70AD. This fact is obvious because God brought those tragedies on Israel to chasten them and did not fight on their behalf. This time however, God is gathering all the nations against Jerusalem to enter into judgment with them. Here is the same event again in Zechariah chapter 14:

"Behold, a day is coming for the LORD when the spoil taken from you will be divided among you. For I will gather all the nations against Jerusalem to battle, and the city will be captured, the houses plundered, the women ravished and half of the city exiled, but the rest of the people will not be cut off from the city. Then the LORD will go forth and fight against those nations, as when He fights on a day of battle." Zech 14:1-3

Again we see very clearly that the Lord is going to gather all the nations against Jerusalem and He Himself is going to fight against them and destroy them. These events have not come to pass in history, but are now beginning to appear on the global horizon. All the words of the prophets spoken about Israel, Jerusalem, and the nations have come to pass literally, and with great accuracy. Therefore, this final scenario is no different. The Gentiles have worked out their "Road Map" which they are determined to force upon Israel, but it will lead to their own demise. They are stumbling over their stumbling stone - the Jewish people. In their humanism and arrogance, they are determined to make Israel commit political suicide by giving up more of their God-given land, including their ancient and eternal capital. However, they have seriously miscalculated and will soon find out who it is they are dealing with. Consider this verse from the prophet Joel:

"For behold, in those days and at that time, when I restore the fortunes of Judah and Jerusalem, I will gather all the nations and bring them down to the valley of Jehoshaphat. Then I will enter into judgment with them there on behalf of My people and My inheritance, Israel, whom they have scattered among the nations; and they have divided up My land." Joel 3:1-2

Notice the Lord says, "In those days and at that time when I restore the fortunes of Judah and Jerusalem," He is very specific. Only one generation can qualify for this and it is the one we are living in. We are in those days and are living at that time. God restored the fortunes of Judah and Jerusalem nearly seventy years ago. He gathered them from all the nations and in 1948 they became a nation again in Judah. And in 1967 they were restored to their ancient capital. Since then the fortunes of Judah and Jerusalem have been burgeoning. Who can dispute this? Yet, the very day after the State was created in 1948, the armies of at least five nations came to destroy it. But the baby state just born soundly defeated them, even taking more of the land. They were attacked again in 1956, 1967 and 1972 and each time the Lord fought with them, putting their enemies to flight. Since that time they have been fighting a war against terrorism that the whole world has been drawn into. This war will continue until it ends in Jerusalem. God is using it as a hook in the jaws of the Gentile armies to gather them for destruction. They have already concluded that there will be no peace on the earth until they have made peace in Jerusalem. Their plan is to divide up the land and the city of God (Mt 5:35). This plan has already been agreed to by an Israeli prime minister. It is written down in the so-called "Road Map" and is regarded now as a sort of international law that will be pursued and executed, regardless of the Israeli or Gentile leadership that emerges. Unfortunately there is no remedying this situation. The sins of the nations toward Israel and their dividing up of His land, not to mention their other evils, have already piled up to heaven. The judgment has already been decreed millennia ago. Consider these words of Isaiah:

"I was angry with My people, I profaned My heritage and gave them into your hand. You did not show mercy to them, on the aged you made your yoke very heavy. Yet you said, 'I will be a queen forever.' These things you did not consider nor remember the outcome of them. Now, then, hear this, you sensual one, who dwells securely, who says in your heart, 'I am, and there is no one besides me. I will not sit as a widow, nor know loss of children.' ....But evil will come on you which you will not know how to charm away; and disaster will fall on you for which you cannot atone; and destruction about which you do not know will come on you suddenly." Isa 47:6-11

These words were spoken against ancient Babylon, the oppressor of the Jews, but it was also spoken against its successors and oppressors throughout the ages. Consider the similarity of this passage in Revelation 18:

"After these things I saw another angel coming down from heaven, having great authority, and the earth was illumined with his glory. And he cried out with a mighty voice, saying, 'Fallen, fallen is Babylon the great! She has become a dwelling place of demons and a prison of every unclean spirit, and a prison of every unclean and hateful bird. For all the nations have drunk of the wine of the passion of her immorality, and the kings of the earth have committed acts of immorality with her, and the merchants of the

earth have become rich by the wealth of her sensuality.' I heard another voice from heaven, saying, 'Come out of her, my people, so that you will not participate in her sins and receive of her plagues; for her sins have piled up as high as heaven, and God has remembered her iniquities. Pay her back even as she has paid, and give back to her double according to her deeds; in the cup which she has mixed, mix twice as much for her. To the degree that she glorified herself and lived sensuously, to the same degree give her torment and mourning; for she says in her heart, "I SIT AS A QUEEN AND I AM NOT A WIDOW, and will never see mourning." For this reason in one day her plagues will come, pestilence and mourning and famine, and she will be burned up with fire; for the Lord God who judges her is strong.'" Rev 18:1-8 NASU Emphasis Mine

This word is spoken against the last world Empire, which is an alliance under the Antichrist (Rev 17:12), identified with the code name Babylon. The prophet Daniel revealed four kingdoms which would oppress the Jewish people: Babylon, Media-Persia, Greece and Rome. The fourth Empire was predicted to fall apart into a mixture of iron and clay and emerge at the end of the age, as a world alliance of ten entities giving their power to Antichrist. This alliance is to have in it all of the attributes of the Empires that came before, and is identified as Babylon, since it was the first (Rev 13:2, Dan 2:38-43). This last great Gentile alliance, which was pictured by Daniel as a beast or monster (Daniel 7:7), will be crushed by the Messiah who will fight for Israel.

Today, we see the fulfillment of these prophecies on the horizon. The nations are franticly working to form an effective global alliance that can end the world's problems and bring "peace and security" (1Thess 5:3). Under the guise of conquering disease, hunger, wealth distribution, "climate change" and world peace, the financial and political elite wish to gain control over the planet. And the Harlot system pushes this agenda riding atop the beast and passing it off as real Christianity when it is in fact just plain old humanism - worshiping the creature rather than the creator. And they are beginning their march to Jerusalem where the divine trap is set. The Lord Almighty has a case against them for how they have treated His people and divided up His land. Indeed, it will be a great slaughter (Rev 19:17-19) as the full weight of judgment for all the atrocities committed against the Jewish people throughout history falls on this generation. Israel will finally be victorious over all her oppressors (Micah 4:11-13), and the Messiah will restore the Kingdom to her.

Parallel Restoration – Israel & the Church

"Therefore repent and return, so that your sins may be wiped away, in order that times of refreshing may come from the presence of the Lord; and that He may send Jesus, the Christ appointed for you, whom heaven must receive until the period of restoration of all things about which God spoke by the mouth of His holy prophets from ancient time." Acts 3:19-21

Throughout the twentieth century as the Lord was restoring Israel to her land, He has also been restoring the church. Chart 16 on page 298 shows the parallel restoration. As God is doing something of great importance with Israel, something of equal significance is happening simultaneously in the church. Stage 1 of the restoration was the discovery of inheritance for both Israel and the church. Stage 2 will bring both into their eternal destinies which are intertwined. Israel is not the church and the church is not Israel. However, notice it is a remnant that enters into the promises. Many Jews will fall away and perish as will many Christians. The church that truly loves Israel and affirms her destiny and call is the True Bride. The one who pulls away from Israel and downplays or ignores her covenant promises is the Harlot. There is taking place at the moment a great sifting of both Israel and the church. The sifting of Israel is over her rejection of Messiah and the stumbling block of the cross. The sifting of the church is about her rejection of the Jews through Replacement Theology and the twisting of God's Word which has led to centuries of Antisemitism. (See chart 16 on page 298)

In 1993-1994 when the Oslo Accords were being signed there was a significant outpouring of revival in the church. The Lord has used this revival to bring His Bride into deeper intimacy and passion for Him. And out of its loins is coming a remnant that is in love with the Bridegroom, keeping Him and His presence their pursuit and passion and following Him wherever He goes. Indeed, the next wave has already begun as God is pouring out a purifying fire among us. This fire will intensify in the days ahead and will bring a separation between those who cling to the Bridegroom and those who have sought to use the "tools" of the Spirit to advance their own agenda. Indeed, the Lord Himself is sending a strong delusion upon the church because of pride and false teaching. They continue to cling to Replacement Theology and do not seem to love the truth but blatantly distort it to suit their own agendas.

"Then that lawless one will be revealed whom the Lord will slay with the breath of His mouth and bring to an end by the appearance of His coming; that is, the one whose coming is in accord with the activity of Satan, with all power and signs and false wonders, and with all the deception of wickedness for those who perish, because they did not receive the love of the truth so as to be saved. For this reason God will send upon them a deluding influence so that they will believe what is false, in order that they all may be judged who did not believe the truth, but took pleasure in wickedness." 2 Thess 2:8-12

The Bride is being adorned with glory. She is becoming completely devoted to her Bridegroom, longing for His appearing. She is learning to put away striving and human effort and to do only what she sees the Father doing. Both the Bride and the Remnant of Israel are about to experience a supernatural deliverance. On the other hand, the nations are being mobilized by the enemy to wage war on Israel and a spiritual war on the Bride. Those in the church that have made solving the world's problems their focus and attention are unknowingly adopting the agenda of the Antichrist. Both the Beast and the Harlot are coming to maturity and can now be seen in the world. They refuse to accept the truth of Scripture regarding Israel's restoration and they scoff at End-Time teaching. A strong delusion from the Lord has been released and a great sifting is underway. This great End-Time sifting of the church, the nations, and Israel, appears to have begun in earnest in the year 2000.

The Sifting of the Church

"But the Spirit explicitly says that in later times some will fall away from the faith, paying attention to deceitful spirits and doctrines of demons, by means of the hypocrisy of liars seared in their own conscience as with a branding iron…" 1 Tim 4:1-2

"For the time will come when they will not endure sound doctrine; but wanting to have their ears tickled, they will accumulate for themselves teachers in accordance to their own desires, and will turn away their ears from the truth and will turn aside to myths." 2 Tim 4:3-4

The church is called to be a Bride made ready for the Bridegroom.[61] Her passion and pursuit is to be of Him and His presence. Bringing others to Him should be her commitment and dedication but not her preoccupation. Love for Him is to consume her as she eagerly awaits His return. Her hope is not in her ability to change the earth but on His promise to come back for her. This is the true apostolic teaching - the true apostolic emphasis.

"Husbands, love your wives, just as Christ also loved the church and gave Himself up for her, so that He might sanctify her, having cleansed her by the washing of water with the word, that He might present to Himself the church in all her glory, having no spot or wrinkle or any such thing; but that she would be holy and blameless. Eph 5:25-27

Consider Paul's concern for the Corinthians.

---

[61] Eph 5:25-27

"For I am jealous for you with a godly jealousy; for I betrothed you to one husband, so that to Christ I might present you as a pure virgin." 2 Cor 11:2

Today however, many are rising up within the church, calling themselves apostles and leading His bondservants astray. The Scriptures clearly warned us that this would happen and we have known it. However, it has been hard to imagine that it would come on such a grand scale and with such ease that so many Christians and pastors would be swept off their feet. But this is exactly what is happening.

Something Did Happen in the Year 2000

It is beginning to seem like in the year 2000 war was declared on the church from within. Just as we were experiencing an incredible wave of refreshing, filling us with His love and power, the Harlot church began to emerge from within our very own ranks. Perhaps the "Hyper Grace Movement"[62] and the "Emerging Church Movement"[63] are the most dangerous since they promote heretical teachings that are leading to large scale apostasy. However, there are other theologies that have experienced a resurgence with the dawn of the twenty first century that are also deeply troubling. They may not necessarily lead to apostasy, but they are nonetheless toxic when it comes to the authority of Scripture and one's ability to discern between the True Bride and the Harlot. These are, "Preterism," and "Dominion Theology" which is also known as "Kingdom Now."[64]

It should not surprise us that there is an avalanche of false teaching and false teachers at the end of the age. This was prophesied by the Messiah Himself. Those of us who know we are at the end should take comfort in this as we fight the good fight of the faith. This is what the John apostle warned:

---

[62] See Appendix 3
[63] See Appendix 4
[64] See Appendix 5 and 6.

"Children, it is the last hour; and just as you heard that antichrist is coming, even now many antichrists have appeared; from this we know that it is the last hour. They went out from us, but they were not really of us; for if they had been of us, they would have remained with us; but they went out, so that it would be shown that they all are not of us." 1 John 2:18-19

It is absolutely astonishing to see how false teachers have become so popular and gained such ground, so much so that hardly anyone is confronting them. Something in them is awry as they twist the Scriptures and deceive people. They take the true doctrines of the faith and distort them replacing them with doctrines of demons, and the church is eating it up. And of course, they mock those of us who believe Jesus is coming soon. Peter warned us of this, and it is clear from his writing that he was referring to believers, since only they would speak of creation or "the fathers."

"Know this first of all, that in the last days mockers will come with their mocking, following after their own lusts, and saying, 'Where is the promise of His coming? For ever since the fathers fell asleep, all continues just as it was from the beginning of creation.'" 2Pet 3:3-4

Peter also identified two types of people who confuse and distort End-Time teaching - the untaught and the unstable.[65] The untaught distort Scripture because they do not have the background or training necessary to interpret it correctly. They are simply missing the context and information required to unlock passages or interpret revelation. They have either not been taught or they have been taught wrong.

The second group that distorts Scripture, according to Peter, is the unstable. The unstable have a propensity to twist the truth or spin it in such a way that it promotes their agenda or inner motive of the heart. This is a serious warning for all who teach the word to consider. It is not merely about some troubled souls who cannot

---

[65] 2 Pet 3:14-16

overcome temptation or sin. It is addressing the ones who preach and teach the Bible but are operating out of some inner conflict or woundedness. This inner instability is distorting their perspective and leading them to erroneous conclusions and revelations that will ultimately result in derailment for them and their followers. They may have started well, but over time, this inner instability led them to force conclusions on Scripture that were complimentary to their "ministries." They began to take license and liberty with verses, distorting their context and meaning because it was advantageous to their agenda.

Make no mistake about it, the condition of our heart and the healthiness of our soul will determine the soundness of our teaching. In addition, what we teach will have a profound effect on our practice as well. Wrong teaching will lead us to wrong conclusions and wrong conclusions can lead down the wrong path. How many good people have gone astray because they neglected the inner issues of the heart? How many good men and women have gone astray because they would not listen to the gentle rebuke of another and took their own perspective too seriously? This is a vital truth and one that all teachers, and especially those who make confident assertions about eschatology, must understand. In the same way, those who say that one's position on End-Times or the Rapture is not important, are making a colossal mistake and throwing away the compass and revelation of God's Word given to guide them through the difficult canyons ahead. They are assuming that "so long as we love the Lord it doesn't matter." By this, they are already embracing error. The End-Time revelation contained in God's word is not just for debate and discussion. It is intended to guide us in faith and practice and to ensure that we have the correct stance at the end of the age.

The end of the age is a time of great sifting and testing and indeed, it has already begun. Those who are not aware of this are nonchalantly paddling their little boats toward the great Niagara.

They may think all is fine and dandy but a rude awakening is coming. The Scriptures tell us that God will send a strong delusion in the last days and that the Antichrist will deceive all who have the ability to receive error. Anyone who has had to deal with error and deception in their own life, or the life of a friend or colleague, knows how easily it can creep in. And, though it is the result of something wrong in the heart, it can be brought on by wrong teaching or unhealthy reactions to something with which we disagree. Bad teaching sows bad seed in the heart that can latch on to some area not yielded to Christ. One has to prepare inwardly as well as outwardly for the Lord's return. We need to keep our spirit, soul and body blameless until His coming.[66] How easy it is to become discouraged and take our eyes off Christ. How easily we can become arrogant, adopting some new plan or "revelation," and dismiss those who do not "get the vision." This kind of arrogance can set us up for failure and deception.

Being Too Nice to Confront Evil

Whenever one brings up the issue of false teaching, there are many who immediately flinch. Any thought of false teaching or Christian celebrities being confronted is "negative" to them. They find the thought of challenging the message of anyone who "loves Jesus" as divisive and against the Father's love. Of course we know there are many who sow division and strife in what they write, particularly on the internet. The so-called Heretic Hunters are everywhere with poison on their lips. However in reaction to them the church seems to be refusing to confront anything no matter how outrageous it is. Surely this is not the attitude of leaders who are caring for Christ's sheep.[67] It certainly wasn't the attitude of the apostles who publicly admonished God's people, often mentioning names. In fact, in one of Paul's letters which was read publicly, two women were rebuked and told to get along (Phil 4:2). Indeed, when it comes to false

---

[66] 1Thess 5:23
[67] John 21:15

teaching the Scriptures are very strong. Consider the following verses.

"Now I urge you, brethren, keep your eye on those who cause dissensions and hindrances contrary to the teaching which you learned, and turn away from them. For such men are slaves, not of our Lord Christ but of their own appetites; and by their smooth and flattering speech they deceive the hearts of the unsuspecting." Rom 16:17-18

"This command I entrust to you, Timothy, my son, in accordance with the prophecies previously made concerning you, that by them you fight the good fight, keeping faith and a good conscience, which some have rejected and suffered shipwreck in regard to their faith. Among these are Hymenaeus and Alexander, whom I have handed over to Satan, so that they will be taught not to blaspheme." 1 Tim 1:18-20

"...preach the word; be ready in season and out of season; reprove, rebuke, exhort, with great patience and instruction." 2 Tim 4:2

"Watch yourselves that you do not lose what we have accomplished, but that you may receive a full reward. Anyone who goes too far and does not abide in the teaching of Christ, does not have God; the one who abides in the teaching, he has both the Father and the Son." 2 John 8-9

The Apostles of the Lord seemed to have this idea that they were protecting the church. Therefore, they confronted everything that was off whether it was absolute heresy or simply somebody saying something that is false. And they did this without being, critical, judgmental, or legalistic. They knew that false teaching would produce bad fruit, and that God's people should be protected from it. But today however, one can hardly confront anything without being labeled divisive. Believers find it shocking when anyone disagrees with their celebrities. It's the spirit of Hollywood among us. They have no use for theology and almost never read anything scholarly. Consequently, people just make up their own doctrine without checking the Scriptures. And rather than confronting what is false, they will often promote it because of the popularity of the speakers and their ability to draw crowds. It is no wonder that the church is in such a time of sifting and testing. Indeed, we have created the perfect environment for false prophets to flourish. When will we catch on? When will we speak the truth in love to one another? When doctrine is promoted throughout the world that is false, we not only have a right but a responsibility to confront it publicly. And if it is dangerous we must mention names. How else will people know what we are talking about? Do we expect them to discern everything on their own? Hardly! That is not the attitude of a true pastor or shepherd but merely political correctness masquerading as godly behavior. We must speak the truth in love and stop being children tossed here and there by the craftiness of those who call themselves apostles and prophets. If you love the truth, you will value correction. If you do not value correction, then you do not love the truth. It is possible to love one another while still confronting false teaching and/or simply disagreeing with direction or emphasis. If what we are teaching is true then scrutiny will only prove it. If it turns out to be wrong, shouldn't we turn away from it?

Chapter Twelve
Anticipation

"Now there is in store for me the crown of righteousness, which the Lord, the righteous Judge, will award to me on that day-and not only to me, but also to all who have longed for his appearing." 2 Tim 4:8 NIV

I grew up in the Irish Midlands on a small farm as the youngest of six children. Every year, about seven or eight miles away, the races took place. I do remember horses galloping and people shouting, but for me, that was only a small part of the fun. You see, there were booths with games and all kinds of shows and fun things for kids, not to mention lots of fruit, ice cream and candy. It was the only thing of its kind in the area. I will never forget how we saved our pennies all year long. Everything we earned (and it wasn't much in those days), was saved for the races. I did not get an allowance, but I did have a chance, once in a while, to help the neighbors on their farms and get a shilling or two. And as the days got closer to the event, I can still remember the anticipation and the longing I felt. It was better than Christmas.

Today I don't long for the races anymore. But as a believer in Jesus Christ, I have no greater longing, no greater anticipation than to see His face. The thought of His return in my lifetime sends chills up and down my spine. Imagine, seeing Him in all His glory setting foot on the mountains of Jerusalem and being next to His side. Just picture being with Him every day and gazing on His beauty and majesty, not to mention His wonderful rule coming to Earth. The thought of being with Him for all eternity and finding the true purpose for all of creation is unimaginable. My brain can't even comprehend being in the very presence of the Father and looking at Him face to face. Doesn't that excite you? Doesn't it make your heart beat faster? Jesus our Bridegroom is coming to take us to Himself. He is coming soon and He is coming here!

Paul was longing for Jesus' appearing, and he expected every Christian to do the same. And why shouldn't we, if we love Him. If we have come to know Him and abide in His love, how could we not be longing for Him to come? Indeed, Paul tells us that even creation itself is longing for his appearing.[68] How much more so should we who are His Bride - His beloved? We should be longing for our wedding consummation. And the knowledge that it is just a few years away should cause us to be feverish with anticipation. This is how the early church lived and what motivated them to suffer so much. They were so consumed with passion for Him that it lit the world on fire. This is what drove them to preach the gospel and gather in the harvest. And they ignited their followers with the same longing for His appearing.

Hope Deferred

"Therefore, prepare your minds for action; be self-controlled; set your hope fully on the grace to be given you when Jesus Christ is revealed." 1 Peter 1:13 NIV

This is the admonition of the apostle Peter. He told us to prepare our minds, to be self-controlled, and to set our hope completely on the return of Jesus. We are being exhorted to make a decision to focus our minds on the hope set before us, which will propel us forward. What a different perspective Peter had than most pastors and preachers today. Imagine telling people to set your whole focus on Jesus coming. How often we hear preachers say things like; "Don't focus on End-Times," "Stop thinking about that all the time," Just get on with the business of living for Jesus," "You're too

---

[68] Rom 8:22

heavenly minded and no earthly good." But the early church felt differently. They loved Him and lived for Him. And the hope of His soon return was their primary preoccupation. They put all their eggs in one basket. "Jesus is coming soon and we need to be ready to meet Him," they said. Their whole hope was in His return. Anticipation of it was their greatest motivation. Listen to what Paul had to say:

"Set your minds on things above, not on earthly things. For you died, and your life is now hidden with Christ in God. When Christ, who is your life, appears, then you also will appear with him in glory. Col 3:1-4 NIV

To set your mind on something is to focus fully on that thing. This is the same as what Peter said. We are told not to focus on our life here, for we have died and are now hidden. We are to focus instead on Jesus being revealed to mankind in glory and us with Him. This is not some ethereal revealing in heaven after you die someday. Neither is it the manifesting of Jesus' character in me, as important as that is. No, it is the visible appearing of Jesus Christ being revealed to the world, and us with Him. This is where our focus should be and what we are to be thinking about constantly. Imagine that! How different the church would be if this were the case. How exciting church life would be if we really caught a glimpse of His appearing and understood it as real and not just church doctrine. What do you think would happen if we really believed Jesus was coming in a few years? Would it change the atmosphere in the church? Would it make us nicer, holier, and more evangelistic? I think so! And I'm inclined to think the devil agrees, because he tries so hard to keep this message out of the pulpits and off the shelves. "Nobody really knows," he says. "He may come someday, but don't worry about it now, it's a long way off." "There is much more important stuff to think about." But when we fall for these lies, we are robbed of the great hope which is set before us; and the destiny which should energize our souls.

Perhaps you have never considered that the devil is behind these excuses. But since they are the antithesis of what Scripture exhorts, there can be no other alternative. Our blessed hope is His soon appearing. The Bible is very clear about that. All who love Him and long for Him, watch for it and look for it with great expectancy. Serving Him should be a delight and advancing the kingdom a joy, but not because of deferred hope. On the contrary, our hope spurs us to godly living and reminds us of the reason we are here.

"For the grace of God has appeared, bringing salvation to all men, instructing us to deny ungodliness and worldly desires and to live sensibly, righteously and godly in the present age, looking for the blessed hope and the appearing of the glory of our great God and Savior, Christ Jesus." Titus 2:11-13

How tragic it is when new believers discover the hope of Jesus' soon return, only to have some preacher or pastor replace that hope with uncertainty or confusion. How many Christians visit the pews week after week for their Sunday fix, because the hope they once had has been deferred.

"Hope deferred makes the heart sick, but a longing fulfilled is a tree of life." Prov 13:12

Hope deferred is hope that has been put off or postponed. This is precisely what the church is doing with End-Times. They are putting it off and postponing it for a later time. And in the process, they are quenching the hope of God's people worldwide and causing them to trust in human effort, rather than His appearing which alone can save us. But the Bride of Christ is waking up and trimming her lamp. She has heard the voice of the Bridegroom. She has made sure to fill her flask with the oil of the Spirit. She refuses to let her hope be dampened and soon, very soon, her longing will be fulfilled.

Fear of Disappointment

So many pastors and teachers refuse to consider that we are the last generation before He comes, because they are afraid of being wrong. They will not consider any eschatological time frame, because to do so, in their minds, is to disillusion God's people. It is an understandable reaction, but it is the wrong attitude. Believers who set false dates, because of deception, should be obvious to the discerning. Indeed, if pastors are trained and not disillusioned themselves, then they should be able to correct false teaching. On the other hand, as we have seen, not all who set dates or make mistakes with their prophetic calculations are deceived. Indeed, many are merely trying to understand what God is doing in their generation. They miss it because they have built their prophetic timetable on a faulty premise. They are missing some or all of the Lost Keys. They misunderstand the heart of the Hebrew prophets due to centuries of false teaching that has mystified and frustrated their eschatology. But false teaching is false teaching and it always leads to wrong conclusions. The same is true for every subject of Scripture.

When one has been fed false information and has based his actions upon it, disappointment is unavoidable. Therefore, not teaching the truth of eschatology because people have been disappointed by false predictions is unscriptural and irresponsible. To deprive the church of the hope of End-Time prophecy through fear that people will become deceived or disillusioned is to give in to a satanic plot that keeps people in darkness. It is to renege on our responsibilities as pastors and leaders. Why not train people? Why not teach them to look for Him? Why not teach them to understand the signs of the end and let them swell with anticipation? The hope before us doesn't disappoint, does it? On the contrary, it spurs us on.

"And hope does not disappoint us, because God has poured out his love into our hearts by the Holy Spirit, whom he has given us." Rom 5:4-5 NIV
If we make a mistake and the Lord does not appear when we expect,

will we become disillusioned? Will we stop looking? Is that what's really going on in the church? Surely God will show us where we went wrong or how we misinterpreted. Our hope will not disappoint us because our hearts have already tasted of His glory. Will those who love Him let go of their hope? Will you, pastor? Will you, Bible teacher? If the first century Jews had to be adjusted in their understanding by divine intervention, then why can't we? And can't we correct our own teaching if need be, or be corrected by others? What's the real reason we are so afraid of this subject? I am not suggesting that we should not be concerned about accuracy in teaching. On the contrary, handling the Scripture accurately is a cause dear to me. But won't dialogue and discussion on End-Times challenge us to a greater accuracy?

Everything we see and understand with regard to End-Time prophecy points to this generation as the last one of this age. This could be wrong perhaps, but not likely. The End-Time scenario, as foretold by Scripture, has not become foggier in the last century. Rather, it has become clearer. Therefore, since we have the more sure prophetic word that has been opened up and made clear to us, we would do well to pay attention and let the morning star of expectancy rise in our hearts.[69]

The repeated warnings about deception in the last days are not intended to keep us from discerning the time or longing for His appearing. Rather, they are emphasizing the real peril of following after man. Have not all those who became disillusioned over false dates been victims of this deception? The false signs and wonders spoken of in the Olivet Discourse, and elsewhere, are intended to draw people after the Antichrist and false messiahs, rather than the true Messiah. These warnings were not intended to rob from us the guidance of the prophetic word or the earnest expectation of His coming. To use them for this purpose is to misuse them.

---

[69] 2Pet 1:19

264 | P a g e

Promoting Purity

"But we know that when he appears, we shall be like him, for we shall see him as he is. Everyone who has this hope in him purifies himself, just as he is pure." 1 John 3:2-3 NIV

We often hear today that to focus on the end of the age and the coming of Christ is immature or irresponsible. To watch the signs, or be a student of biblical prophecy regarding End-Times is usually equated with foolishness or a lack of character. As a result, if you teach on the subject, you are presumed to be unconcerned about Christian purity or holiness. But the above Scripture says the exact opposite. It is those who have this hope that are more concerned with purity and holiness both in themselves and others. The clear implication from this verse is that those who long for His appearing must and will take this matter seriously. It is also clear that the hope of His soon return is a key motivator to live holy and godly in this present age. Therefore, when there is a lack of holiness in the church, it is not a result of the teaching of End-Time prophecy, but rather a lack of teaching on the importance and necessity of holiness. Far too often believers are told to just "accept Jesus" and not what He expects of those who love Him. Also, many are now preaching that God doesn't care about sin anymore and repentance of any kind is legalism. But as we have already seen, He is coming for a spotless Bride, who loves Him and lives for Him. Those who have rejected His call to purity will not partake of His glory. When He comes we must be found by Him to be holy and blameless. This is the clear teaching of Scripture as the following verses attest.

"For he chose us in him before the creation of the world to be holy and blameless in his sight." Eph 1:3-4 NIV

"May God himself, the God of peace, sanctify you through and through. May your whole spirit, soul and body be kept blameless at the coming of our

Lord Jesus Christ. The one who calls you is faithful and he will do it." 1 Thess 5:23-24 NIV

"So then, dear friends, since you are looking forward to this, make every effort to be found spotless, blameless and at peace with him." 2 Peter 3:14 NIV

"I charge you to keep this command without spot or blame until the appearing of our Lord Jesus Christ." 1 Tim 6:13-14 NIV

"Pursue peace with all men, and the sanctification without which no one will see the Lord." Heb 12:14

It's All About Love

The above passages make it clear that we must concern ourselves with purity and holiness if we are to be among those waiting for Him. This does not suggest that we must earn His righteousness, but we must be clothed with it lest we be found naked. We cannot arrive at this place of sanctification by human effort, yet there is a responsibility on our part. We cannot say, "We have prayed the prayer and that's all that matters." We must learn to appropriate His grace, mercy, and forgiveness, and walk it out. This does not mean we will never stumble, but that our lives are given to Him in obedience to His will. Jesus gave His life for us. He offered Himself up for us out of love. For us to do less for Him and withhold our lives from His sanctifying grace and power would be to not love Him, and reject His invitation. Those who love Him cannot but live for Him. It is all about love. Though fear of the Lord will keep us safe, those who have matured in their love are not afraid of judgment,[70] because they are motivated and captivated by love. There is no greater motivation in the entire universe. To know Him is to love Him. To love Him is to live for Him. To disobey Him is to deny Him. This does not mean that we cannot sin and fail Him. However, if anyone sins there is an advocate with the Father, Jesus

---

[70] 1John 4:18

Christ the righteous.[14] Thank God for the blood. But this is not a license to sin or walk in impurity. On the contrary, it is the enablement not to do so. If we love Him we will not live this way. When He comes for His Bride He will be coming for those who have chosen Him over this world and what it has to offer. He is coming for those who are longing for His appearing and eagerly awaiting Him.

"...so Christ also, having been offered once to bear the sins of many, will appear a second time for salvation without reference to sin, to those who eagerly await Him." Heb 9:28

No one who is eager for His coming will stay very long in sin. No one who walks in sin will be eager for His appearing. This is the reason we must let them know it is soon. Some would say that if we just tell them to obey Him and walk in love and righteousness, they will be ready. Perhaps! But not to tell them about His soon coming is to deprive them of the impetus, the motivation to live for Him. Sure, we love Him even though we have not seen Him, but we long for Him because we will see Him. And our longing for Him will cause us to prepare ourselves for His arrival. May the Lord bring this longing to the fore in the church! May He awaken the prophetic word in our hearts! May we fix our eyes on Him and His appearing! May we follow Christ who, because of the hope set before Him, endured the cross and despised the shame! And may the Bride of Christ rediscover the Lost Keys and once again embrace the living hope that is set before her! Let us rise in anticipation as overcomers in these challenging End-Times!

Appendix 1
12 Reasons Why this is The Final Generation

1. The restoration of Israel to the land — 1948- Fig Tree Blossoms - Acts 3:21 - restoration of all things spoken by the prophets of Israel

2. Restoration of Jerusalem to Israel - Gentile dominance of Jerusalem ends - 1967
   - ➤ The generation to see these things will see all of it (Jesus) - Luke 21
   - ➤ Restoration of Israel to God is underway

3. The History of Gentile empires dominating Israel, as revealed to Daniel, is in the final stages.
   - ➤ 10 nation alliance - ten toes - ten horns - little horn Antichrist - Daniel 2 & 7
   - ➤ Rev 17:12 - Revived Roman Empire - WEU 10 nations create post for Beast with Recommendation 666
   - ➤ Forming of the 7th head of the RRE or EU treaty to admit Israel

4. The making of a covenant with Antichrist - peace treaty - "Road Map to Peace" is the hottest item for all the nations - Israel is ready to sign and commit apostasy - Dan 9:27

5. The Gospel of Jesus Christ has been preached to all the nations beginning in Jerusalem - small number of tribes left will be reached within a few years although it is not necessary for the prophecy to be fulfilled - Mt 24:14

6. The advent of Globalism - Global Governance - EU - UN - Banking, Commerce - New Religious Globalists - Rev 13:7, 16-17, 17:1-8

7. Rise of Anti-Semitism - war on Israel - radical Islam - global terror - all nations believe the problem is Israel & Jerusalem - all nations against Jerusalem - Zech 12:3, 14:2

8. Outpouring of the Holy Spirit upon the church - continued increase of His presence and restoration and revelation - separation of a remnant

9. Alliance of Gog & Magog - Middle Eastern Muslim nations aligned with Russia as per Ezekiel 38 & 39

10. Existence of technology - weaponry - atomic bomb - media - satellite - necessary to fulfill last generation prophecy

11. Rise of earthquakes

12. 7th Millennium to begin in this generation per literal reading of the Bible and adding of time - prophecies to be fulfilled in 7th Millennium - Hos 6:1-2

   ➤ Third Millennium after 70AD - Luke 13:32
   ➤ Third Day - the Day of the Lord - Reign of Messiah

Appendix 2
The Hyper Grace Movement

Have you heard of the "Grace Revolution?" "What is it?" you ask. Is it like the Arab Spring? Well, not exactly. Yet, according to some of its leaders, it will have a profound an effect on the Body of Christ as those recent uprisings have had on the Middle East. It is not a "gentle reformation," they insist, but a "true revolution." A separation between what they call "grace teaching" and "law teaching." A revolt against the "religious legalism and hypocrisy of those who mix law and grace," thereby binding believers in condemnation and bondage, or so they say. According to some, it is sweeping the globe as churches and preachers are joining the ranks daily. Nevertheless, what is it really about and why would it be bad? Is not grace the divine favor of God - the empowering of the Holy Spirit to do what we cannot do and be what we cannot be on our own? We are justified by grace, sanctified through grace, and glorified by His grace. Indeed, "Of his fullness we have all received and grace upon grace" (John 1:16). What then can be wrong with a revolution of grace? Is it any wonder that the ranks are swelling? Who could possibly find fault with it? Is not the gospel of Christ itself the gospel of grace? Did not Jesus come to bring us into grace and Paul say that those who receive the abundance of grace will reign in life? What then is wrong with the revolution and why are pastors and leaders speaking out against it? The answer is actually quite simple. It is contained in the following Scripture:

"For (or because) *the Law was given through Moses; grace and truth were realized through Jesus Christ." John 1:16*

The above text says Jesus did not appear bringing grace only and neither does it say there was no grace before He came. What it clearly says is that for or because (Gr. OTI) the Law came through Moses, grace and truth were realized (or came) though Jesus Christ. It does not say that Moses brought the Law but Jesus brought the grace, as is the standard reading. There is no but in the sentence. The Law given by Moses is not being contrasted with or against the grace of Christ but shown to be the preparation for the grace of Christ. Nonetheless, Christ did not bring grace only but He also brought truth. The truth brought by Christ is as essential to us as the grace brought by Christ. We cannot have one without the other. Grace without truth is not really God's grace but something entirely different. Therefore, the problem with the "Grace Revolution" does not actually have to do with grace but the "truth" that accompanies it. To have a true grace revolution we must have a truth revolution as well. Thus, we must take a closer look at the message of this movement and compare it to the truth brought to us by Jesus.

A Brief Summary of "Hyper Grace"

Before we begin, let us understand that this "Grace Revolution," also known as "Hyper Grace," does not claim to have a new release of grace from heaven, or a fresh outpouring of the Holy Spirit. Rather, it claims a new or "restored gospel" that has been purged of commandments and requirements, which it believes will revolutionize the church. According to this message, the Law given by God is the enemy of grace, and if the believer is truly walking in grace there can be no mention of commandments or requirements. The Christian is free from the Law since he died with Christ and has become a new creation. He is now exclusively under grace where there is no law or requirement. He is, in fact, the very righteousness of God and is no longer to receive any condemnation or even conviction, which they perceive to be the same thing. Thus, there is no need for him to repent ever again, since Christ has taken away all of his sins, past, present and future and has not even a record of them. All the believer needs now is education. He just needs to know who he is and get his thinking changed and he has arrived. This is the essence of the "Hyper Grace" message, although there is much more to it as we shall see later.

Fly in the Ointment

As we examine this relatively new message, we immediately see that there is much about it that is true. That of course is the problem. If it did not have a good chunk of truth, most people would not fall for it. It is also why it is so dangerous- because so much of it is true, and even refreshing, that it snares the untaught and unsuspecting. However, the mixture is lethal, yet it is not the grace in the mixture but the error combined with it that will lead to ruin. The all too common plot in detective mysteries reminds us that if you want to poison someone, you must hide the poison in something the victim is eager to consume – where he would least expect it to be. What better than something sweet, something that he cannot resist. Thus, the best place for the enemy to hide his lies at the present is in the grace message we are all consuming. It is the proverbial fly in the ointment – the Achilles heel of the Revival Movement. It is the place where the church is weakest, since it has distorted the Biblical understanding of Law and Grace from its early days. Consequently, when pastors and teachers confront it they often sound like they are backpedaling because their own understanding of Law and Grace is skewed. Thus, they are easily portrayed as the defenders of tradition and the Law - the "legalists" who have kept us in bondage all these years. In addition, when the message of grace is cloaked in a promise of freedom from "religion" and rules, this young "postmodern" generation of Biblically-challenged, six-month ministry school "equipped" revolutionaries, find it irresistible. Nevertheless, God has a plan in all this. He is flushing something out - bringing it to a head in these last days.[71]

---

[71] Excerpt from "Grace Gone Wild" by PJ Hanley

Appendix 3
The Emerging Church Movement

"The emerging church (sometimes referred to as the emergent movement) is a Christian movement of the late 20th and early 21st century that crosses a number of theological boundaries: participants can be described as evangelical, post-evangelical, liberal, post-liberal, charismatic, neocharismatic and post-charismatic. Participants seek to live their faith in what they believe to be a "postmodern" society. Proponents of this movement call it a "conversation" to emphasize its developing and decentralized nature, its vast range of standpoints and its commitment to dialogue. What those involved in the conversation mostly agree on is their disillusionment with the organized and institutional church and their support for the deconstruction of modern Christian worship, modern evangelism, and the nature of modern Christian community."[72]

Emergent Church is a very post-modern movement. Post-modernism basically says that there may be truth, we just can't know it. They would say that truth may indeed come from God, but we just can't know what it is. So we embrace mystery.

Emerging church leaders want to remake Christianity in favor of a new "postmodern," "enlightened" version. They look on the revelation contained in the Bible as an "ongoing story of redemption." They disdain orthodoxy of any kind and emphasize orthopraxy. I'm sure you are thinking that I am speaking about a fringe group. I wish I were. Unfortunately, they are gaining a large following in many of today's Evangelical and Charismatic churches. They have had the most success with those who were hurt in the church and those who are trying to adjust to the so-called "postmodern era."

---

[72] Wikipedia

The Emerging Church is either denying or distorting, the trinity, the nature of God, the fatherhood of God, the deity of Christ, the cross, the judgment of sin, the authority of God's Word, and the resurrection.

Appendix 4
The Resurgence of "Kingdom Now" or "Dominion Theology"

For years I had thought that the Reconstructionism and Dominionism of Rousas J. Rushdoony[73] had become obsolete. This theology of the church taking over the world and establishing "The Kingdom" was popular for a while in the USA, particularly during the Reagan years when it looked like Christians were rising to the top and had the impetus to overcome social ills. But since then, particularly with the liberals in power, it seemed to have been abandoned by all but a fringe. However, since the year 2000 came and went without incident, it appears that a number of Charismatics became disillusioned and adopted a form of Post-Millennialism or Partial-Preterism. And as a result, teachings on "Kingdom Now" and "Dominion Theology" have come to the fore.

Now I realize that many of you will not know what a Preterist or a Pre-Millennialist is. By the way, if you are a pastor or a leader this is nothing to be proud of. In any event, Pre-Millenialists believe that Jesus is coming bodily to Earth before the Millennium begins and that the events outlined in the book of Revelation as well as the Olivet Discourse (MT. 24) are yet future. Partial Preterists on the other hand, believe that all of these events have already been fulfilled in 70 AD or thereabouts, and that since then we have been in "The Kingdom Age" with a small portion at the end of the book of Revelation yet future. The focus then of Preterists has to be "Kingdom Now" since they are going to hand the "Kingdom" over to Jesus, presumably when the work is complete.

Partial Preterism
There are at least two kinds of Preterists, Partial Preterists and Full Preterists. It seems Partial Preterists have modified Preterism

---

[73] http://en.wikipedia.org/wiki/Rousas_John_Rushdoony

slightly, perhaps to be covered by the Nicene Creed. For Preterists, the Olivet Discourse (Mt 24, Luke 21, Mk 13), and most of the book of Revelation (except the last couple of chapters), were all fulfilled in the first couple of centuries. All of the prophecies concerning Israel's regathering were fulfilled with the return from the first Babylonian exile. So there is now no Day of the Lord Tribulation, no Armageddon, no Antichrist, no Seventieth Week or Last Shemitah Cycle, no Revived Roman Empire, no Last Days, no bodily First Resurrection, and, of course, no State of Israel as a work of God's regathering. Besides the devil was bound in 70AD and Jesus came in the clouds to pour out vengeance on those "wicked Jews" and destroy the "wicked city" of Jerusalem. Partial Preterists though, say there is still another coming at the end of the Millennium which they claim we are either in or bringing in. In this way they pretend to be like Pre-Millenniumists but their second coming could be a thousand years from now. This appears to be the only difference between Partial and Full Preterism. According to Preterists, Jesus cannot come until the church has taken over the world and reigned for an undetermined amount of time. Then the "end" will come when He appears and takes the Kingdom, handing it over to the Father. Some of them consider this "end" to be near since Mt 24:14 has almost been fulfilled. But since the end being referred to by Jesus in Mt 24:14 is the Abomination of Desolation in verse 15, and they believe that Mt 24 has already been fulfilled in 70AD, it's hard to fathom how their minds work. But this is how it is with almost everything that Preterism teaches. I honestly don't know how anyone could call the last 2000 years the "Reign of Christ." But this teaching is gaining momentum among us! This paper is not a full treatment of the doctrine of Preterism (such material has been written),[74] but there are two foundation Pillars of Preterism as I see it, 1) Replacement Theology, and 2) Private or non-literal interpretation of Scripture.

---

[74] "Has Bible Prophecy Already Been Fulfilled?" Dr. Thomas Ice, http://www.pre-trib.org/articles/view/has-bible-prophecy-already-been-fulfilled

Replacement Theology

There are many references in the writings of the Hebrew prophets regarding the destruction and scattering of Israel and her regathering from the ends of the earth at the end of the age. The Preterists consider these verses to have been fulfilled in the return from Babylon when only a small number of Jews returned. They also consider the Last Days to have ended in 70 AD, which was the period of the destruction of Israel and not a regathering from all the nations. The prophets were very specific when they prophesied the final return, making it clear that Israel would be surrounded by all nations, but this last time God would fight for them and they would be victorious (Mi 4:11-13, Is 41:8-16). But even if we accept the view that this was fulfilled by the return from Babylon as the Preterists say, what are we to do with Zechariah who prophesied after the return from Babylon? He said that all the nations would come against Israel and Jerusalem to destroy it but the Jews would be victorious as God fights for them. When was this prophecy fulfilled? When did all the nations come against Jerusalem and when were they destroyed?

"On that day, when all the nations of the earth are gathered against her, I will make Jerusalem an immovable rock for all the nations. All who try to move it will injure themselves. On that day I will strike every horse with panic and its rider with madness," declares the LORD. "I will keep a watchful eye over the house of Judah, but I will blind all the horses of the nations. Then the leaders of Judah will say in their hearts, 'The people of Jerusalem are strong, because the LORD Almighty is their God.' On that day I will make the leaders of Judah like a firepot in a woodpile, like a flaming torch among sheaves. They will consume right and left all the surrounding peoples, but Jerusalem will remain intact in her place. The LORD will save the dwellings of Judah first, so that the honor of the house of David and of Jerusalem's inhabitants may not be greater than that of Judah. On that day the LORD will shield those who live in Jerusalem, so that the feeblest among them will be like David, and the house of David will be like God, like the_Angel of the LORD going before them. On that

day I will set out to destroy all the nations that attack Jerusalem. Zech 12:3-9 NIV

This doctrine of Preterism was invented by a Jesuit priest to counter Reformation Eschatology. It relies, of course, on the rejection of Israel (Replacement Theology) which has been the theology of those who persecuted the Jews throughout the centuries. Replacement Theology celebrates all the words of the prophets concerning the literal destruction of Israel and Jerusalem, but robs and steals all of the prophecies of her restoration making them non-literal and applying them only to the church.

It is very clear in the New Testament that the first century church did not share this view, and it is equally clear from history that the second century church did not share it either. But the Preterists have a way out of that. It is by seeing the early church as "Primitive" and they being more mature and enlightened.

"But if some of the branches were broken off, and you, being a wild olive, were grafted in among them and became partaker with them of the rich root of the olive tree, do not be arrogant toward the branches; but if you are arrogant, remember that it is not you who supports the root, but the root supports you." Rom 11:17-18

1. Private or Non-Literal Interpretation of Scripture

"But know this first of all, that no prophecy of Scripture is a matter of one's own interpretation, for no prophecy was ever made by an act of human will, but men moved by the Holy Spirit spoke from God. But false prophets also arose among the people, just as there will also be false teachers among you, who will secretly introduce destructive heresies, even denying the Master who bought them, bringing swift destruction upon themselves." 2 Peter 1:20-2:1

Now we will examine this scripture from 2 Peter again, this time focusing on the context which is clearly End-Time teaching. The whole book is about false teachers who lack character, who have gone astray from the faith and are saying, "Where is the promise of His coming?" Peter tells us that the parousia (presence, coming) and revealing of Jesus to the world in glory and majesty, which was prophesied by the prophets (1:19), is coming even though some think it is taking too long. He also calls this parousia the Day of the Lord.

"But the day of the Lord will come like a thief, in which the heavens will pass away with a roar and the elements will be destroyed with intense heat, and the earth and its works will be burned up."2 Peter 3:10

The Day of the Lord judgment which is coming upon the world is a primary theme of the prophets of Israel (Joel 2:31, Is 2, 13:9-13, many more). Incidentally, it is not the time of destruction upon Israel which took place in the first century. It is a time of judgment on the earth when all of the wicked will be destroyed.

"The sun will be dark when it rises and the moon will not shed its light. Thus I will punish the world for its evil and the wicked for their iniquity…" Isa 13:10-11

Peter of course being a good student of the prophets knew this and affirms it in Chapter 2, verse 9.

"….then the Lord knows how to rescue the godly from temptation, and to keep the unrighteous under punishment for the day of judgment…" 2 Peter 2:9

Now regarding the words of the prophets, and all Scripture for that matter, Peter says that it is not a matter of one's own private interpretation. This means that the words of the prophets have a literal meaning which cannot be taken away or reinterpreted by us. The literal and plain meaning of the authors of the Bible is not to be overwritten by anyone. This was the practice of these false teachers in the first century and it is the practice of many in our day as well. Though it is clear that there is often a prophetic truth to be gleaned from a passage or a moral application to be made, there is never a license or justification to make a change in the plain literal meaning of the author. The only time we can interpret a passage non-literally is when the text makes it clear that it is <u>not</u> to be taken literally. This really is not difficult to understand. Text has to have a literal meaning and the rules of language insist that words have a literal meaning and application. They cannot be altered or translated as something other than what was written and intended by the author. But those who use their own private interpretation can make the Scripture say whatever they want. This was the practice of the Gnostic false teachers in Peter's day and it is the predominant way in which the Bible is interpreted today. It is also the primary reason we have so much confusion in the church.

There are scores of passages in the Bible relating to Israel's scattering throughout the world as punishment for their sins, and equally as many about their regathering from all the nations at the end of the age, and being restored in their relationship with God. Who in the church will deny that this scattering took place? Who denies that Israel was punished and scattered by the Lord? Let us examine just one verse:

"I will lay waste your cities as well and will make your sanctuaries desolate, and I will not smell your soothing aromas. I will make the land desolate so that your enemies who settle in it will be appalled over it. You, however, I will scatter among the nations and will draw out a sword after you, as your land becomes desolate and your cities become waste." Lev 26:31-33

I have never heard anyone claim that the church was scattered because of sin and a sword drawn out after them. Of course not! Please notice that this is a scattering to the nations and not just to Babylon and that their sanctuaries (plural) are made desolate. This includes both first and second Temples. Now let us read one of the countless restoration passages that appear side by side with the scattering ones.

"Therefore thus says the Lord GOD, 'Now I will restore the fortunes of Jacob and have mercy on the whole house of Israel; and I will be jealous for My holy name. They will forget their disgrace and all their treachery which they perpetrated against Me, when they live securely on their own land with no one to make them afraid. When I bring them back from the peoples and gather them from the lands of their enemies, then I shall be sanctified through them in the sight of the many nations. Then they will know that I am the LORD their God because I made them go into exile among the nations, and then gathered them again to their own land; and I will leave none of them there any longer. I will not hide My face from them any longer, for I will have poured out My Spirit on the house of Israel,' declares the Lord GOD." Ezek 39:25-29

Just as God promised to scatter Israel, which He did in 70AD, He also promised to bring them back (Notice it's a scattering to all the nations and not just Babylon). If the first promise is for Israel, then how is the second one for the church? How can Israel be the natural descendants of Jacob in one passage and the church in another? How can the literal meaning be valid in one and invalid in the next? Indeed, everywhere "Israel" or "Jacob" or "Judah" is mentioned and words are spoken about them, it has to apply to the nation of Israel. There is no such thing as a "Spiritual Israel" in these passages. There can't be. No such concept was ever introduced by the Hebrew prophets. All their words came to pass literally and what is left will also come to pass literally. Who has a right to change the meaning of "Israel" and "Jacob" to "The Church?" Listen to the words of Jeremiah:

"Thus says the LORD, who gives the sun for light by day and the fixed order of the moon and the stars for light by night, who stirs up the sea so that its waves roar; the LORD of hosts is His name: if this fixed order departs from

before Me," declares the LORD, "then the offspring of Israel also will cease from being a nation before Me forever." Jer 31:35-36

According to Jeremiah, Israel and the natural offspring of Jacob will always be a national entity before the Lord – forever. Thus Israel can never be the church and the church can never be Israel. Neither can Israel become a part of the church since this would obliterate her national identity.[75]

All of the scattering words concerning Israel end on a positive note of regathering - all of them. The Hebrew prophets all declare that Israel would come out on top, reconciled to God and the Messiah, and would never again be driven from their land, but would dwell securely in it and that God Himself would be among them. There are countless passages on this. Those who say that these prophecies were fulfilled with the return from Babylon, or annulled in the first century cannot hold on to them or apply them to themselves. God said that Israel would always be a nation (state) before Him (Jer 31:36), but they say no. But even if this were to be the case, which it is not, then they must discard the whole of the Prophets and all of Moses since most of what they contain refers to a literal Israel. They can of course hold on to a few Psalms and Proverbs and some of the moral Law if they wish. But they have no right to take something that does not belong to them and reinterpret it. Well they can do that, but it has no authority for them, no more than a work of fiction.

Now let's go to the New Testament. What about the city of Jerusalem? Consider this verse:

"…and they will fall by the edge of the sword, and will be led captive into all the nations; and Jerusalem will be trampled underfoot by the Gentiles until the times of the Gentiles are fulfilled." Luke 21:24 NASU

---

[75] For more on this subject see "Israel Awakening" by this author or "Prophetic Destinies" by Derek Prince

Jerusalem in this verse means literal Jerusalem, and not New York or Los Angeles (on this the Preterists agree). Now Jesus here states that the Jews would be scattered to all the nations and that Jerusalem would be trampled underfoot by Gentile rulers until the time of their domination ended. But this very statement requires a regathering of Israel, since if the Gentiles are no longer dominating it then it must be administered by Jews. This of course happened in 1967 as God had restored Israel to their land after almost two thousand years. Astonishingly, Preterists believe that the modern state of Israel is of no significance. Since they were done with Israel in the first century, its existence today cannot be acknowledged as an act of God. Thus they are set up for the Anti-Semitism of the last days. Furthermore, since they believe that all of the prophecies regarding Israel and Jerusalem and the Last Days were fulfilled in the first century, or thereabouts, then all of the New Testament passages about Biblical prophecy are also null and void and meaningless today. Thus we must also lay aside all of the Olivet Discourse, the book of Revelation, 1st and 2nd Thessalonians, 2 Peter, most of Philippians, and any other teaching on End-Times found in the Gospels and Epistles, since it has already been fulfilled. Also, most of 1 John since it is about the world passing away and the Antichrist. Now our Bible has become quite small indeed, but it is the Bible not only of Preterists but many in the church today. Also, since literal Israel is a topic in many of the remaining passages, and they have been reapplied to the church, how reliable can they be? I know some will be very offended by this statement, but it is just a logical deduction. In fact, I know a man who has decided to teach only those passages to his people since he claims the others are "irrelevant."

Dangers of Post Millennialism and Partial Preterism
1. **Replacement Theology**
   Partial Preterists and Post-Millennialists believe that God is finished with Israel and that all the promises of Israel (the good

ones) are now for the church. They will say they love Israel, but in the same way they love Ireland or Japan.

2. **They place no value on watching for Jesus' return** since He cannot come back until they have taken dominion of the earth. Therefore they will never teach or emphasize the Lord's return.

3. **Everything is going to get better until the church takes over.** Thus they do not recognize the reality that the world is becoming more and more Antichrist. This presents a severe danger of deception and sets them up to not recognize the Day of the Lord when it comes and to even be found working with the Antichrist.

4. **Since it tends to apply Scripture in a non-literal way**, with most of the literal passages already being fulfilled, it opens the door for a private, pick and choose application and interpretation of Scripture.

5. **It places incredible pressure on the church to take over the world and "disciple nations"** (a distortion of Mt 28) rather than winning and discipling souls for Christ. Such pressure can cause believers to justify, as it did in the past, human efforts at world dominance or even violence as in the crusades.

6. **Since they believe God's judgment to be past and do not believe in the coming Antichrist**, they are in danger of being deceived by him believing their agenda to be the same.

7. **It may cause many to become disillusioned** when they see the world continue to reject Christianity despite all their efforts to the contrary.

"For they themselves report about us what kind of a reception we had with you, and how you turned to God from idols to serve a living and true God, and to wait for His Son from heaven, whom He raised from the dead, that is Jesus, who rescues us from the wrath to come." 1 Thess 1:9

The Seven Mountains Mandate

The Seven Mountain Mandate is the idea that the church must win, take over or influence the so called Seven Mountains of Culture. These are defined as business, government, media, arts and entertainment, family, religion and education.

The Seven Mountain Movement and its objectives appear to be sweeping the church today. Many Pre-Millennialists have adopted it as a means of influencing and evangelizing nations. If it is seen in this light, and the goal is to do the work of the kingdom until Jesus comes, then there is little problem with the idea of influencing the so called seven spheres of culture. Indeed all sincere Christians want to win souls and have an impact on their cities and nations for the kingdom of God.

There is however, considerable confusion among Pre-Millennialists and many who are presenting the 7M Mandate as to where they stand on eschatology, or with regard to the mixing of Post and Pre-Millennial views. The 7M Mandate is used by many of its key proponents to promote Dominion Theology and Post-Millennialism. Indeed, they are very clearly advocating it. Others see it as a means to awaken Christians to evangelism and increase their influence for the kingdom. The 7M Mandate however, is generally not presented as a strategy to influence culture but to take it over. Indeed, the rallying cry is to "Take the 7 Mountains" and "Rule the 7 Mountains" and "Be the head and not the tail." Phrases such as "Social Transformation," "Reaching the tipping point," "Becoming a change agent" and "Taking our cities for God" have a Post-Millennial view of the Great Commission. In fact, if the role of the church in the days ahead is to take over the 7 Mountains of culture, then we can envision the future, before Christ returns, in the following way.

> **Government** - One World Government controlled by the church.
> **Religion** - One World Church controlling all religion and ruling the world.
> **Business** - The One World Church and One World Government will control all world finance.
> **Family**-All families will be Christian and follow God's laws as taught by the One World Church.
> **Education** – The word of the church will go forth from …?
> **Media** - The World Church network only.
> **Arts & Entertainment** – Sanctified Hollywood

When I consider the above scenario I can only think about the Dark Ages when the church was in control or the Tribulation when the Harlot Church is in control. I have to ask the following questions:
> Is a One World Church led by a hierarchy of apostles a good thing?
> Is there any evidence that it worked before?
> Is the church capable of governing the world since it does such a poor job of governing itself?
> What will we do with criminals?
> Who will lead such a World Church that has "taken the Mountain of Religion?"
> What will we do with all the other religious adherents who will not embrace Christianity?

Does Your Eschatology Matter?
Many Premillennialists are flirting with the Kingdom Now Movement because of the promises to win cities and nations and bring the whole world into the Kingdom. It all sounds great!

Indeed, it seems to be such a noble goal no one would want to interfere with it. Who can allow something as "boring" and "lifeless" or "divisive" as theology to get in the way? This is the argument that is being raised up in our time. But this thinking is flawed. Theology matters a great deal. Indeed, we follow what we believe and what we believe determines where we will end up. If the goal is to take over the Seven Mountains then whatever way we can do that will eventually be deemed ok. However, the end never justifies the means – never. The church will rule the earth and the heavens with her heavenly Bridegroom, but only as she submits to Him and follows His will. She cannot seize the Kingdom on her own. If she does she will not be seizing His Kingdom but her own. Jesus was promised the Kingdom by the Father.

"Ask of Me, and I will surely give the nations as Your inheritance, and the very ends of the earth as Your possession. You shall break them with a rod of iron, You shall shatter them like earthenware." Psalm 2:8-9

If Jesus had merely come to bring the Kingdom He could have followed this verse and taken it by force. After all, didn't the Father promise it to Him and wasn't that therefore God's will? This is the kind of reasoning some Seven Mountain teachers use. If Jesus had done that it certainly would have been a good thing, but would it have been the will of the Father? Yet, think of all the good it would have done, and all the lives it would have saved and He would not have had to endure the cross. Do you think He was tempted to do this? He most certainly was. Indeed the devil knowing this temptation offered it to Him on a silver platter. There was of course one little hitch - compromise yourself and worship satan. Jesus had His chance to infiltrate and seize the Kingdom. After all what's one little bow? Once He got up He had the Kingdom and could have done with it whatever He willed. But Jesus, who would do nothing that was not in union with the Father, declined this Kingdom Now offer and said, "Get behind Me satan." And if the church today had any sense they would do the same. Now this offer is being made to the Queen just as it was made to the King. It is a great sifting and testing. Will she accept or decline? You see she has to have this test. In past history she did not understand and now she does. She must knowingly make a choice. She is destined to reign but on the throne with Jesus and not on her own (Rev 3:21). But after all, isn't it God's will for her to reign – to be the head and not the tail? Is it just merely a timing issue? Did He not say He would give her the Kingdom and after all, look at all the good it will do and all the lives it will save and she won't have to suffer. Can't she just hand it back to Him afterward? What will she decide to do?

"The Spirit Himself testifies with our spirit that we are children of God, and if children, heirs also, heirs of God and fellow heirs with Christ, if indeed we suffer with Him so that we may also be glorified with Him." Rom 8:16-17

"If we endure, we will also reign with Him; if we deny Him, He also will deny us..." 2Tim 2:12

"He who overcomes, I will grant to him to sit down with Me on My throne, as I also overcame and sat down with My Father on His throne." Rev 3:21

Jesus clearly taught us that whoever humbles himself will be exalted and whoever exalts himself shall be humbled. The overcoming Bride walks with Jesus, abiding in His love and longing for His appearing.[76] The result of her relationship with Christ is fruitfulness and ministry. Instead of an earthly focus, she is ravished with love for the heavenly Bridegroom and her sights are set on Zion's Holy Hill. This is the Bride of Christ whose eyes are fixed on His beauty and whose heart is purified by His love. She longs for the Rapture, not just so she can escape suffering, but because His presence has become her all and all. To be with Him is her passion and to reign with Him her inheritance and reward.

---

[76] 2Tim 4:8

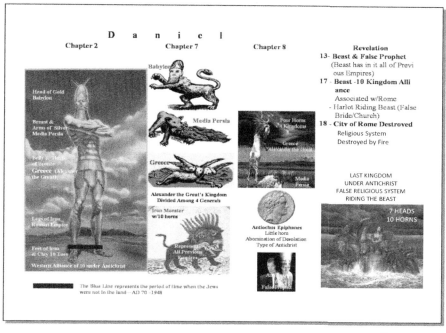

Chart 1

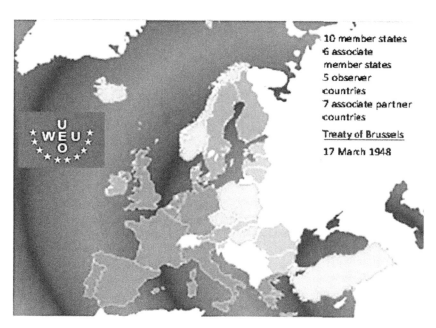

Chart 2

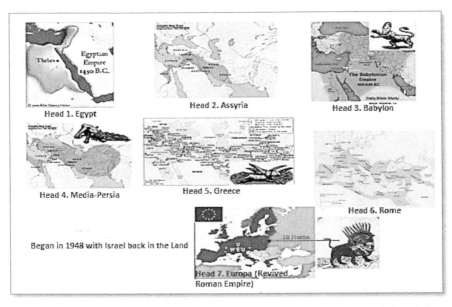

Head 1. Egypt

Head 2. Assyria

Head 3. Babylon

Head 4. Media-Persia

Head 5. Greece

Head 6. Rome

Began in 1948 with Israel back in the Land

Head 7. Europa (Revived Roman Empire)

10 Horns

Chart 3

Daniel's 70ᵗʰ Week
Last 7 years of Age

Dan 9:27

Peace
Treaty

Abom

Jesus

ARMAGEDDON X

X ————————————————————————— X —————————— ↑

Peace & Security
1 Thess 5:3

Great Tribulation
Mt 24:15, 2 Thess 2:3-4

THE APOSTASY

THE DAY OF THE LORD

"And he (Antichrist) will make a firm covenant with the many for one week, but in the middle of the week he will put a stop to sacrifice and grain offering; and on the wing of abominations will come one who makes desolate, even until a complete destruction, one that is decreed, is poured out on the one who makes desolate."

Chart 4

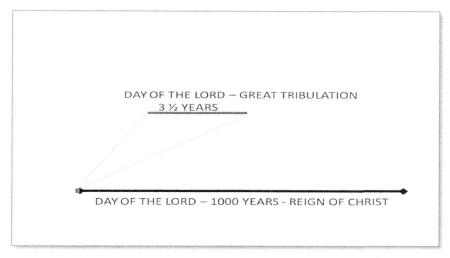

Chart 5

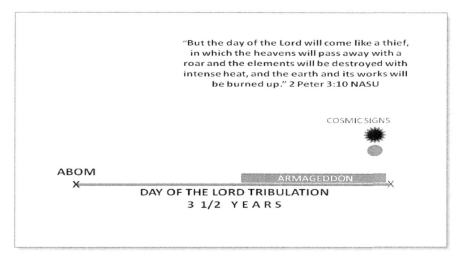

Chart 6

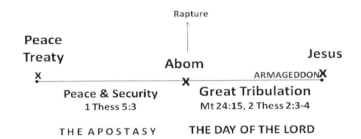

Chart 7

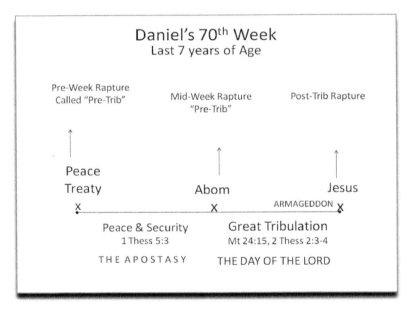

Chart 8

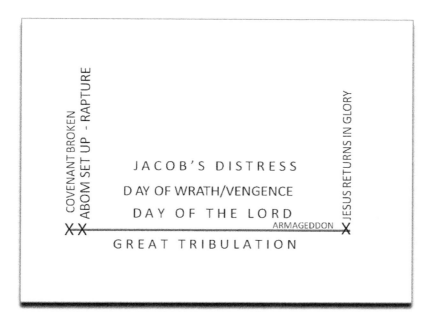

Chart 9

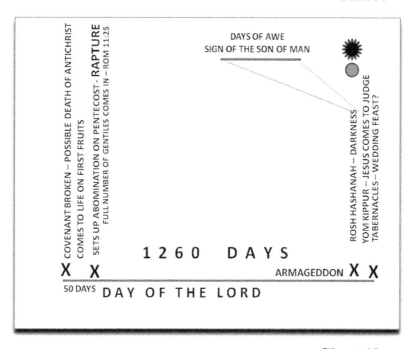

Chart 10

1ST SEAL – ANTICHRIST

2ND - RED HORSE – WAR

3RD - BLACK HORSE FAMINE

4TH – PALE HORSE – DEATH

5TH SEAL – MARYTRS

6TH SEAL – GREAT EARTHQUAKE – COSMIC SIGNS – END OF TRIBULATION

Chart 11

Chart 12

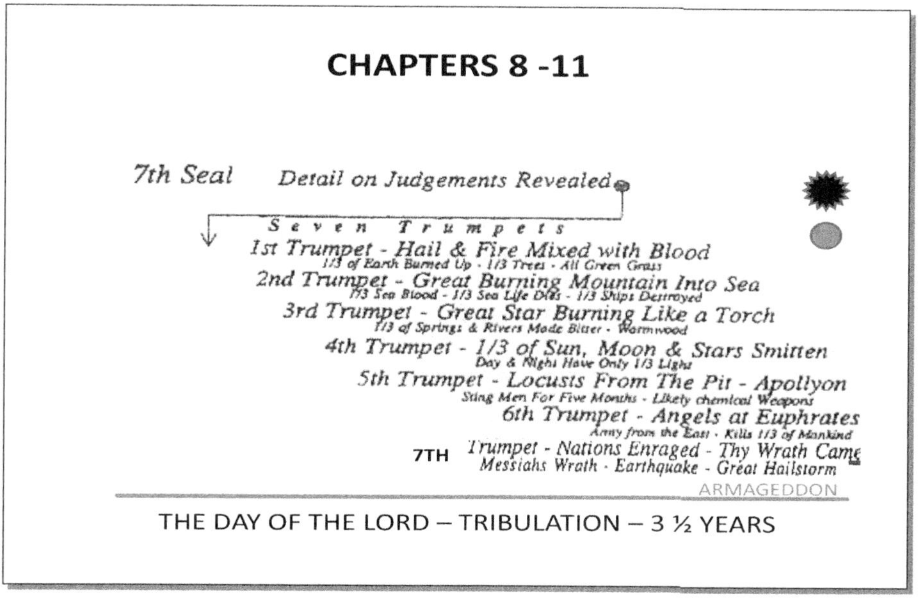

CHAPTERS 8 -11

7th Seal   *Detail on Judgements Revealed*

S e v e n   T r u m p e t s

1st Trumpet - Hail & Fire Mixed with Blood
1/3 of Earth Burned Up - 1/3 Trees - All Green Grass

2nd Trumpet - Great Burning Mountain Into Sea
1/3 Sea Blood - 1/3 Sea Life Dies - 1/3 Ships Destroyed

3rd Trumpet - Great Star Burning Like a Torch
1/3 of Springs & Rivers Made Bitter - Wormwood

4th Trumpet - 1/3 of Sun, Moon & Stars Smitten
Day & Night Have Only 1/3 Light

5th Trumpet - Locusts From The Pit - Apollyon
Sting Men For Five Months - Likely chemical Weapons

6th Trumpet - Angels at Euphrates
Army from the East - Kills 1/3 of Mankind

7TH *Trumpet - Nations Enraged - Thy Wrath Came*
Messiahs Wrath - Earthquake - Great Hailstorm

ARMAGEDDON

THE DAY OF THE LORD – TRIBULATION – 3 ½ YEARS

Chart 13

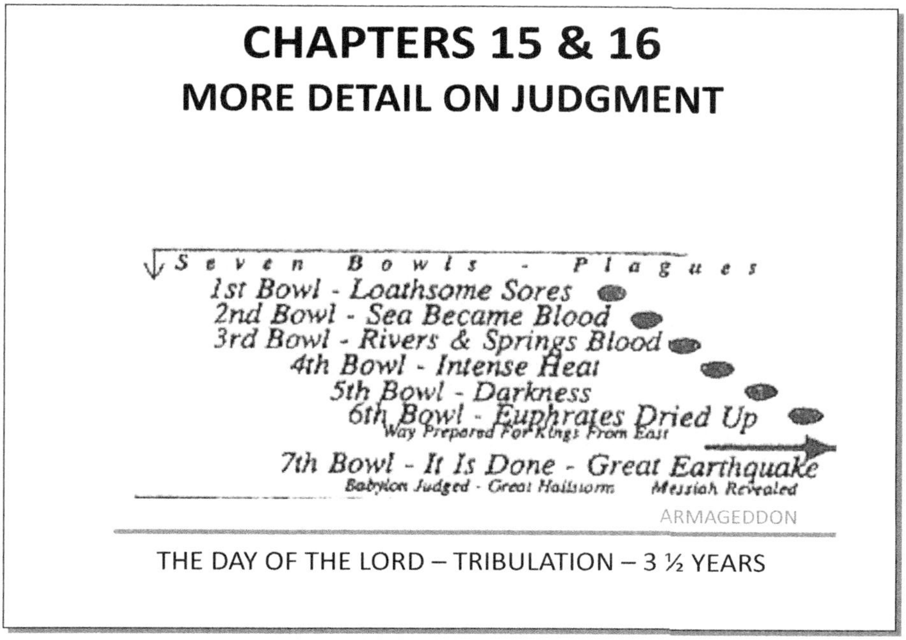

CHAPTERS 15 & 16
MORE DETAIL ON JUDGMENT

S e v e n   B o w l s   -   P l a g u e s

1st Bowl - Loathsome Sores
2nd Bowl - Sea Became Blood
3rd Bowl - Rivers & Springs Blood
4th Bowl - Intense Heat
5th Bowl - Darkness
6th Bowl - Euphrates Dried Up
Way Prepared For Kings From East

7th Bowl - It Is Done - Great Earthquake
Babylon Judged - Great Hailstorm   Messiah Revealed

ARMAGEDDON

THE DAY OF THE LORD – TRIBULATION – 3 ½ YEARS

Chart 14

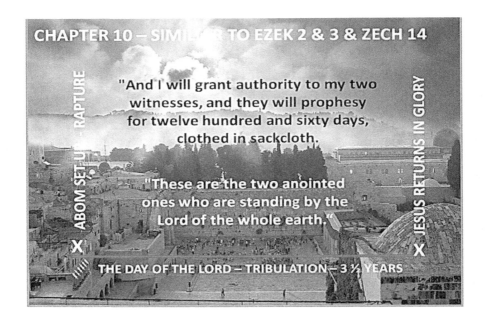

Chart 15

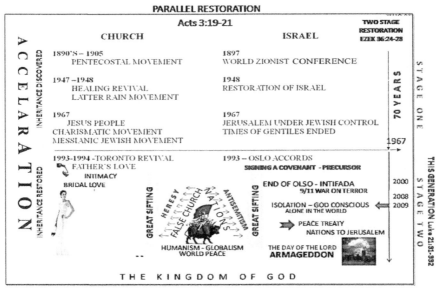

Chart 16

Printed in Great Britain
by Amazon

33418221R00165